COMMUNITY DEVELOPMENT
A critical approach

Margaret Ledwith

Consultant Editor: Jo Campling

This paperback edition published in Great Britain in November 2005 by

The Policy Press
University of Bristol
Fourth Floor
Beacon House
Queen's Road
Bristol BS8 1QU
UK

Tel +44 (0)117 331 4054
Fax +44 (0)117 331 4093
e-mail tpp-info@bristol.ac.uk
www.policypress.org.uk

© Margaret Ledwith 2005

Reprinted 2006, 2007

British Library Cataloguing in Publication Data
A catalogue record for this book is available from the British Library.

Library of Congress Cataloging-in-Publication Data
A catalog record for this book has been requested.

ISBN 978 1 86134 695 7 paperback

A hardcover version of this book is also available

Margaret Ledwith is Reader in Community Development at St Martin's College, UK.

Cover design by Qube Design Associates, Bristol.
Printed and bound in Great Britain by Henry Ling, Ltd, Dorchester.

For Grace

Contents

Tables and figures

Foreword

Margaret Ledwith's book is one that must be read by scholars, students and community activists, indeed, by all civic-minded individuals. She offers an eminently readable theory and practice for making democracy work from the bottom up, community by community, in an age when corporations and governments are weakening popular rights and undermining social needs. In her chapters, she models the approach she recommends, wonderfully merging conceptual and practical matters in regard to community development. Few books of scholarly merit move so seamlessly between theoretical and practical matters as does this one. Her thoughtful chapters offer a searching review of the literature while also pulsing with the author's own experience in community activism. In these ways, the pages connect scholarship, practice and autobiography to the tenor of our troubled times. With exemplary compactness, my colleague Margaret Ledwith rethinks community organising, critical pedagogy and feminism within the context of globalisation and British politics on the one hand, while reflecting on the legacies of two philosophical landmarks of the last century, Paulo Freire and Antonio Gramsci. Such comfortable travelling from autobiography to philosophy to history and to social justice activism is the outcome of her own productive years as an activist and scholar.

What a pleasure it is to read her continuing contributions now, nearly a decade after I first met Margaret in Omaha, Nebraska, at the third annual Pedagogy of the Oppressed Conference in April 1997. Before and after that gathering, an international debate has been underway about the very questions she takes up in this volume, into which it makes a major and hopeful statement.

As this book makes clear, we live in complex times which require complex thinking from the bottom up to deal with the global policies being imposed from the top down. Hard-won rights of working families are eroding as quickly as the environment itself. What is sometimes called the 'social contract' is being rewritten unilaterally now by multinational conglomerates who have wielded enormous power since the end of the Cold War and the emergence of a borderless one-world market. A *religion of the marketplace* has emerged whereby market forces are considered too sacred to be touched by local and social concerns; human needs that contradict market needs are fast becoming expendable; indeed, it appears that the market religion is superseding regional planning, community desires and elected governments at all levels. As vast power collects in the hands of a few world businesses, how can communities, citizens and families educate and organise themselves to protect their political rights, their livelihoods, homes, neighbourhoods, children, health and environment? The wealthy who benefit greatly from this new world order live protected from the consequences of their own policies – with their guarded and gated residences, their private pristine vacation retreats, their private concierge medical care, their private health clubs, their private jets, yachts, and limos to ferry them about.

Unlike the privileged, the great bulk of the world live in communities undermined by policies favouring the wealthy and the corporations. This book is written for them. All those who work for democracy and social justice, who oppose racism and sexism and favour solidarity across difference need to learn from each other about our successes and failures in educating and organising for transformation. A great deal is at stake and this book helps us know how to do our work better.

Ira Shor
Professor, City University of New York Graduate Centre

Acknowledgements

I wish to acknowledge the ways in which my analysis has become more incisive due to the lived experience of:

Wendy Derbyshire, White community activist and organic intellectual, who continues to stimulate my thinking on the intersection of class and gender.

Paula Asgill, Black activist and critical educator, who shared with me her insights into the complexity of gender and 'race' over the years before her sudden and premature death in May 2005.

As well as the many other people who have shared their life stories and their different 'ways of knowing' with me.

Glossary

Action/reflection: the foundation of community development praxis, where our knowledge base is developed through reflection on action, and our subsequent action is informed by this analysis.

Civil society: in Gramscian theory, civil society is the site in which the dominant ideas of the ruling class invade our minds persuading us that their way of seeing the world is *common sense*. The institutions of civil society which engage us in life – the family, media, schools, religious organisations, community groups, and so forth – play a role in getting us to consent to ideas that favour the already privileged in society.

Codifications: in Freirean pedagogy, these are representations of familiar local situations that stimulate critical debate leading to consciousness of the structural sources of oppression in society. They can take the form of photographs, video, drawings, drama and so on.

Communitarianism: a view of community as a homogeneous unity in which values of mutuality and reciprocity are seen as natural and lead to self-help and social cohesion, founded on the ideas of Etzioni, in particular. This is not only a denial of conflict and competing interests in community, but it dilutes the radical concepts of community development into a model of self-help rather than liberation.

Conscientisation: translated from the Portuguese, *conscientização*, Freire used this concept for the process of becoming critically aware of the structural forces of power which shape people's lives as a precondition for critical action for change.

Critical alliance: these are strategic alliances across difference, which are built on the collective strength of diversity in mutual collective action for social justice.

Critical analysis: refers to the theories and conceptual tools with which to analyse practice so that subsequent action is targeted at the source, not the symptoms, of oppression and therefore has the potential to bring about change for social justice.

Critical consciousness: involves the "dynamic between critical thought and critical action" (Shor, 1993, p 32). This is the stage of consciousness needed for the empowerment to collectively act in relation to the wider contexts of power from local to global.

Critical pedagogy: refers to that type of learning which is based on a mutual search rooted in a "profound love for the world and for people" (Freire, 1996, p 70). It is a democratic process of education which encourages critical consciousness as the basis of transformative collective action.

Cultural invasion: is a Freirean concept which captures the way that the values, beliefs, ideology, cultural norms and practices of a dominant culture are superimposed on the culture of those it oppresses. It links to Gramsci's concept of *hegemony*.

Dialogue: in Freirean pedagogy, is a mutual, respectful communication between people which engages the heart and mind, the intellect and emotions, which Freire saw as the basis of praxis.

Dichotomous thought: refers to a binary, either/or way of seeing the world that defines one thing in relation to its opposite, with a subject/object power implicit in the relationship, for example, working-class/middle-class, male/female, White/Black.

Difference: is shorthand for the wide range of social differences that create our identities, and which are related to the process of discrimination, for example, 'race', class, gender, faith, ethnicity, age, sexuality, 'dis'ability and so forth.

Discrimination: refers to the process by which people are disadvantaged by their social identity and therefore given unequal access to rights, resources, opportunities and power. Its consequence is oppression, and "it is a major obstacle to dignity, equality and social justice" (Thompson, 2003, p 78).

Empowerment: people have their dignity and self-respect restored through empowerment, which is the consequence of critical consciousness: the understanding that life chances are prescribed by structural discrimination, an insight which brings with it the freedom to take action to bring about change for social justice.

Enlightenment: this is the philosophy that developed in western Europe in the 17th and 18th centuries, which rejected previous supernatural ways of making sense of the world in favour of an objective, rational, unemotional, scientific knowledge embedded in masculinity.

Environmental justice: calls for action to redress exploitation of the environment by capitalism which is destroying biodiversity and causing climate change, endangered species, pollution and degradation of land and water resources. The impact is experienced disproportionately by already disadvantaged communities and poorer nations, and so is inextricably linked to social justice.

False consciousness: refers to the unquestioning view of the world in which subordinate groups accept their reality in passive and fatalistic ways, leaving the power and privilege of dominant groups unchallenged.

Feminism: feminist theory in community development places patriarchy as an oppressive force alongside that of class and 'race', seeking to create a diverse world where peace, cooperation, participation and sustainability offer a force to change the essentially exploitative system created by capitalism.

Globalisation: refers to the acceleration of capitalism's global reach by the most powerful systems in the West, exploiting the most vulnerable people and environments in the world for economic gain, and invading other cultures with a western worldview which reproduces discrimination on a complex global level.

Hegemony: concepetualises the ways in which one class maintains dominance over the rest of society by a subtle system of coercion and consent. Coercion is maintained through the law, police and armed forces, and ideological persuasion, Gramsci's important contribution gives insight into the way that our minds are colonised by dominant ideas through the institutions of civil society – the family, religious organisations, schools, and so on.

Magical consciousness: is Freire's concept for a fatalistic, disempowered and passive way of seeing the world

Metanarratives: are theories which attempt to explain universal, collective experience, but in doing so reduce diversity to a naively simplistic unity, subsuming difference shaped by gender, 'race', ethnicity, age, sexuality, 'dis'ability, and so forth.

Naive consciousness: is Freire's concept for partial empowerment which relates to the symptoms of oppression, engaging with single issues rather than the underlying roots of injustice.

Narratives: people's personal stories contribute to collective narratives, which express the hopes and fears, needs and strengths that are the basis of community development theory and practice.

Neoliberalism: refers to a free market non-interventionist state which emphasises the individual, and justifies the deregulation of trade and finance.

New Labour: maintaining the neoliberal principles of a free market, the Third Way politics of the Blair government, influenced by communitarianism, locates community/civil society as the interface between people and the state, building its modernisation agenda on community partnerships.

New Right: an ideology which supported a free market economy rooted in a politics of individualism, associated with Thatcherism in the UK.

Oppression: is the outcome of discrimination. While categories of discrimination can be seen as class, 'race', gender, ethnicity, and so forth, the forms of oppression which result are classicism, racism, sexism, xenophobia, and so forth, which are mostly expressed at a cultural level (Thompson, 2003).

Participation: true participation is achieved in community development through the empowerment of people to engage in collective action for justice and democracy from a critical perspective.

Pluralist community work: believes that there is a multiplicity of competing power bases in society, mediated by the state, and that community work is only capable of ameliorative small-scale neighbourhood change and piecemeal reforms.

Positivism: is the basis of sociology's claim to a scientific paradigm which measures human behaviour, often in a decontextualised way and with little concern for the more intangible intuitive, emotional or feeling aspects of being human. People are perceived as objects in either/or categories based on dichotomous thought. This is a consequence of the Enlightenment's emphasis on rational thought and a consensus view of society (Dominelli, 1997).

Praxis: a unity of theory and practice, which, in community development, involves theory generated in action, the link between knowledge and power through critical consciousness which leads to critical action.

Prejudice: can be seen as the expression of discrimination at a personal level in overt or covert ways, and involves judgmental attitudes which are based on stereotyping and resist reason or evidence (Thompson, 2003).

Problem-posing: the essence of Freirean pedagogy: people are encouraged to ask thought-provoking questions and "to question answers rather than merely to answer questions" (Shor, 1993, p 26). This calls for strong democratic values as the basis of a mutual, transformative learning context where educators expect to be co-learners.

Radical community development: is committed to the role of community work in achieving transformative change for social and environmental justice, and develops analysis and practice which move beyond symptoms to the root causes of oppression.

Social justice: for radical community development social justice aims to create equal worth, equal rights, opportunities for all and the elimination of inequalities reinforced by poverty (Commission for Social Justice, 1994).

Notes on the author

Margaret Ledwith lives in Lancaster where she is Reader in Community Development at St Martin's College. She has worked for many years in community settings in Scotland and North West England. Vietnamese refugees in Montrose, North East Scotland, challenged her thinking and changed her direction. David Alexander and Ralph Ruddock, critical adult educators, introduced her to the conceptual tools to analyse power and privilege in the world, but the most critical experience of all was when these theories came together with everyday lives. The privilege of seven years as a community worker in Hattersley, among the harsh realities of the lives of local people, did more than anything else to sharpen her understanding of power and oppression in society today. This was the context in which her search for praxis finally became a unity: where theory came alive in everyday experience, and made sense. Now, the benefits of these insights give authenticity to her teaching, research and publishing and her ongoing commitment to social justice and environmental justice. Her theoretical analysis is embedded in that of Paulo Freire and Antonio Gramsci, from which it develops into a Freirean-feminist pedagogy as a basis for reclaiming the radical agenda for community development.

Opening thoughts

Radical community development

In our times, we face escalating crises of justice and sustainability on a global scale. Social divisions cleaved by poverty erode people's human rights both within and between countries to an unjustifiable level. The environment is increasingly depleted by consumer lifestyles that neglect a responsibility to live in balance with the natural world. Never has there been a more important opportunity for community development to redefine its radical agenda and to engage with injustice in the process of change.

The ideas that are woven through this book are based on five vital points, which I would like you to bear in mind:

- Radical community development is committed to collective action for social and environmental justice.
- This begins in a process of empowerment through critical consciousness, and grows through participation in local issues.
- A critical approach calls for an analysis of power and discrimination in society.
- The analysis needs to be understood in relation to dominant ideas and the wider political context.
- Collective action, based on this analysis, focuses on the root causes of discrimination rather than the symptoms.

Community development begins in the everyday lives of local people. This is the initial context for sustainable change. It is founded on a process of empowerment and participation. Empowerment involves a form of critical education that encourages people to question their reality: this is the basis of collective action and is built on principles of participatory democracy. In a process of action and reflection, community development grows through a diversity of local projects that address issues faced by people in community. Through campaigns, networks and alliances, this action develops a local:global reach that aims to transform the structures of oppression that diminish local lives. A critical approach calls for a unity of theory and practice (praxis). Informed by anti-discriminatory analysis, and in a symbiotic process of action and reflection, critical analysis deepens in relation to practical experience. In this way, theory is generated in action, and in turn action becomes more critical through analysis. Inspired by a vision of a more just, equitable and sustainable world, this aspiration is not only a possibility, but a necessity.

There is an urgency for community development to reclaim its radical agenda. "We cannot go on the way we have been doing based on the way we have been thinking ... the resultant human tragedies will fuel misery and violence, as well as further ecological damage" (Reason, 2002, pp 3-15). In these ways, the practice of a more just society starts in the personal everyday experiences that shape people's lives. It builds on grassroots community activism, developing projects that are based on sustainable living, local economies and human values, but reaches out in alliance to change the root causes that give rise to discrimination.

The process of community development is based on confidence, critical consciousness and collectivity, consciousness being the linchpin between the two. Confidence grows as people begin to question their reality, and act together for change. Collective action grows in strength as individuals form groups, groups identify issues and develop projects, and projects form alliances that have the potential to become social movements. This process is cemented together by what is popularly referred to as social capital (Putnam, 2000): the connections between people that are based on values of trust, mutuality, reciprocity and dignity, and which result in conviviality, compassion and cooperation. A critical engagement with community resonates outwards in common humanity for people facing injustice everywhere. People perceive that they are part of a greater unity, a more coherent whole, rather than alienated fragments without the power to change the issues that are affecting their lives. In this sense, social capital becomes transferable and transformative. The hopelessness that gives rise to anger or apathy becomes a more dignified and determined hopefulness. A world held in common is one in which we are able to reach across all aspects of difference to act together on issues that are wrong. In these ways, an altered way of 'knowing' the world (epistemology) results in changed ways of 'being' in the world (ontology).

The full collective potential of community development is not being realised. This is due, in large part, to the divide between theory and practice that results in "actionless thought" and "thoughtless action" (Johnston cited in Shaw, 2004, p 26). This tendency to emphasise 'doing' at the expense of 'thinking' renders community work vulnerable to the manipulations of the state. Gary Craig captures some of the consequences of this in current times:

Community work is too often drawn into the latest fashions of government policy agendas because that is where the funding is, rather than developing and maintaining a clear analysis to inform action. Increasingly, the emphasis on training seems to be on skills to the exclusion of thinking about the theory and politics of community work (at both micro and macro levels): there remains a paucity of good literature to help students think through the implications of their work. Government, on the other hand, has implicitly recognised the lessons of the CDPs [Community Development Projects] in that it now provides an employment base which is fragmented, short-term and insecure. I think that practice is dominated by the policy and political context rather than creating it. (Craig, in Shaw, 2004, p 42)

In response to this fundamental problem, that is the theory:practice divide that gives rise to state domination rather than grassroots liberation, this book develops a critical analysis for a radical approach to community development practice that has social justice and participatory democracy at its heart. It leaves the reader in no doubt about what it is, how to analyse it, and how to 'do' it! As I have stressed, the key to this approach lies in praxis: the unity of theory and practice, action and reflection, thinking and doing. In order to achieve this, every stage of the process is rooted in the strong ideological base that informs community development. Democratic values of respect, dignity, reciprocity and mutuality together form a practical framework for checking the validity of everything we do in the name of community development, from personal encounters to global action. I will refer to this as an *ideology of equality*. Through this ideological lens, our skills are shaped and our theories evolve. It provides consonance, a system of checks and balances that ensures that we remain true to our purpose throughout every aspect of our work. This is the critical pedagogy of Paulo Freire re-visioned for our current times.

The use of personal narratives to reveal the political nature of our lives is fundamental to Freirean pedagogy (Freire, 1972). In reflection on experience, we engage in what Freire saw as a process of "denunciation and annunciation": the "act of analyzing a dehumanizing reality, [and to] denounce it while announcing its transformation" (Freire, 1985, p 57). This narrative approach also engages with feminist pedagogy locating the *personal as political* by linking voice to narrative through "little stories" (Griffiths, 2003, p 81) that make the vital connection between the deeply personal and the profoundly political.

My personal journey to praxis

In order to understand the relevance of ideas, it is important to understand the ways in which they have been germinated. My own story is one of a quest for praxis to give my practice a critical dimension. My questioning started early on when, as a child, I knew that some things were just not right but did not get any satisfactory answers. As a young teacher in the classroom, I saw issues of power acted out before my eyes. Some children in my care had their life chances enhanced by privilege and others were subordinated, their confidence diminished, their expectations lowered (Shropshire and Middleton, 1999). I could see that the vastly different identities of the children I taught were shaped by their early experience far more than the innate 'cleverness' by which they were judged for academic success by the state. I could also see that the competitive nature of education confirmed failure in those whose self-esteem already faltered in the face of the harshness of their lives outside the school building.

Take, for instance, Jennifer O'Leary's story. She was just six when her father left, and her mother put their three children into a local children's home. The daughter of Jennifer's 'houseparents' at the children's home was Yasmin Jones. They were both in my class. Yasmin assumed superiority; she needed that sense of self to survive. She was a child of mixed heritage in a racist society. Jennifer's brothers, Dermot and Devlin, were in classes older and younger than Jennifer. Every Friday, Dermot would stand on the outer step of the classroom anxiously looking for his mother who had told him that one weekend she would come and get them back.

As a young teacher, in these ways, I witnessed hegemonic forces shaping personal lives in my classroom. Yet, my teacher education had told me this was an apolitical space, decontextualised from the real world. Alan, a colleague, rubbed his hands together in the staff room at the beginning of each new academic year proclaiming, "Well that's got that lot sorted out: these will make it and those don't stand a chance". Life chances prescribed in the first decade by an agent of the state acting unconsciously, Alan played his part well. His words resonated inside me, and teacher education not having provided me with any answers, I got involved with the beginning of the national adult literacy campaign seeking to put right the damage done by schooling.

Later, I found myself in Scotland working with Vietnamese refugees traumatised by the rejection of the Western world as they floated adrift on the South China Sea. They changed my worldview with their stories of giving birth on rusty landing craft, of being separated from children, of hope and hopelessness. They taught me more about life than I could ever teach them, and I was desolate in the knowledge that, in the West, they would be at the bottom of an unjust system, their hopes dashed. After this experience, my search led me to Edinburgh University and a Master's degree in community development.

It was David Alexander, the adult educator, whose passion in relation to Antonio Gramsci and Paulo Freire had a profound impact on me. At the same time, emerging feminist theory offered critiques of these two thinkers that exposed their patriarchal assumptions. Feminist ideas inspired me as a woman on both an intellectual and emotional level. In similar vein, Peter Mayo (2004, p 10) refers to the "fusion of reason and emotion" contained in Freire as touching people in a holistic way that reaches beyond the limitations of the intellect. This was a critical time for me. I found a greater synthesis of action and reflection, of doing and thinking, of theory and practice and it gave me a glimpse of the potential of a more coherent, integrated praxis. The hegemonic function of schooling, which had eluded me for so long, was starkly exposed. My naïvety shocked me; these ideas were so obvious I could not believe they had failed to come to me naturally. Of course, it is not quite as simple as that. Gramsci (1971) emphasised the insidious nature of *hegemony*, the power of dominant ideas to infiltrate our thoughts as *common sense* when they make no sense at all, and the role of critical education in raising consciousness.

A more critical consciousness not only changed the nature of my understanding of the insidious nature of power, but it changed my engagement with the world. I saw the world in different ways, naming power and discrimination in action. This is the point at which I entered a decade of my life spent in grassroots activism in Manchester. My work in community development was at first located in the multicultural context of the city, followed by a very different experience in Hattersley, a largely White Manchester 'overspill' or 'peripheral' estate.

A critical approach

Community development begins in the everyday reality of people's lives by "extraordinarily re-experiencing the ordinary" (Shor, 1992, p 122). It is a praxis that locates the silenced stories of those who are marginalised and excluded at the heart of any theory of change for social justice. Their stories are the basis of our theory and our practice. In a process of action and reflection, theory builds from experience. Praxis is the synthesis of theory and practice to a point where they become a unity, where theory develops in action. The key to this process is problem-posing or *problematising* (Freire, 1972). People are encouraged to ask thought-provoking questions and "to question answers rather than merely to answer questions" (Shor, in McLaren and Leonard, 1993, p 26). This critical approach to community development exposes structures of power and the way these impact on personal lives. However, critical consciousness is not liberating until it becomes a collective process for change. Freire did not believe in self-liberation:

> Liberating education is a social process of illumination.... Even when you individually feel yourself most free, if this feeling is not a social feeling, if you are not able to use your recent freedom to help others to be free by transforming the totality of society, then you are exercising only an individualist attitude towards empowerment or freedom. (Freire, in Shor and Freire, 1987, p 109)

The body of knowledge that informs community development praxis grows in dynamic relation with changing communities, changing contexts and changing knowledge. The way that we understand our world shapes the way we live in our world. It is by challenging the way we see the world that we open ourselves to new worldviews, new possibilities for creating a world that is just, sustainable, and non-violent, and this new understanding, in turn, changes the way we live our lives.

These opening thoughts give you a glimpse of some of the critical aspects of my story. The relevance of this narrative approach is that it gives you insight into the personal experiences that are woven through my ideas, illuminating the points I make, and grounding them in lived experience. Human inquiry is a lived experience, and is an integral component of community development. I see action and reflection as a process of search, of research, of curiosity and a desire to understand, driven by a commitment to change things for the better. It begins in lived reality, in context, and it reflects the whole tangled complexity of life. It explores different ways of knowing; it also challenges the authority of knowing and relocates authenticity in the reality of people's lives, giving silenced voices the right to be heard.

All this may sound chaotic in its complexity, but there are theories, conceptual tools and models that help make sense of the process. In contributing to a body of knowledge that is based on countering discrimination, exploitation and injustice, we push beyond the constraints of our limited understanding to explore new possibilities. Breaking free from a controlled and controlling view of the world, one that we are taught to see as inevitable, we make the choice to step into uncharted territory. This is not only liberating and challenging, but at times frightening and unpredictable. The important point to remember is that it carries the hope that a more socially and environmentally just future based on participatory democracy is a possibility.

A critical approach to community development begins in people's lives in community, but reaches beyond the symptoms of injustice to the root causes by making critical connections between personal experiences and the oppressive political structures that perpetuate discrimination. Collective action is the process by which people join together to bring about change. If we fail to take our practice beyond the good work that goes into local issues and local projects, we fail to realise this potential, and our work is good but not transformative; it is making local lives easier, tolerable, more pleasant, but is not addressing the root source of the problems that give rise to injustice.

Let me illustrate my point. If, in my practice in community, I notice that there are an increasing number of people sleeping rough or in temporary accommodation, and I work with the local community to set up a night shelter and a soup kitchen, this is good practice, but not transformative. It is not transformative because it is dealing with the symptoms but failing to reach the causes of the problem. My analysis is not going deep enough to identify the reasons that give rise to this escalating social problem, and the temptation is to stop at the project stage where it remains a local issue. Consequently, the forces generating the problem will continue unabated. To address structural oppression, collective action, through networks and alliances, harnesses collective power beyond local issues to movements for change at national and global levels.

There is much good practice evidenced in community development, but its weaknesses lie in it i) remaining local, and ii) having a propensity to divide theory from practice. Do I hear some of you say that this is impossible given the constraints that keep us working with short-term funding, within the parameters of government policies, using indicators that are imposed from outside and limit and fragment our practice? I remind you that, as a profession, we have always been targeted to change things for the better but not rock the boat too much; it is the nature of the ambivalent relationship between community work and state (Shaw, 2004). This limits our practice to tokenism, and it fails our professed aim to achieve social justice. Gary Craig puts his finger on the button when, as I said earlier, he names the way in which we have become "dominated by the policy and political context rather than creating it" and have allowed ourselves to be preoccupied with "skills to the exclusion of thinking about the theory and politics of community work" (Craig, in Shaw, 2004, p 42).

Community development needs to redefine its critical potential within the current political context if it is to realise its social justice intention. The body of knowledge that informs community development needs to grow in dynamic equilibrium with the rapidly changing political context, and we need to engage with and contribute to that body of knowledge if we are to achieve a political analysis worthy of action for a just and sustainable future. This book contributes to a radical, anti-discriminatory practice that is capable of transformative change.

A critical approach to practice calls for reflection on action, and the use of critical questions keeps us focused:

- How is your practice influenced by an anti-discriminatory analysis?
- In what way are dominant ideas and national policy changes impacting on the diverse lives of local people?
- What evidence is there that your practice contributes to change for social justice and environmental justice?
- How can you extend collective action beyond the boundaries of community to build national, international and global alliances?

In order to develop a critical approach to practice, I attempt to weave a greater synthesis of theory and practice through this book. Throughout, I choose to emphasise the diverse political nature of the categories 'White' and 'Black' by using capital letters. In the same way, I emphasise the socially constructed nature of 'dis'ability and 'race'. I hope the ideas I share engage you and inspire you to go into the world with new determination.

ONE

Why empower?

A brief history of radical community development

Let us begin this exploration by considering the roots of radical practice. Community development began its theoretical life in Nigeria between 1927 and 1949 with the work of Batten, who was critical of the use of community development for colonial domination (Popple, 1995). British community work emerged much later from the charity work of the Anglican Church and the university settlement movement. This was prompted by the suffering created by urban poverty, and tended to be philanthropic rather than revolutionary. It was based on a Victorian ideology of self-help that gave rise to the cooperative movement, adult education (the Workers' Educational Association was established in 1903), friendly societies and trade unions (Dominelli, 1990; Popple, 1995).

A move away from benevolent paternalism towards a philosophy of liberation led to a change in class and gender consciousness that gathered momentum as the 20th century progressed. For example, Sylvia Pankhurst adapted ideas of self-help from Jane Addams' Hull House, the settlement in Chicago that Addams had modelled on Toynbee Hall. With her group, the East London Federation of Suffragettes, Sylvia Pankhurst set up a cooperative toy factory to provide employment, with a creche based on progressive theories of education through play. The Gunmaker's Arms was transformed into a health clinic for mothers and babies, renamed The Mother's Arms. And during the First World War, 1914-18, when rents soared, she got involved in community action, supporting families to occupy empty houses. Similarly, in Glasgow, the Women's Housing Association organised a mass tenants' strike to coincide with threatened industrial action, causing the government to regulate rents (Rowbotham, 1992). Collective action became a tool of women's suffrage and of the National Unemployed Workers' Movement throughout the early years of the 20th century, culminating in the General Strike of 1926.

In response to concerns about escalating unemployment in the inter-war years, community centres were built on new housing estates with the aim of creating greater unity by integrating marginalised groups. So, much as the university settlements confronted middle-class philanthropy with working-class need, community centres were seen to offer a form of social work intervention to ease unrest and disaffection. In the 1950s, UK community work practice became influenced by theory that emerged from North America based on the work of the Canadian, Murray Ross. This inspired a new approach to neighbourhood and interagency work (Popple, 1995). The theory and practice of community work in the UK became more coherent in the following decade.

Community work began to emerge as a distinct occupation with a strong educational component in the 1960s, following the Younghusband Report (1959), which identified community organisation as a key component of social work, based on the North American model. Community organisation was seen as an approach that supported people to define their own needs and identify ways in which these may be met. Based on Younghusband's definition, Kuenstler (1961) presented the first collection of community work material directly relevant to the British context, in relation to social need and current practice at the time. This was the beginning of British community work as we know it today.

The term 'community development' gradually became applied to community work that was based in local neighbourhoods. In 1968, the Gulbenkian Report, based on research into the role of community work in the UK, located community work at the interface between people and social change (Calouste Gulbenkian Foundation, 1968). It defined community work as a full-time professional practice based in neighbourhoods, which helped local people to decide, plan and take action to meet their needs with the help of outside resources. Within that, key components were improving the delivery of local services, developing interagency coordination, and influencing policy and planning (Calouste Gulbenkian Foundation, 1968). In its broadest sense, the report recommended that community work be a recognised part of professional practice for teachers, social workers, the clergy, health workers, architects, planners, administrators and others with a community-based service. There was a fundamental split in the recommendations between educationalists, who saw community work as essentially adult/community education, and others who placed more emphasis on planning and service delivery. In contrast, Scotland, particularly after the publication of the Alexander Report in 1975, has chosen to place much greater emphasis on community development as community learning (Scottish Education Department,

1975). In the final outcome, despite concerns expressed by community workers, the Gulbenkian Report chose to gloss over the contradictory and political aspects of the work (Craig et al, 1982; Popple, 1995).

A number of other influential reports were published around this time; including that of the Seebohm Committee (Seebohm Report, 1968), which recommended the expansion of community work, particularly as a dimension of social services provision, and the Skeffington Report (Skeffington Report, 1969), which recommended increased public participation in urban planning.

Community work rose against what it saw as "the social control functions of both the welfare state and the state sponsored caring professions. Community work presented itself as a radical alternative to social work, which it caricatured as 'soft policing'. Similarly, youth work was dismissed as a means of simply keeping working class kids off the streets. The welfare state, it was suggested, was designed to contain rather than cure poverty" (Jacobs, 1994, p 156). It is this commitment to get beyond the symptoms to the root causes of oppression that defines radical community work.

This was a time of transition and change: 1968 is widely acknowledged as a critical juncture in world history, described by Popple (1995, p 15) as a year of "revolt, rebellion and reaction throughout the world". It was a year when civil disobedience erupted in the form of 'race' riots, student demonstrations, civil rights marches and anti-Vietnam protests, and which witnessed the assassinations of Martin Luther King and Robert Kennedy. At the same time, there were significant developments in community work practice: the Urban Programme was set up in 1968, and the Community Development Projects emerged from it in 1969. The Urban Programme was a Labour government response to social unrest around unemployment, immigration and 'race' relations, to allay tension generated by Enoch Powell's 'rivers of blood' speech; the Community Development Projects targeted 12 communities in poverty based on an analysis of Keith Joseph's "cycle of transmitted deprivation" theory (Rutter and Madge, 1976, p 3). The grassroots experience of the impact of poverty on people's lives led the project workers to reject this reactionary theory in favour of radical/structural Marxist analyses of discrimination. The translation of Gramsci's *Prison notebooks* and Freire's *Pedagogy of the oppressed* into English had an immense impact on community work praxis, as did Alinsky's *Reveille for radicals*, well-thumbed copies of which poked out of the pockets of any activist at the time. In these ways, the theory and practice of radical community work came together.

The distinct approach of the profession began to be recognised and expansion took place in both the voluntary and statutory sectors, but as the 1970s progressed there was more emphasis on state sponsorship with the inevitable consequence that community workers were increasingly located in a contradictory position – working with local people to demand better public services at the same time as being employed by the local state which provided those services. Since that time, there has been a split between the radical agenda, which believes that community work is a locus of change within the struggle for transformation of the structures of society that are the root cause of oppression; and the pluralist agenda, which believes that there is a multiplicity of competing power bases in society, mediated by the state, and that community work is only capable of ameliorative small-scale neighbourbood change and piecemeal reforms. The radical tradition, including class, feminist and anti-racist models of practice (for example, M. Mayo, 1977; Craig et al, 1982; Ohri et al, 1982; Dominelli, 1990), built its knowledge base on critical consciousness and what are termed 'hard issues' of social justice and sustainability. The pluralist agenda rejected a wider political analysis to focus on skills and local 'soft issues' such as interagency work and service delivery (Henderson and Thomas, 1980; Thomas, 1983; Twelvetrees, 1991).

Working in and against the state, revolution or reform, has presented an ongoing tension for community work, with the state as both employer and oppressor. After the election of the Thatcher government, the anti-state approach of radical community workers became an increasingly ineffective mechanism with which to challenge the declining social democratic consensus and the reactionary ideology of the New Right (Lees and Mayo, 1984). Waddington (1994, p 6) referred to the Conservative government's moralising ideology in which "'enterprise' replaced 'greed' in the political lexicon, and the cultivation of 'national unity' … disguised the active reinforcement of social divisions".

Prior to this, Cockburn's (1977) challenge was that community work's function as state-sponsored activity is one of defusing escalating conflict by diverting energy into forms of participation that give an illusion of democracy. In reality, this serves the interests of the state by maintaining the status quo. This identified a potential contradiction where the community worker could be unconsciously acting in a placatory way to further the interests of capital. Waddington (1979) responded by arguing that community work's quest for a just socialist society is inextricably bound up with the state, and that analyses of that relationship must be central to our practice. Blagg and Derricourt (1982) entered this debate, advocating that we move beyond a crude anti-state approach to identify a conflict model that operates within the state to counter consensus models of community work practice promoted by the Gulbenkian, Seebohm and Skeffington Reports, and perpetuated in the more pluralist approaches of the Henderson and Thomas tradition (Barr, 1991).

Barr (1991, p 129) quotes Peter Marris's analysis, which slices through these positions to state:

> So long as government policy and community action justify themselves by the same ideals, community action has scope for influence on government's own terms, even if its ideology is in other ways radically opposed to the assumptions of government.... Movements for change are empowered by the convergence of social ideals expressed in principles of action ... [and we need] to incorporate into those struggles a demand for effective, open, collective planning, as a crucial part of carrying out any practical ideal of social justice.

Within this model, as Barr (1991, p 129) notes, "the state, particularly given its planning powers, remains a target for influence but can also be a partner for change". With this in mind, and more than a decade later, with the state courting community partnership, where is the evidence of radical community work practice?

The political context

Beveridge and the post-war consensus on welfare

In times of war, the external threat and the state's need for healthy soldiers always improve the collective will for a healthy nation and this provided the consensus for the Beveridge Report, the basis of the modern welfare state. Based on principles of cooperation, there was a "pooling of risk so that the fortunate shared the cost of supporting the less fortunate" (Morris, 1994, p 43). Wartime Britain received the Beveridge Report with optimism. Public reaction was so enthusiastic that there were queues outside the London branch of HMSO from the night before publication – and it rapidly sold out. Beveridge was based on three guiding principles: first, the opportunity for revolutionary change afforded by the war context; second, an attack on the five giant evils – Want, Disease, Ignorance, Squalor and Idleness; and third, cooperation between the state and the individual (Timmins,

1996). Beveridge was hailed as a national hero, even though we would now say that his approach to welfare "hid the giants Racism and Sexism, and the fights against them, behind statues to the Nation and the White Family" (Williams, 1989, p 162). The post-war Labour government implemented these welfare reforms, and state consensus sustained expansion well into the 1970s.

Despite its high ideals, the Beveridge Report's aims were never fully realised. In the early 1960s, Peter Townsend and Brian Abel-Smith 'rediscovered' the nature of poverty in the UK by defining relative poverty, its prevalence and its impact (Mack and Lansley, 1985). Television documentaries such as *Cathy Come Home* heightened public awareness of social problems, and in time new pressure groups, such as the Child Poverty Action Group and Shelter, were formed.

The New Right emerged as an intellectual and political power, as both a product of the global economic recession after 1973 and as a reaction to the expansive welfare spending of the 1960s. "It posed a clear ideological challenge to the conventional wisdom and forced a range of important and neglected issues back to a central place in the analysis of the role of the state in welfare" (George and Wilding, 1994, p 15). As economic growth faltered, the perceived burden of the welfare budget increased and the New Right rhetoric of the 'welfare scrounger' took hold. The age of individualism and 'trickle-down' theories was born and gave an ideological backdrop for the welfare revolution that was to follow.

The New Right and Thatcherism

Under Thatcherism, Britain of the mid-1980s was characterised by the full and unmitigated ascendance of New Right politics, an ideology that supports a free market economy rooted in a politics of individualism. This did not occur in a vacuum. The welfare state ideology survived in the collective consciousness into the 1980s, but the context for change was set by a world economic recession and the welfare burden of escalating unemployment. However, in a democracy change has to be accompanied by popular consensus, and one of the ways of achieving this is to use negative imagery. New Right rhetoric, blaming the victims of poverty, painted evocative stereotypes of the 'welfare scrounger' that divided the poor into deserving and undeserving. This was sewn into the minds of the people with such images as Norman Tebbit's 'on yer bike' approach to job searching; and the demonisation of single parents by Peter Lilley's rendition to Parliament of Gilbert and Sullivan: "I've got a little list, I've got a little list of young ladies who get pregnant just to jump the housing list." These divide and rule politics set people in poverty against each other.

This conceptual paradox, one of need set against greed, made an immediate impact on communities. Social welfare became perceived as a burden rather than a collective responsibility and a moral right. Notions of collective social responsibility, which had formed the bedrock for the post-war welfare state, gave way to a competitive culture driven by consumerism. The 'Thatcher revolution', fuelled by social, political and economic change, was committed to a "dismantling of the protective elements of state welfare, to breaking the power of the organised labour movement and to a reaffirmation of market forces that would bring poverty and unemployment to unprecedented levels" (Novak, 1988, p 176).

At the same time as a welfare revolution was being paved, a politics of *common sense* persuaded the British people to see the Miners' Strike of 1984-85 as an attempt to undermine democracy and liberty: an enemy of the state. Only in the course of time have the dirty tricks of the state been exposed as venting full power on the National Union of Mineworkers – the issue being not the economics of coal, but the right to organise (Milne, 1994). Margaret Thatcher perceived her hair's breadth victory as a triumph over collective organisation, and it gave her government a head of steam to bring in other major reforms. For instance, the 1986 Social Security Act promised welfare reforms unsurpassed since Beveridge, but the results were devastating, forcing vulnerable groups further onto the margins of society while the rich got richer (Cohen et al, 1996). This transfer of wealth from the poor to the rich created massive social divisions, with children becoming the single group most vulnerable to poverty (Oppenheim and Harker, 1996). Under Thatcherism, social reforms devoured rights and reduced benefits for some of the most vulnerable groups in society. These risks of poverty were further exacerbated by class, ethnicity, gender, age and 'dis'ability, "yet to suggest that poverty is evidence of structural rather than personal failing is to swim against the modern-day tide of individualism" (Witcher, in Oppenheim and Harker, 1996, p vii).

As a society, we became complicit, allowing the most vulnerable to be exploited in the interests of the powerful. "Between the 1980s and 1990s, the number of people who could objectively be described as living in poverty increased by almost 50 per cent" (Gordon and Pantazis, 1997). There was a massive transfer of wealth from the poor to the rich, with the income of the wealthiest tenth of the UK population being equal to that of the poorest half (Goodman et al, 1997). The indictment of this period is the way that poverty targeted children.

One in three children in Britain was growing up in poverty in the UK by 1997, an enormous increase from one in ten in 1979 (Flaherty et al, 2004).

The Third Way and New Labour

The neoliberal ideology that emerged as Thatcherism also developed during the same period through Reagonomics in the US, the Pinochet regime in Chile, and the International Monetary Fund (IMF) and World Bank programmes in the developing world (P. Mayo, 1999). Neoliberal political philosophy embraces: a free market economy, minimal government, economic individualism, acceptance of inequalities, moral authoritarianism, nationalism, low ecological consciousness and the welfare state as a minimal safety net (Giddens, 1998). "It is now also a feature of parties in government which have been historically socialist" (P. Mayo, 1999, p 2). Based on the premise that traditional socialism is obsolete, the Third Way has interested intellectuals and politicians not only in the UK, but in the USA, Continental Europe and Latin America.

In the UK, the Third Way is associated with the politics of New Labour, the dawn of which was the landslide election of the Blair government in 1997. A subtle change of emphasis took place. While maintaining the neoliberal principles of a free market, the Third Way located community and civil society as the interface between people and the state. This marked a distinct shift from Thatcher's attempt to convince us that there is no such thing as society. Not long after his election, Prime Minister Blair wrote: "we all depend on collective goods for our independence; and all our lives are enriched – or impoverished – by the communities to which we belong.... A key challenge of progressive politics is to use the state as an enabling force, protecting effective communities and voluntary organisations and encouraging their growth to tackle new needs, in partnership, as appropriate" (Blair, 1998, p 4). This new approach to government was informed by the thinking of Anthony Giddens (1998). New Labour combined strands of communitarianism: community as a life with meaning based on the mutual interdependence of individuals, and the role of the state in partnership with community in creating a quality of life. For the first time, we find the language of partnership with community, of bold anti-poverty statements, of a preoccupation with regeneration projects, of widening access to education. In this context, community development has more policy recognition than it has known before. But radical community development is concerned about the capacity of these policies to follow through to make a sustained difference to the lives of people in poverty when policies and practice are flawed by the absence of a structural analysis of inequality and injustice. In addition, the rhetoric of communitarianism, that of autonomous, flourishing communities founded on mutuality and reciprocity, takes on an edge of state authoritarianism. Zero tolerance policing, punitive approaches to asylum seekers, and on-the-spot fines for anti-social behaviour are indicative of policy approaches that circumvent a bottom-up empowerment model to impose top-down interventionist approaches to community (Calder, 2003).

In 1997, the Blair government inherited poverty and social divisions that had escalated during the 1980s under Thatcherism. At Toynbee Hall, in March 1999, Tony Blair delivered a speech on the legacy of Sir William Beveridge, the unanticipated high spot of which was his own personal and political commitment to end child poverty within 20 years. Going public on poverty was applauded by the social justice lobby, and a social policy programme was set to tackle child poverty, unemployment, neighbourhood deprivation and inequalities in health and educational achievement. For example, the Child Poverty Action Group found themselves for the first time working with a government that acknowledged the unacceptability of such high child poverty rates, and was encouraged by the abundance of anti-poverty policies directed at children and poor families. But, just below the surface, there are clear contradictions that exist between the interests of the state and the rights and responsibilities of parents. As Tess Ridge (2004) rightly points out, a state interest in children as future workers leads to policies that are qualitatively different from those that are concerned with creating better childhoods:

> Children who are poor are not a homogeneous group, although they are often represented as being so. Their experiences of being poor will be mediated by, among other things, their age, gender, ethnicity, health and whether or not they are disabled. In addition, children will interpret their experiences of poverty in the context of a diverse range of social, geographical and cultural settings. (Ridge, 2004, p 5)

The pledge to end child poverty by 2020 was ambitious: nevertheless the target of cutting child poverty by a quarter by 2004-05 seems to be on target on a before-housing-costs basis, and just a little short on an after-housing-costs basis. The half-term target of a 50% reduction in child poverty by 2010 will be harder to meet (Flaherty et al, 2004). Targeted anti-poverty strategies have, between 1997 and 2001, moved the UK from the highest child poverty rate in the European Union (EU) to fifth highest (Hills and Stewart, 2005). This clearly leaves much room for improvement when ending child poverty is "vital for the effectiveness, as well as the justice, of UK society" (Dornan, 2004, p 3). In spite of the generosity of the new tax credits, poverty for working lone parents, the majority of whom are women, remains high in relation to European levels, reflecting the gendered nature of poverty (Hills and Stewart, 2005). The links between women's poverty and child poverty are crucial to understanding that tackling women's poverty is fundamental to the success of any child poverty strategy. According to Ruth Lister's (2005) analysis these can be grouped around two main issues: those related to women's role as the main carers of children and managers of poverty; and those related to women's position in the labour market related to child poverty. While it is to be commended that child poverty has been put on the political agenda, and there is some welcome evidence that redistributive policies may possibly meet the initial government targets, there is real concern from campaigning bodies, like the Child Poverty Action Group, as to whether the will to continue this commitment is strong enough to propel it forward towards its 2020 goal (Platt, 2005).

Of particular relevance to community development is New Labour's swing from the business approach to regeneration of Thatcherism to what is known as the 'new localism' approach to modernisation based on community partnerships. New Labour inherited 'divided Britain': "There was an increasing concern about so-called 'worst neighbourhoods', with concentrations of poverty and worklessness and the associated problems of high crime and disorder, diminishing and dysfunctional services, empty housing and environmental decay" (Lupton and Power, 2005, p 119). In 1998, the newly formed Social Exclusion Unit (SEU) produced a report, *Bringing Britain together*, in which about 3,000 neighbourhoods were identified as having high levels of poverty, unemployment, poor health and crime, with poorer service delivery, poorer quality schools, fewer doctors' surgeries, fewer shops, and high levels of litter and vandalism. This marked the beginning of a very different policy approach that focused regeneration on poor neighbourhoods, and in 2000 the National Strategy for Neighbourhood Renewal was launched. The New Labour vision was that "within 10-20 years, no-one should be seriously disadvantaged by where they live" (SEU, 2001 cited in Lupton and Power, 2005, p 120). The main area-based programmes have been the Single

Regeneration Budget, Education Action Zones, Health Action Zones, New Deal for Communities, Sure Start, Excellence in Cities and Employment Zones, from which a plethora of initiatives has emerged aimed at reducing worklessness and crime, improving skills, health, housing and environments, and lessening social divisions. These are informed by underlying concepts, such as exclusion, multiculturalism, social capital and community, within the overriding idea of *community cohesion* as a general principle for improving the quality of life in communities. Burton (2003) identifies a divide here between rhetoric and reality, with progress hampered by the gap between theory and practice. Evidence points to the fact that community involvement is not working in practice; that "public involvement in neighbourhood regeneration work has yet to live up to its own ambitions" (Burton, 2003, p 29). In a review of the limited research evidence, he concludes that community involvement strategies are "poorly conceived, inadequately resourced and developed far too late in the cycle to be very effective" (Burton, 2003, p 28). He refers to the tokenistic nature of the process, which is supported by my own research in which a local activist identified: i) unequal power relations in partnerships, ii) top-down agendas, and iii) inappropriate funding criteria as key issues that not only hampered community development, but destroyed the enthusiasm of local activists. "Some improvements do seem to be happening, although it is not clear that they are shared by all poor neighbourhoods; indeed, some may be getting worse" (Lupton and Power, 2005, p 127).

It is too early to assess the real impact of the National Strategy for Neighbourhood Renewal, and it could be that further improvements follow. It cannot be denied that the focus on neighbourhoods is a welcome and innovative policy change, but "'neighbourhood renewal' cannot be tackled only within individual neighbourhoods, [it] depends on broader policies and economic developments" (Hills and Stewart, 2005, p 336). There are many flawed aspects to the way that policies are engaging with community, but before their lack of success results in a swing back to externally imposed agendas, it is imperative that we become more rigorous in researching better ways for bottom-up approaches to engage with this top-down willingness for partnership: "there will be no sustainable change unless communities themselves are given the power and responsibility to take action" (M. Taylor, 2000, p 48).

The need for critical approaches to community development is reflected in Gary Craig's reference to *ideological confusion* (1998, p 2). If we are uncritical in our practice, we may find ourselves naïvely supporting policies that emphasise *participation* as a further erosion of rights in favour of responsibilities, rather than a process leading to social justice and equality. The end result of this would be a continued transfer of resources away from the most vulnerable communities, with an increased emphasis on local self-help as an inadequate response to the structural forces of discrimination. Let us take a look at the political changes and the power of the ideas that have distracted us from a social justice analysis.

Globalisation

The process of globalisation has accelerated, resulting in oppression and exploitation on a grander and more complex scale. Neoliberal globalisation is the "market-organized and imposed expansion of production that emphasizes comparative advantage, free trade, export orientations, the social and spatial divisions of labour, and the absolute mobility of corporations" (Fisher and Ponniah, 2003, p 28). In other words, we find ourselves in a world where capitalism has re-formed on a global level, exploiting the most vulnerable people and environments in the world in the interests of the dominant and privileged. It is a form of corporate capitalism where the most powerful systems of the West not only dominate the world economically, but invade other cultures with a Western worldview that works on political, cultural, racial, gendered, sexual, ecological and epistemological differences. In the name of a free market economy, not only is labour exploited in the interests of capital (class), but the same structures of oppression that subordinate groups of people according to 'race', gender, age, sexuality, faith, ethnicity and 'dis'ability are being reproduced on a global level.

> Neoliberal globalization is not simply economic domination of the world but also the imposition of a monolithic thought (*pensamento unico*) that consolidates vertical forms of difference and prohibits the public from imagining diversity in egalitarian, horizontal terms. Capitalism, imperialism, monoculturalism, patriarchy, white supremacism and the domination of biodiversity have coalesced under the current form of globalization (Fisher and Ponniah, 2003, p 10).

Wealth is increasingly transferred from poor to rich countries by exploiting the labour and resources of the developing world in order to feed the consumerist greed of the West. The consequence is increased divisions both within and between countries, with the new phenomenon of corporations becoming wealthier than countries, for example the global dominance of Microsoft. Globalisation presents anti-discriminatory practice with increasingly complex, interlinking and overlapping oppressions that are poorly understood and therefore infrequently challenged. In this way, poverty becomes increasingly convoluted, and oppression becomes distant and even more concealed. It is not possible to take a critical approach to community development without having an analysis of the way in which all communities are inextricably linked on this global dimension.

Current debates related to radical community development

In 1996, Ian Cooke called for a re-evaluation of radical community work in relation to the changing political context in order to get beyond "the current lack of clarity and direction which hinders the further development of a coherent radical practice" (1996, p 7). He identified two major causes for a change in the radical agenda at the time: i) the Conservative government's approach to a free market economy and the simultaneous acceleration of globalisation, and ii) the decline of the Labour and trade union movement in favour of a more fragmented pressure group politics with the emergence of new social movements. Let me remind you that the key distinguishing feature of radical, as opposed to pluralist, practice is the political consciousness that unites people in collective action beyond the boundaries of neighbourhood to engage in wider structural change. Cooke, together with other key critical theorists (Allman, 1999, 2001; Hill, McLaren, Cole and Rikowski, 1999), advocates a political analysis that unites a politics of difference within the centrality of class.

> If radical community work requires a mission statement for the nineties and beyond then we could do worse than the words of Sivanandan (1989): "... to open one's sensibilities out to the oppression of others, the exploitation of others, the injustices and inequalities meted out to others – and to act on them, making an individual/local case into an issue, turning issues into causes and causes into movements and building in the process a new political culture, new communities of resistance that will take on power and capital and class." (Cooke, 1996, p 22)

At the same time as the debates around the future of radical community work raged, communitarianism (Etzioni, 1995, 1997) found expression in the political agenda of New Labour as a way of linking neoliberalism with *community* as a key component of its political project, locating a contradiction between its free market approach, which is a direct threat to community, and its emphasis on community and civil society.

Essentially, this preoccupation with community is founded on a conglomeration of ideas that are driven by the desire to create "a new moral, social and public order based on restored communities, without puritanism or oppression" (Etzioni, 1995, p 2). Communitarians claim to understand the functioning of a real community. They hold two fundamental beliefs: i) that normal human relationships only thrive through trust, cooperation and mutuality, and ii) that this gives rise to increased social cohesion in which democracy flourishes, promoting a more egalitarian society. They consider that conscious citizens understand the significance of shared values and attitudes driven by the social nature of being human (Dixon et al, 2005).

Etzioni (1995, 1997) builds his theory on the notion that individuals, once their own needs are met, have a responsibility to meet the needs of others through the institutions of civil society – the family, schools and a range of community organisations – through a system of values based on reciprocity and mutuality. In this way, individual rights and collective responsibilities are held in balance. Robson finds the notion of having both freedom and autonomy as nonsense in a modern Western democratic state, and nothing more than an expression of the coercion/consent of civil society as defined by Gramsci. He refers to the "rediscovery" of civil society within a communitarian ideology as "the almost total neglect of Gramsci as an authority" (Robson, 2000, p 14). From a Gramscian perspective, civil society, far from being a collective spirited expression of citizenship as rights and responsibilities, is the site in which the dominant ideas of the ruling class infiltrate people's thinking by ideological persuasion – a more powerful force than state coercion. Robson feels that the communitarian definition masks the way in which a "belief in the individual as a free and independent being with unlimited rights has been translated into a question of relative rights and unlimited responsibilities" (Robson, 2000, p 129). More than this, he warns that "subordinating or reducing social problems to an insistence on the need for rights to take second place to the stranglehold of 'responsibility' to the wider community is tantamount to a demand for an acceptance of an extension of the regulation of human behaviour" (Robson, 2000, p 134). His challenge is that the communitarian view of family and community is not based on reality. "The 'community' today is a complex matrix of intense competition between contesting groups, often class-based, struggling for a slice of the social and financial cake" (Robson, 2000, p 132). Similarly, Dixon et al (2005) identify a contradiction in communitarian philosophy in the gap between its aspirations and community reality. Rather than a unity of values, the reality is that competing worldviews give rise to different perceptions of community, human nature and individual identity that result in differing ways of engaging in community. Communities are heterogeneous contexts that "feature a complex paradigm of diverse opinions and attitudes, emotional reactions and sentimental attachments, which are discernible in the wide variety of social networks that exist in a specific locality" (Dixon et al, 2005, p 13). The community worker, within this model, faces the challenge of developing a unity of purpose across difference and diversity from which empowerment and democratic participation can lead to social change for the common good.

In summary, the thrust of Dixon et al's (2005) critique of communitarianism is that it embraces a naïve conception of the unity of community, whereas in reality there are diverse, competing worldviews. From a radical perspective, Robson (2000, p 13) takes this further, arguing that radical language has been incorporated into communitarianism and diluted as part of "more moderate approaches to social and political change ... [suggesting] not so much an acceptance of a new and revolutionary idea as much as a desire to draw such ideas closer to the breast of the dominant democratic order". His thesis is that these are reactionary politics in the guise of progressive politics, which locate us all as "'stakeholders' in a rediscovered, repackaged 'civil society'" rather than the centrality of community as a site of social change (Robson, 2000, p 14). Not only does he challenge New Labour for naïvely 'rediscovering' civil society and packaging it in the rhetoric of transformative change, but he says that the activists, the former revolutionaries "who discarded 'class' for the new battalions of 'communities', drew heavily on the rhetoric of their past, translating it into a form of politically acceptable 'community speak' as they in turn sought justification for the new relationship with the state. Civil society became the basis of social transformation and 'social partnership' – a vague alliance of those at the base and those who manage the superstructure – as the means of acquiring that civil society" (Robson, 2000, p 15).

Robson (2000) faces us with the co-option of radical community work. The professionalisation of community action has given rise to a new type of worker who has replaced critical Freirean concepts, such as *conscientisation*, with *sustainability* and *social inclusion*. This marks a subtle move that elevates material outputs over critical outcomes. At the same time, an emphasis on skills, training and managerialism has further obscured critical thought for surface-level activities that create the comfortable illusion of making a difference.

An incisive debate on the fine line between an ideology of self-help and radical practice is presented by Berner and Phillips (2005). Their fundamental premise is that *participation*, a radical concept, has been co-opted into mainstream theory and diluted in potential, together with other related concepts, such as *decentralisation* and *empowerment*. Their warning is that the shift to self-help obscures the social justice argument for redistribution of resources, failing "to adequately serve the needs of the poor, succumbing to a neo-liberal wolf dressed up as a populist sheep ... the community self-help paradigm needs to be refined by a recognition that the poor cannot be self-sufficient in escaping poverty, that 'communities' are systems of conflict as well as cooperation, and that the social, political and economic macro-structure cannot be side-stepped" (Berner and Phillips, 2005, p 20). Buying into the argument that redistribution of resources is degrading to the poor, undermining their self-esteem, we give free rein to the forces that privilege few and marginalise many: "self-sufficiency, the idea that 'left to their own devices' (and their current resources) poor communities would lift themselves out from poverty just fine, makes for an attractive myth but a regressive policy" (Berner and Phillips, 2005, p 23). In accord with Dixon et al (2005), and with Robson (2000), they propose that naïve interpretations of *community* that assume unity and reciprocity are created by *outsiders* who "see homogeneity and harmony where there is complexity and conflict" (Berner and Phillips, 2005, p 24).

Forces of exploitation and discrimination permeate communities, and if we overlook this then we fail to see the role of community development in the process of change for social justice. The depoliticisation of self-help places the responsibility for tackling poverty onto the very groups which are most targeted by oppressive forces, denying the reality of structural power that penetrates communities and perpetuates poverty. "Empowerment means *changing* the relationship between the rich and the poor, not the false option of 'breaking' it.... Empowerment cannot be depoliticized" (Berner and Phillips, 2005, pp 26-7). Self-help plays a role in the process of empowerment through critical consciousness, but it is not an alternative solution to the redistribution of unequally divided resources. Critical consciousness is the key to strong, analytic, coherent, cooperative anti-poverty action on the part of poor communities. The danger is that if we accept analyses of communities as homogeneous, not only is this naïve and obscures the reality of life in community, but it provides a smokescreen for the forces of structural inequality:

> The idea that poor communities can 'develop themselves' – if it means that they require no redistribution of resources, if it means that heterogeneity and inequity *within* communities can be glossed over, if it means that the macro structures of wealth and power distribution can be ignored – is flawed to the point of being harmful. It harms calls for realistic levels of funding for tackling poverty; it blurs the divergent needs of the heterogeneous poor, and masks those of the poorest; and it risks legitimizing inequity, reinforcing the complacent view that the poor are poor because they have not helped themselves.... To expect 'communities' to be havens of cooperation is utterly naïve; to treat them as homogeneous will further marginalize those most in need. Poverty and wealth are opposite sides of the same coin. The wealthy cannot withdraw from the lives of the poor, and the poor cannot withdraw from the lives of the wealthy – sustainable solution will require either partnership or confrontation. (Berner and Phillips, 2005, p 27)

In summary, civil society and its relation with the state are central to the rapid processes of change in which we find ourselves launched without a critical analytic rudder. If we unconsciously accede to the co-option of the radical agenda, we steer a dangerous, thoughtless course. In the UK, within a decade the language of partnership, participation and sustainability has become the order of the day, blurring the role of the state in relation to civil society in a blanket of politically acceptable rhetoric imported from the radical agenda of community work. This creates the illusion of us all being on the same side, while the state adopts an increasingly authoritarian interventionist position. Civil society is a site of progressive politics that embraces different and often conflicting interests, but holds the future for participatory democracy and equality (Deakin, 2001). The changing nature of relationships between the family, the community and the state has led to what Giddens (1998) identified as a new relationship between individual autonomy and collective solidarity. Tom Collins (2002, p 92) argues that the *generative politics* propounded by Giddens, which exists in the "space that links the State to a reflexive and mobilized society at large", is not in reality participatory, and that civil society should be recognised as part of the state apparatus coercively reaching into social groups and geographical areas that have previously been elusive. So, in these changing times, communitarianism and New Labour agendas present community as a homogeneous unity, as a given, implicitly reducing progressive politics to "the discovery, or the imposition, of what was already there, or what should have been. This is precisely to deny the scope for political transformation – for community in the sense of a project" (Calder, 2003, p 6). To counter this popular trend, it would be more critical to approach community as a *project*, something yet to be achieved, "not a thing, not a structure to be built, and then nailed down in stasis. It is, rather, a process" underpinned by participatory democracy; "the political and moral precondition of a just, participative and genuinely inclusive public life" (Calder, 2003, p 6).

Social justice and poverty

During the 18 years of the Thatcher/Major governments, "the British … lived under a regime whose leaders [did] their best to eliminate the word poverty from the English language, along with all talk about inequality and social injustice" (Donnison, 1998, p 196). John Smith, then leader of the Labour Party, established the Commission on Social Justice in 1992 on the 50th anniversary of the Beveridge Report. It defined four core elements for social justice (Commission for Social Justice, 1994):

- the equal worth of all citizens;
- the equal right to be able to meet their basic needs;
- the need to spread opportunities and life chances as widely as possible;
- the requirement that we reduce and where possible eliminate unjustified inequalities.

The Commission for Social Justice (1994) and the Rowntree Report (Joseph Rowntree Foundation, 1995) argue that the social divisions created by poverty jeopardise the long-term stability of the economy by undermining social cohesion. It is precisely this juxtaposition of the economy and community that pinpoints a fundamental contradiction in New Labour politics: on the one hand a commitment to participation and partnership in community, and on the other the primacy of the free market, the very mechanism that gives rise to the divisions that perpetuate social injustice. "It is this yoking together of the economic and the social which has formed the kernel of one powerful critique of neoliberalism" (Oppenheim, 1998, p 12).

Social justice is a contested concept. Donnison (1998) proposes that a good society is one in which everyone acts justly and not one that rewards individual gain and personal advantage. He emphasises how change creates new opportunities and poses new dilemmas, making it vital that we "stand from time to time outside the evolving patterns of moral values enshrined in the conventional wisdom" (p 190) and redefine what we mean by 'good'. John Rawls' (1971, 2001) theory of justice has made the biggest single contribution to the social justice debate. He argues in depth that a just and morally acceptable society rests on two fundamental principles of justice: the right of each person to have the most extensive basic liberty compatible with the liberty of others, and that social and economic conditions be open to all and to everyone's advantage. Rawls, in the course of time, came to accept that "his principles were not universal and timeless, but socially embedded" (Donnison, 1998, p 190). And, in his later work, *Justice as fairness*, Rawls rejects that the two principles can be met within a capitalist welfare state (Rawls, 2001). Gary Craig (undated, p 6) also raises "a major political question about the degree to which social justice is compatible at all with the operation of a market economy" as a free market economy reinforces the structures of exploitation and discrimination that social justice is committed to countering. Yet, in the government review of funding initiatives that support community capacity building, community development is clearly central to building civil renewal with social and environmental justice as core values (Home Office, 2004).

Social justice, in relation to community development, needs analyses based on inequality, oppression and exploitation, and action based on participatory democracy. In relation to critical practice, civil society remains a site of both liberation and domination with a narrow divide between the two. In terms of progressive politics in civil society, the International Association for Community Development in partnership with the Combined European Bureau for Social Development and the Hungarian Association for Community Development sponsored a conference in Budapest in 2004 with representatives from 33 countries coming together to explore building civil society in Europe through community development (Craig et al, 2004). The central thrust lies in the recognition that community development strengthens civil society through the empowerment of local communities in a participatory and democratic way by giving voice to those who are disadvantaged and vulnerable. A coherent, egalitarian ideological approach, set within the context of Europe, offers increased potential for collective action for social justice. This echoes Fisher and Ponniah's call for a universal approach to human rights that is based on new global values. "The key to the development of new values lies in the capacity to produce democratic processes and institutions that will allow for a genuinely international or global dialogue that will articulate a 'universalism of difference'" (Fisher and Ponniah, 2003, p 284). In this way, they argue for liberation through a form of participatory democracy that is built on a new solidarity, one that embraces diversity and grows out of civil society.

Why empower?

Empowerment is a key concept at the heart of radical community development. It is the process whereby we develop the theory and practice of equality. Of course, in order to get to grips with this, critical insight into the way that power in society favours the already privileged, and the way that forces of disempowerment perpetuate these inequalities, is essential. Radical practice "provides a starting point for linking knowledge to power and a commitment to developing forms of community life that take seriously the struggle for democracy and social justice" (McLaren, 1995, p 34).

Communities are contexts for liberation as well as domination, and there is a fine line between the two. For community development practice to achieve an emancipatory dimension, it must be capable of creating a body of practical knowledge grounded in everyday experience in the search for a more just and sustainable world. Our fundamental purpose is not simply to understand our world, but to use that understanding to bring about change. New paradigms, new worldviews, offer new possibilities for being in the world, and a radical agenda calls for a participatory paradigm, a participatory consciousness that contributes to what Reason and Bradbury (2001, p 10) see as part of a "resacralization of the world". In order to do this, we need analyses that help with insight into the nature of knowledge and power. The dominant hegemony, which shapes the way we think and therefore the way we act in the world, and in doing so creates a reality that privileges the already powerful, is one of the greatest obstacles to overcome.

Community development has become distracted from its commitment to social justice by allowing its radical agenda to be diluted by more reactionary theories that lead to ameliorative rather than transformative approaches to practice. This is linked to an ongoing tension in practice that emphasises *doing* at the expense of *thinking*;

and *action* without *reflection* is uncritical. The result is a continuing divide between theory and practice that fails to achieve a critical praxis where action and reflection are a unity. This renders community development vulnerable to more diluted interpretations. Critical approaches to practice involve theory and practice in dynamic with emancipatory action research, so building a body of knowledge based on concepts of justice, equality and democracy.

TWO

The story of a community

The previous chapter traced the history of radical community development, set the political context and explored some of the current debates relevant to the radical agenda in relation to social justice. Let us now move into practice and explore the way in which critical approaches take shape.

Community development is grounded in people's everyday lives. A critical approach to community work calls for insight into the power structures that influence that reality, and one way of beginning that process is the community profile. In Freirean pedagogy, this begins in the narratives of the people and is set within an analysis of poverty as structural discrimination.

Community profiling

> This struggle [for humanization] is possible only because dehumanization, although a concrete historical fact, is not a given destiny but the result of an unjust order that engenders violence in the oppressors, which in turn dehumanizes the oppressed. (Freire, 1982, p 21)

For Paulo Freire, the process of transformation for a just and equal world lies in theory and action, which begins in people's lived reality. He suggests that the impetus for change will not come from the powerful, but will be generated by oppressed people through a process of critical consciousness and collective action. We tend to accept the injustices of our world in unquestioning ways that give rise to false consciousness: seeing the world from a critical perspective involves questioning everyday experience. Both Gramsci and Freire believed that this would not happen spontaneously, that people external to the community provide the catalyst for critical consciousness. Community workers are critical pedagogues working in informal educational contexts in community. Our role, through a diversity of projects, is to create the context for questioning that helps local people to make critical connections between their lives and the structures of society that shape their world. The process is one of action and reflection, and the specific skills and strategies needed for critical practice are addressed in Chapter Three. From this beginning, people generate their own theory and determine their own action. Every project that we undertake has this core of critical pedagogy running through it, giving rise to new ways of seeing the world and leading to new ways of being in the world.

Community workers are privileged to be accepted into people's lives in community, and with this privilege comes a responsibility to develop relationships that are mutual, reciprocal, dignified and respectful. These underlying values emerge from an ideology of equality, and they shape every aspect of our practice, determining the way that we plan and conduct specific projects. The beginning of the process of community development lies in listening, valuing and understanding people's particular experiences. It also involves analysing how these experiences are linked to the forces of power that are embedded in the structures of society, and understanding how these forces reach into communities to impact on personal lives. The ideas of Gramsci on hegemony offer insight into this process, and are discussed in Chapter Six.

Community is a complex system of interrelationships woven across social difference, diverse histories and cultures, and determined in the present by political and social trends. This calls for community workers to have an incisive analysis of the changing wider political context and the historical issues that have helped to shape the present. One way into this understanding is through a community profile conducted in partnership with the community. Other types of profiling (social audits, needs assessments, community consultations) may have other political agendas and may not reflect the purpose of community development. The community development approach is based on an implicit assumption that "the organisation and structures of society cause problems of powerlessness, alienation and inequality. To achieve greater equality and social justice, resources and power must be redistributed" (Haggstrom, cited in Hawtin et al, 1994, p 35). A community development approach to community profiling is to have the voices of the people at its heart, and to weave together everything that is affecting people, including the way that they feel about their lives in community. This becomes more useful when it is set in comparison with other communities, in the local area, nationally and internationally.

Research is integral to community development praxis; it is the way in which practice is kept relevant to the changing social and political context. Research in community development is set within a participatory paradigm and its approach is referred to as *participatory*, *collaborative* or *emancipatory* action research, concepts that are closely allied but with subtle differences of emphasis. As a reminder of the social justice intention of community development, I prefer to use the term 'emancipatory action research'. It has a clearly defined ethical code and purpose that are consonant with community development practice. A more detailed definition can be found in Chapter Four. All research of this nature, including a community profile, needs to reflect feeling and thinking, theory and practice, local and global dimensions as an integrated whole in order to develop a critical praxis. Traditional approaches to research are based on positivism, and result in rational, scientific methods of measuring human behaviour that treat people like objects and deny the less tangible feeling aspects of being human. If we fall into a positivist approach to research that encourages research *on* people rather than *with* people, we will certainly overlook vital aspects of community life. For instance Hustedde and King (2002, p 338) refer to an "increasing interest in the emotional life of communities as a neglected aspect of community development" and argue the case for a community's faith in the soul or spirit as critical to a flourishing community. This is a counter-force to a society built on Western rational thought, and is akin to the more integrated approach to life of indigenous cultures:

> Soul is often linked to the beauty, mystery and forces of nature. In essence, soul is part of the world of creation. It can be part of the bonds of solidarity and capacity in community … it is about deep meaning and quality relationships. Soul thrives on paradox. It is about mystery – the presence of something profound that cannot be grasped by science or the boundaries of human language; it is something that's non-linear. The great wisdom traditions argue that soul is not about values and ethics but about a deeper reality that penetrates the illusion of the external world. We see soul when non-dominant cultures and people speak their value judgements (emotions) of compassion, forgiveness, understanding, and hope amidst despair. (Hustedde and King, 2002, p 340)

These are the qualities that are implicit in popular concepts like social capital and community cohesion, and are of vital importance in the process of community development.

The community profile could provide you with your first project in a community: a chance to involve local people in researching their own stories, beginning the process of critical consciousness. If there is a history of community development in your community, you should check whether a profile has been carried out previously. As a local-authority-employed community worker in Hattersley, a Manchester 'overspill' housing estate in Tameside, I found that although there was not a community profile as such, there was a massive amount of archive material. This came in the form of an extensive supply of newspaper cuttings and photographs collected by community workers and activists, and it painted a picture of the creation of the community. Newspaper articles covered early community action against the inadequate infrastructure in place to support a community of 10,000 people, as well as the problems with damp housing from the outset, hence its label 'the forgotten town'. In the council offices, I found minutes of meetings and percentage (mid-term census) surveys that offered more formal evidence of Hattersley's development. Local authorities conduct research on communities, but do not always involve or inform community workers or activists. I was astonished to find a recent percentage survey had been undertaken, of which neither the community development team nor the community forum was aware. It was only by going to the council offices to ask about documentation on Hattersley that I discovered this valuable information. In addition, and to my further surprise, I found that Peter Townsend, the leading national authority on poverty, had been commissioned by Tameside Council on behalf of the Greater Manchester Boroughs to undertake a poverty analysis (Townsend, 1988). This was vital information for our work. When we examined the Townsend analysis we were shocked at how skewed the census data became with the ameliorating effects of the wealthier wards within which Hattersley fell. With some gentle persuasion, the statisticians in the council offices disembedded the Hattersley data by using local enumeration districts (smaller units of analysis than wards). The picture that emerged was of a community that was among the most impoverished and disenfranchised in the country.

Structuring a community profile

The community profile enables you to make critical connections more readily if you juxtapose the voices of local people, statistical evidence, sociopolitical trends and community development interventions in a more structured way:

a) the individual
b) the group
c) the community
d) the structures/institutions of society
e) the wider society (regional, national, global).

This framework should be in place throughout any community activity. It not only helps you to weave the connections that take your analysis deeper, but in turn it provides a tool of reflection that you can use in practice, working with local people to frame specific questions that elicit a more critical picture of the forces impacting on community life. In these ways, you extend the potential of your practice to a more critical approach where people begin to question the nature of their lives and make connections with the structures of society that marginalise and oppress. (This is the essence of Freirean pedagogy and is discussed in more detail in Chapters Three and Five.)

Participation is the basis of community development practice, and it is important to ensure, in terms of anti-discriminatory practice, that this is representative of the diversity of the community. By this, I mean that we need to understand the ways in which community life is heterogeneous: experience is shaped according to social difference. The term *difference* is a shorthand for the way in which our identity is formed from our class, gender, ethnicity, 'race', faith, age, sexuality, 'dis'ability and many other aspects of our being that affect our life experience. If the profile of a community is conducted from an external, or even an internal but single, perspective, it will not tell an accurate story of the lives of the people across all their difference and diversity. This is discriminatory practice. We may only hear the loudest voices or only notice those with whom we most identify, and this gives a distorted perspective of community life. I give a deeper analysis of *difference* in Chapter Eight.

Where to look for information

Statistical data

Increasingly, current statistics are available via the Internet and this offers a useful beginning. You will find demographic, housing and socioeconomic profiles as well as information on schools, policing and crime, transport and local government details – try www.upmystreet.com. For local authority information, including neighbourhood profiles and committee minutes, try www.open.gov.uk.

A national census is undertaken the year after the turn of each decade, and for information based on a ward analysis you will find details on demography including ethnicity, health, economic activity and housing/households, which are compared with overall data for the borough as well as the national average. For England and Wales, go to www.statistics.gov.uk; for Scotland, www.gro-scotland.gov.uk; and for Northern Ireland, www.nisra.gov.uk. For a history of your community and general background material, go to the Informal Education (Infed) website, www.infed.org, and access their 'search the web' page. This website provides the largest collection of theory and practice papers in a single resource directly relevant to community development.

Involving people

First, you and your profiling group will need to have skills based on listening, valuing and dialogue. It is important to remember that the voices of local people, in all their diversity and all their roles, are central to this project. Perhaps your profiling group could capture the essence of this by providing cameras and getting people to take photographs of what is important to them in their daily lives. You could work with a writing group to capture community life in story and poetry. Your team could develop research skills through the discipline of noticing, using journals based on noticing events, encounters and conversations as they happen (Mason, 2002). Maybe you could develop a display of photographs, archive material, stories and poetry that would stimulate other people to get involved in the research. For instance, we had a reminiscence group of older residents who worked together with local schoolchildren for a radio programme. The children began by introducing popular playground games, and this stimulated cross-generational discussion about local life and its similarities and differences over time.

How will you motivate people to act together? How will they perceive a community profile as relevant to their lives? Whom are you going to contact and where will you find them? Are there active community groups already in existence? Are there key people you can contact? Should you hold a public meeting? How will you make sure the people who join you are representative and diverse? Communities are not homogeneous; there will be conflicting interests, sometimes marked by violence and hostility. For instance, how will you deal with sensitive issues like domestic violence, racism and homophobia? If these sensitive issues are swept under the carpet, we become complicit in their perpetuation.

The questions posed for the community profile should always be determined in partnership with the community. By setting your own questions, you will inevitably be framing their world through your eyes. The process of constructing the profile, once you have established a working group, will be life-changing for the people involved and will form the basis of further community development practice. The important questions can be developed through problem-posing. This can be done by capturing an aspect of community life in drawing, photography, film, drama, music or writing. This focuses the group and stimulates discussion, the community worker facilitating the process by asking questions rather than giving answers. In other words, you create a learning context in which the group can explore its ideas about its own community more critically. Here are some ideas, using the structure set out above, with which to begin the problem-posing process.

a) The individual

As community workers, we listen to the deepest feelings of the local community. Freirean pedagogy involves listening with compassion to people's fears, worries, hopes, resentments and joys. What are their deepest concerns? What most affects their lives? These emotions are the key to the motivation to act. The act of listening, of giving people your full attention, is empowering in itself. It takes people's experience seriously.

b) The group

What unites people in their current experience? What are the different interests represented between groups? How active are groups in the community? What are the successes people have achieved by uniting in groups? We should always build on the strengths and the experience of the community.

c) The community

What makes people feel a sense of belonging to the community? How do people feel about living here? What has united people in their history and culture? What diversity is there within local culture? Are differences celebrated? What are the skills that people have? What is the local economic base? Has this changed? Who does the unpaid work in the community? What are the resources that exist in the community? What are the resources that are, or could be, available to the community from outside? What are the collective concerns for the community? How positive or confident is the community to act on its own behalf?

d) A structural analysis

How do local statistics compare with the local authority, region or country as a whole? How do the diversity and difference in your community compare with the country as a whole? To what extent are the issues affecting your community in line with wider social trends? In what way do current policies benefit/discriminate against local people? How relevant and efficient is service delivery? What plans are in place for developments? How might these benefit or act against the interests of the local community? Do local people feel that they are taken seriously? What environmental policies and issues impact on the community?

e) The wider society

In this section, think local to global. Who represents local people in local and national government? Are there other leaders who act on behalf of the community to influence decisions? What changes are there in dominant ideology, and how it is affecting the local community? What wider social trends are reflected in the community? What links does the community have with wider, European or global, movements and trends? What environmental policies and issues affect the local community?

Presenting the profile

However you present your profile, the community must feel that it belongs to them, that it represents them in the most accurate way possible, that it is empowering and that they are proud of it. How will it become a working document? Will you have a community launch to celebrate its findings? Will this include a video, photograph and graphic display of the findings as part of a social event? Could part of it be displayed on a community noticeboard for a wider audience? How will you use it to stimulate action in the community? How will you use it to stimulate critical thinking in the community? How will you integrate theory and practice? If you fail to weave theory and practice together, your work is likely to reflect unconscious prejudice and discrimination. One useful tool that might aid a critical approach to the profiling process is the model of critical praxis.

Model of critical praxis

The purpose of models is that they help to simplify complex situations. In their simplicity they can help us to understand significant interrelationships and, more than this, "by constructing a model we gain additional understanding by virtue of the whole being greater than the sum of its parts" (Thompson, 1995, p 21). In this way, models play an important role in critical reflection by helping us to move towards a complete rather than a partial understanding. We are more able to locate the root sources of an issue, to develop relevant forms of practice and, in turn, through the process of reflection, to contribute to theory.

Dominant ideologies are powerful and persuasive, and it is important to remember that those of us who are struggling to free our own thinking are products of the same social and political context, and thus are subject to the same forces. Western thought is dichotomous and increasingly fragmented and alienating in nature (Reason and Bradbury, 2001). By this, I mean that we are taught to see life in relation to opposites: either one thing or another, for example rich/poor, Black/White, male/female. It is a hierarchical perspective that is built on superiority/inferiority, thus lending itself to domination and oppression (hooks, 1984; Spretnak, 1997). Contradictions and complexity are not within its scope.

Alternative worldviews, different ways of seeing the world, can help to move us towards a vision of wholeness: a reintegration of the self; strength in diversity; and a symbiotic relationship with the environment. This provides a model based on harmony rather than violence, on cooperation rather than competition, on need rather than greed. Today, we have much greater awareness of difference and diversity, giving insight into the experience of oppression in all its complexity. From here, the shift has to be towards interconnectedness across difference: the thread of humanity is held together by each individual and the quality of humanity is determined by mutual responsibility to this whole. A commitment to liberation and justice requires new ways of thinking about social reality from a critical perspective that embraces both social and environmental justice: "future participation will mean a very different experience of the self, an ecological self distinct yet not separate, a self rooted in environment and in community" (Reason, 1994, p 37).

The model of critical praxis I present (see Figure 2.1) is the result of my own reflections on practice over time. It worked for me by locating internal and external forces in community, and in doing so presented me with a more critical understanding of how these impact on local lives. This gives a much clearer insight into the ways in which community development has to work both inside and outside community in order to transform the root sources of oppression. A critical approach to community development calls for a framework within which smaller projects can be seen as contributing to a bigger whole. Otherwise, community workers can be either sucked into impotence and despair or respond with palliatives that are incoherent in the long-term quest for social justice. This is the spirit in which I offer the model of critical praxis.

The model aims to locate power and domination within a social and political framework, and gives an idea of the way in which subordination is reinforced. In juxtaposition to this is *critical consciousness*.

Figure 2.1: Model of critical praxis

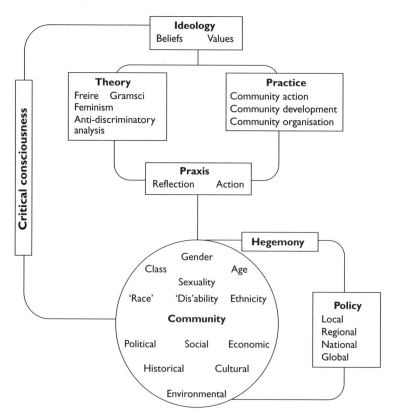

The two come together at the interface of *community* and *praxis*. The model indicates two major circuits: one I have labelled *hegemony* to denote the ways in which ideological consent is gained in order that we accept the policy decisions that govern us; the other I have labelled *critical consciousness* to indicate an alternative way of seeing life based on equity and justice. These two circuits overlap in *community*. Let us follow my journey round the model.

Starting in ideology, I developed certain beliefs and values that were based on my experience and perceptions of the world (epistemology). These are always in process and have reformed many times. They are constantly re-examined in relation to my engagement with the world (ontology). As a community worker, I cannot make sense of my practice without having conceptual tools of analysis. Of these there are many, but I have chosen to name Freire, Gramsci, feminism and anti-discriminatory analysis as prime areas of thought which have profoundly influenced me in my search for a theory of transformative change. In much the same way, these theories would make little sense without my experience.

Practice includes the stages of development in community, so here I have included *action*, *development* and *organisation* as reminders that community development adopts different approaches at different stages. These come together in *praxis*, the synthesis of *action* and *reflection*. Here, it is important to mention that this journey is not carried out in isolation. In *praxis*, my journey comes together with others in the quest for *critical consciousness*: making sense of the world in order to transform it is a collective experience. I share my thinking and ideas in dialogue with people in *community* as we move forwards in mutual inquiry and action. The dynamic between ideas and experience takes us deeper into the process of *conscientisation*. It locates understanding in experience, rather than in a decontextualised intellect, and this is the basis of collective action.

This dynamic, between ideas and experience, is not sterile: it is contextualised in *community*, which is in itself in dynamic with *hegemony* – the way in which our minds are colonised by the persuasiveness of dominant ideas. It is vital to recognise that hegemony is flexible and in constant reformation in relation to its context. In my years as a community worker, the dominant ideology transformed with the ascendance of New Right thinking. It demanded rigorous reflection in order to make sense of such a radically changing political context. I found myself witnessing a community restructuring its identity in the face of persuasive New Right ideology under Thatcherism, and one example was the way in which local people began to express increasing disregard for working-class solidarity as individualism took hold. The impact on the community was dramatic. This is precisely why my journey needs to engage with *hegemony*.

On the model, the impact of local, national and global changes is seen in relation to *community*. If my praxis had developed in relation to community alone, failing to recognise the impact of outside forces, it would have been incomplete and much more likely to follow a self-help rather than a critical approach to practice. The lives of the people with whom I worked were permeated by a dominant thinking that persuaded them to passively accept the policy changes that marginalised them further, causing massive suffering. *Critical consciousness* is not possible without an analysis of *hegemony*. The two come together in *community* and are the basis of *critical praxis*. In this way, the journey towards critical consciousness is rooted in an analysis of the lived experience of people in their communities, within society.

Participatory democracy, poverty and social justice

This section continues the discussion on poverty and social justice that began in the previous chapter in relation to changing political contexts and changing ideologies. Here its focus is set in relation to a critical approach to community profiling:

> We live at a precarious moment in history. Relations of subjection, suffering dispossession and contempt for human dignity and the sanctity of life are at the center of social existence. Emotional dislocation, moral sickness and individual helplessness remain ubiquitous features of our time ... democracy has become ... subverted by its contradictory relationship to the very object of its address: human freedom, social justice, and a tolerance and respect for difference. (McLaren, 1995, p 1)

Social justice embraces a range of ways of being in the world that are not seen as *deviant* from the norm – young, old, 'dis'abled, single, lone parent, lesbian, gay, all faiths and none, and so on. If a just society is one in which people are treated with equal dignity and respect, where different cultures are embraced, where different abilities are valued, and where everyone is enabled to reach full potential, then injustice can be seen as a violation of these values.

Discrimination gets embedded in the structures of society through poverty:

> The ultimate cause of poverty is an imbalance of power. This imbalance plays itself out through the most powerful having a disproportionate control of the society's resources, at the expense of the least powerful. Poverty, the consequence, is a lack of financial resources, pure and simple. Other explanations that are from time to time offered, such as labour market problems, benefit inadequacy or behavioural explanations are the mediators which make powerlessness lead to poverty. Establishing the causal chain is critical: unless the causes are properly understood policy makers will not be in a position to design effective responses. (Flaherty et al, 2004, p 2)

As I have stressed, it is of vital consequence for community development that community workers have a critical analysis of poverty and the way that it works in the interests of discrimination if we are to contribute to change for social justice. We need to get angry about poverty and the suffering it creates in serving the interests of the privileged. This section offers you a discussion of the critical links between poverty and power in relation to community.

Debates have raged long and hard around *absolute* and *relative* poverty: *absolute* definitions are based on a minimum standard of living and a person's biological needs for food, water, clothing and shelter as basic rather than *relative* to a broader socially and culturally acceptable standard of living (Oppenheim and Harker, 1996, p 7). Often we hear arguments that justify inequalities as inevitable, an argument that Marcuse dismisses as "the regulation of free competition among unequally equipped economic subjects" (Marcuse, 1991, p 1).

Peter Townsend's (1979) extensive study of *Poverty in the UK*, based on a major survey that he carried out in 1968-69, was hailed as a seminal contribution to understanding relative poverty and its impact on citizenship. Mack and Lansley (1985) built on the work of Townsend and brought the debate on relative poverty into public consciousness by attempting to measure poverty using the opinions of society as a whole rather than 'experts'. Asking a cross-section of people to prioritise life's necessities, a public consensus on acceptable living standards was determined, anything below which would define poverty. London Weekend Television commissioned MORI, survey specialists, to design and conduct the survey. "The survey established, for the first time ever, that a majority of people see the necessities of life in Britain in the 1980s as covering a wide range of goods and activities, and that people judge a minimum standard of living on socially established criteria and not just the criteria of survival or subsistence" (Mack and Lansley, 1985, p 53).

There was a massive consensus across social classes to support this view, with more marked differences defined according to political affiliation: "Conservative supporters are much more likely to blame the victim and much less likely to identify injustice" (Mack and Lansley, 1985, p 209). The surprising consequence of this research was the extent to which the general public supported the idea of redistributing wealth to create a more equal society.

The concept of human rights is central to the poverty debate: "people should have a right to an income which allows them to participate in society, rather than merely exist" (Oppenheim and Harker, 1996, p 11). As a community worker during Thatcherism, without an understanding of the persuasive power of *hegemony* I would have lacked the conceptual tools to understand how, in a wealthy democracy, it was possible to create a situation whereby the rich became richer and the poor became poorer. Let us explore some of the factors that contributed to this in relation to child poverty.

Child poverty in particular

Child poverty is an indictment of our times. During the 1980s, we became a more divided society than at any other time this century. From 1979, with the ascendance of New Right politics, the rhetoric of the 'welfare scrounger' took hold, and the UK witnessed a massive transference of wealth from the *poor* to the *rich*, reinforced by policy changes informed by this value base. As marginalisation and exclusion escalated, poor people were told to tighten their belts and wait for the trickle-down effect. As we can see from these statistics, wealth did not trickle down but continued to advantage the already privileged. We need to be concerned about the persistent nature of the trend created at this time, as you can see in Table 2.1.

Under Thatcherism, child poverty escalated from 14% in 1979 to 34% in 1996/97 (Flaherty et al, 2004, p 145), and children replaced

Table 2.1: Marketable wealth, 1979-2001

% of marketable wealth owned by:	1979	1983	1987	1992	1996	1997	2000	2001
Most wealthy 1%	20	20	18	18	20	22	22	23
Most wealthy 10%	50	50	51	50	52	55	55	56
Least wealthy 50%	8	9	9	7	7	7	6	5

Source: Inland Revenue statistics, *Personal Wealth*, 2003, Table 13.5, cited in Flaherty et al (2004, p 216)

pensioners as the single group most at risk of poverty. This left the UK with one of the highest rates of child poverty compared with other countries facing similar economic trends. The Child Poverty Action Group, formed in 1976 from a concern about the levels of child poverty, warned that "the poverty devastating the life chances of children today will have future repercussions for us all" (Witcher, in Oppenheim and Harker, 1996, p vi). The lasting impact of child poverty on adulthood is still poorly understood.

The employment position of the household is an important factor in determining the status of children, with over half of poor children in 1995/96 living in households with no adult in work. Incomes for households with children fell progressively behind those without children throughout the 1980s and 1990s, trends that were obscured for a long time, largely due to the handling of data that emphasised the cost of a child rather than the risks of poverty to the child. In this way, trends accelerated by changes in household formation and re-formation – single adult households, single parent families and families without children – added to changes in employment patterns to mask the enormous impact that poverty was having on children (Gregg et al, 1999).

Growing up in a family in poverty is closely linked to poor educational achievement and reduced chances of employment. We also know that poverty creates ill-health and premature death: for example, children of those in the bottom social class are five times more likely to die from an accident and 15 times more likely to die in a house fire than those in the upper social classes (Flaherty et al, 2004). Yet evidence points to the fact that escalating child poverty during Thatcherism was a political choice rather than an inevitability. Bradshaw (1999), investigating international trends, provides evidence that out of 25 countries only Russia and the US had higher rates of child poverty than the UK. In 16 years, 1979-95, child poverty increased more in the UK than in almost all other industrial countries, and in Europe only Italy had a sharper increase than the UK. Important to note is that this included countries facing similar demographic and economic trends. "Nearly half of all countries had no increase or a reduction in their child poverty rates" (Bradshaw, 1999, p 16).

Even a relatively superficial glance at the statistics reveals that children at risk of poverty correlate with social groups targeted by poverty, a critical factor in this analysis:

- lone parent households;
- low-paid households;
- households without an adult in paid work;

- minority ethnic families;
- 'dis'abled children or those with a 'dis'abled parent.

Also, children who grow up in poverty are more likely to:

- have low birthweight leading to infant death or chronic disease later in life;
- suffer from malnutrition;
- underachieve at school;
- be suspended, excluded or truant from school;
- have low self-esteem;
- have low expectations;
- experience unemployment and low wages;
- for girls, become pregnant in their teenage years;
- for young men, be at risk of suicide;
- die prematurely (mortality);
- suffer from long-term debilitating illness (morbidity).

Critical connections like this provide us with a complex picture of the interlinking dimensions of poverty. The correlations between unemployment, poor mental health, homelessness, school exclusions, children in care/leaving care and the escalation in youth suicide are important critical connections for community development (Howarth et al, 1999); as is the connection between increasing concentrations of poverty on council housing estates (D. Page, 2000); as well as the gendered and racialised dimensions of child poverty that link to growing up in lone parent families and in families of non-White ethnicity, compounded by ill-health and low income (Gordon et al, 2000). We must be concerned with this both in terms of its profound injustice and its cost to society as a whole.

First, we need to recognise what is happening in children's lives, but if we leave it at a personal/local level we fail to notice the ways in which these are social trends that are linked to structural injustice. Our practice is more likely to address the symptoms than the causes. Understanding the complex ways in which divisions of *difference* interact and interweave with poverty to reinforce prejudice and create social injustice is of vital importance to community workers who want to make a difference to people's lives.

Since 1997, the number of children living in income poverty in the UK has fallen by some 500,000 to a total of 3.8 million. Despite this being the lowest level since 1991, it still leaves one in three children growing up in poverty. The racist dimensions of child poverty leave those from minority ethnic families at most risk: 27% of children in White families live below the 60% median (after housing costs), whereas 36% of Indian, 41% of Black Caribbean, 47% of Black non-Caribbean and 69% of Pakistani and Bangladeshi children are growing up in this level of poverty. Similarly, 'dis'abled children or those with a 'dis'abled parent are much more at risk of poverty, inadequate housing and experience of exclusion from public and community services (Flaherty et al, 2004). So, you begin to see that when we make these connections we understand more fully the complex discriminatory dimensions of poverty. Campaigning, research and watchdog bodies such as the Child Poverty Action Group and the Joseph Rowntree Foundation are vital in providing information on current policy and poverty statistics to keep your analyses up to date.

It is vital that these trends are set within wider issues of world poverty and its gendered and racialised dimensions. Peter Townsend, as a critical commentator on world poverty and on behalf of UNICEF, talked about the UK escalation in child poverty as a "neglect-filled Anglo-American model which unless there is massive investment in children we will head for economic catastrophe":

> ... a skewed labour market, the depression of lowest wages, the disproportionate rise in top salaries and wages, the cutting back of progressive taxation, corporation taxes and inheritance taxes, the imposition of heavier taxes like VAT on poorer groups, higher rates of long-term unemployment, the casualisation of labour, the emergence of various forms of self-employment, the abandonment of some social security benefits and the restructuring of others, and the indexing of insurance benefits in payment, like state pensions, according to prices rather than earnings. The key strategies have been those of disemployment, deregulation, cuts in public expenditure and privatisation. The monetarist conception of development has consistently sought to reduce the budget deficit, remove public subsidies, privatise state-owned enterprises, and liberalise trade in the expectation of attracting inward investment from multi-national corporations (MNCs). These tight monetarist 'conditionalities' have led to a catastrophic decline in GDP in Sub-Saharan Africa, Latin America, the Caribbean, Eastern Europe and many of the republics of the former Soviet Union.... No longer can the trend in the poor countries be separated from that in rich countries. The

> problems ... are increasingly the product of economic and
> political powers exercised by the international agencies and
> the MNCs.... There needs to be 'real world' coalitions ... as
> a basis for principled international redistribution.
> (Townsend, 1995, pp 10-12)

His comment was made before New Labour came into power in the
UK and went public on poverty, but the issues remain the same.
Important to remember here is that community development practice
needs to be informed by an incisive analysis of the discriminatory
nature of poverty in society at large, and an understanding of how
these trends affect the communities with which we work. Relative
poverty within a country has a massive impact on issues related to
social exclusion. Setting this within an understanding of world poverty
and environmental justice gives insight into the ways in which the
problems lie with disproportionate levels of personal wealth in Western
societies, which simply cannot be sustained. Therefore, a critical
approach to practice has to be based on the notion of a redistribution
of wealth that reduces the divisions cleaved by poverty that affect the
life chances of people within nations and between nations. Naïve
notions of increasing the levels of consumption of the poorest in our
society will simply accelerate the world crises of sustainability and
injustice.

Anti-poverty practice

Your community profile set within this level of analysis will inevitably
lead to anti-poverty projects. In my own practice, we decided that a
credit union would make a community-wide impact on poverty. Setting
up a community credit union is a long-term project requiring not
only the development of specific skills, but great perseverance and
determination. Information on credit unions and a range of other
local economic projects can be obtained from the New Economics
Foundation (www.neweconomics.org). A discussion on credit unions
and other local economic projects can be found in Twelvetrees (1998).

Women are at greater risk of poverty, and they are largely the ones
preyed on by loan sharks. These predators arrive on the doorstep with
much-needed bales of bedding, clothing, pots and pans – the stuff that
is linked to women's role in keeping the home functioning and the
children healthy. Offers of cash loans come next. Often short term,
these loans carry extortionate rates of interest. In such ways, the women
of the community are carrying the practical responsibility for keeping

families together. It is the women who need to save, need to borrow, and need support for their unrecognised contribution to the fabric of life.

To illustrate my point, I will introduce Hattersley Credit Union. Unsurprisingly, it was the women of the credit union who rolled their sleeves up and transformed the idea into a reality. The men who were involved often wanted symbols of status, like lapel badges. Women shared the vision and rose to the challenge. They developed skills they never dreamt they had. They identified other women from the community and, in this way, the band of volunteers grew. They staffed collection points, pored over the bookkeeping, and assessed people for loans. They were the ones who, in the end, challenged the men: "Stop strutting around looking important. Either roll your sleeves up and get on with it or get out!"

A credit union is founded on cooperation, mutuality and trust, encouraging its members to participate in policy making and to take an active interest in the day-to-day procedures. It is a not-for-profit organisation. After expenses have been covered and reserves have been topped up, any profit is returned to members in the form of a dividend. A credit union is owned by its members and it is run by an elected board of directors. All the roles are voluntary until it gets to the stage where it is able to benefit from employing people. It serves the financial needs of the community by encouraging regular saving to provide a common pool for loans, and education is part of its role. This is the principle of mutuality upon which the system works – savings must remain intact when a loan is taken out, otherwise the pool is depleted.

In 1988, Hattersley was the first registered credit union in the region. As confidence grew, the credit union women played a key role in travelling far and wide to other community groups to support them in establishing their own credit unions. Events and training days were held at Hattersley Community Centre with people attending from all over the region. On a wider scale, contact was made with Northern Ireland credit unions and each year on International Credit Union Day we held a social event for all members linking us into the global credit union movement. This process was immensely empowering. Communities in poverty usually believe that they are alone in their suffering, and the collective action generated by this anti-poverty movement brought confidence and optimism.

Hattersley Credit Union not only offered the lowest unsecured loan rate in the country, but also demonstrated how women act in the face of multiple forms of oppression and discrimination to organise their caring in an alienated world. The Hattersley women involved in the running of the credit union look upon their voluntary work as a job that has developed confidence and skills and in many ways carries more commitment than paid work. It is this 'messy tangle of real life' that Hattersley women roll up their sleeves and get on with.

The credit union has done much to change the negative image of Hattersley. Media interest over the years has portrayed Hattersley Credit Union as an outstanding achievement by local people, challenging the legacy of the 'Moors Murders' in the 1960s, which continued to cast a shadow over Hattersley decades later. The credit union has stood proud on the financial pages of national newspapers and done much to foster a sense of pride in the community, a deeper consciousness of discrimination and collective action and campaigning on poverty.

Why is it that women are so active at grassroots level? Anne Witte Garland suggests that:

> ... since women are traditionally concerned with home and family and community, they're the first to recognise threats to them and to act on those threats ... men are more integrated into the system that creates the threats, and that since women have been excluded from that system historically, they have less to lose than men in fighting for it. (Witte Garland, 1988, p xii)

Hattersley has been ostracised by the surrounding communities since its creation. The 'slum clearance' label, an early polio outbreak and the Moors Murders brought about prejudice on a local level, which reinforced the discrimination of poverty. Yet, still the women rise and sustain the life of the community, just like the women of the mining communities, the women of Northern Ireland or the women of the communities hit by the 1991 riots; they are the ones "who sustain[ed] the personal, public and political lives of these neighbourhoods" (Campbell, 1993, p 321).

Community development is a mutual process. It begins in everyday lives, understanding histories, cultures and values, and listening to hopes and concerns. Any research into people's lives locates the voices of those people expressing their own experience at its core, as the beginning of a process of empowerment and change. This needs to be set within a critical analysis of the way that prejudice and discrimination target specific groups through poverty, making them more at risk than others, and creating a system of domination and subordination, locally, nationally and globally. Identifying the forces that shape people's lives, we are able to make critical connections that form the basis of critical action. The community profile offers a strategy to gather this information together in a systematic way in partnership with the community. The critical connections that weave together through the profile provide a foundation for developing critical consciousness and practical projects. This is the basis of a critical approach to community development that weaves action and reflection, theory and practice, into a unity of praxis.

Doing community development

The most challenging context for a community worker is one in which people have been silenced into apathy; apathy lacks energy. Anger, on the other hand, generates an energy that can be redirected into positive action. Working with Freirean pedagogy, we know that *relevance* is the key to unlocking the energy to act, and relevance is located in people's everyday reality. This chapter introduces the work of Paulo Freire, the Brazilian educator, who has made more impact than any other thinker on community development around the world since the 1970s. Here, I focus in particular on his emphasis on the stories of the people being at the heart of the process of change. I want to consider the skills and strategies with which to begin this process, while remembering to situate it within the bigger political picture.

Introduction to Paulo Freire

Since the publication of *Pedagogy of the oppressed* in the UK in 1972, Paulo Freire (1921-97) has proved to be one of the visionary thinkers of our time for workers involved in the practice of social justice. The most significant contribution of his work is his insight into the political nature of education. For Freire, education can never be neutral: its political function is to liberate or domesticate. In other words, the process of education either creates critical, autonomous thinkers or it renders people passive and unquestioning. By failing to understand this, we fail to recognise the ways in which power and domination are woven through the fabric of our everyday experience. Freire achieves a synthesis of theory and practice that is fundamental to a critical approach to community development. His particular contribution according to Cornel West (Preface to McLaren and Leonard, 1993, p xiii) lies in his "genius ... to explicate in this text and exemplify in his life the dynamics of this process of how ordinary people can and do make history in how they think, feel, act and love. Freire has the distinctive talent of being a profound theorist who remains 'on the ground' and a passionate activist who gets us 'off the ground' – that is, he makes what is abstract concrete without sacrificing subtlety, and he infuses this concrete way of being-in-the-world with a fire that fans and fuels our will to be free".

Pedagogy is critical when situated within an analysis of ideological and structural power. Paula Allman calls for a radical rereading of Freire, stating that "the publication of Gramsci's work in English has been one of the most important influences in preparing us for the rereading and radical use of Freire's ideas" (Allman, 1988, p 99). The complementary nature of the two lies in "Freire's consideration of the political nature of education and in Gramsci's consideration of the educational nature of politics" (Allman, 1988, p 92). Freire cannot be ignored: his ideas echo through generations, continuing to inspire educators as well as generating passionate critique. "Remaining steadfast till the very end to his cherished principles of radical humanization and democracy, Freire has, throughout his life, produced work that provides those who share his political-pedagogical philosophy with resources of hope and a strong sense of agency" (P. Mayo, 2004, p 2).

Freire's approach to critical pedagogy exposes the power and authority of the traditional educator in perpetuating domination. A critical educator works with values of humility and compassion, seeing the educational relationship as one of mutual humanisation with a loving commitment to people at its core. "I could never think of education without love and that is why I think I am an educator, first of all because I feel love" is a remark attributed to Freire a few days before his death in 1997 (McLaren, 2002, pp 245-53). Community workers are critical educators, and as such every aspect of our work encourages the critical questioning of reality. Every educator–learner role defined in relation to critical pedagogy is mutual: it involves a co-learning/co-teaching approach in which the educator also learns and the learner also teaches. Rather than the traditional, authoritarian, top-down pouring of facts from teacher to learner, which assumes an unquestioning power relationship, critical pedagogy is a mutual search based on a "profound love for the world and for people" (Freire, 1996, p 70). This is similar to Gandhi's emphatic declaration to the unemployed mill workers of Lancashire in the 1930s that he loved all the children of the world *as his own*. It is a worldview based on critical compassion. This mutual caring is the basis of dialogue, the foundation of a dialectical approach to learning that, in identifying the contradictions that permeate our lives, moves to transformative action. It calls for critical educators to act in solidarity to transform the ideologies and structures of oppression that continue to create suffering and subordination. Critical dialogue replaces the arrogance of the traditional educator with humility: "For all their competence and authority, teachers must be humble to relearn that which they think they already know from others and to connect, through learning … with their learners' lifeworlds" (P. Mayo, 2004, p 93).

Freire in his life and times

Our lives are shaped by difference, culture, history and the politics of our times:

> Society not only controls our movements, but shapes our identity, our thoughts and our emotions. The structures of society become the structure of our own consciousness. Society does not stop at the surface of our skins. Society permeates us as much as it envelops us. (Berger, 1966, p 140)

In this sense, ideas can only be fully understood in relation to the thinker, contextualised culturally, politically and historically, and, in turn, are only useful if adapted to the changing political and social times. For these reasons, it is important to understand the context from which Freire's ideas emerged. His early experience influenced his thinking profoundly. He was born in the town of Recife in North-East Brazil in 1921 into a middle-class family. As a consequence of the world economic depression in the 1930s, his family was plunged into poverty. This changed state of affairs had a great impact on him: as a child Freire could see the ways that social class barriers were still acted out in the face of starvation, and he was puzzled that people were silenced by their suffering. At the age of 11, he resolved to commit himself to the struggle against hunger so that other children did not have to suffer in the same way. Although malnutrition affected his early schooling, family fortunes eventually improved and he was able to qualify for Recife University.

Brazilian university education was modelled on that of the French, and it was through this system that Freire was introduced to the thinking of Althusser, Foucault, Fromm, Levi-Strauss and Sartre. After the rigours of his schooling, the academic life suited Freire but equipped him with little practical direction. In quick succession, he became a lawyer, a teacher of Portuguese and then an adult educator. In 1944, he married Elza, also a teacher. They became involved in the Catholic Action movement among middle-class families in Recife, locating critical contradictions between the Christian faith and privileged lifestyles. However, radical, democratic ideals were not well received in this petit-bourgeois context. "It proved to be an extremely disheartening experience, as they uncovered strong resistance to the idea that bourgeois families should, for example, treat their servants as human beings" (Mackie, 1980b, p 3). They changed the focus of their work to the poor of Recife, which was a turning point in Freire's life, but not an easy transition. "I said many beautiful things, but made no impact. This was because I used my frame of reference, not theirs" (Freire, in Mackie, 1980b, pp 3-4). Sharing the lives of the people led him to name the *culture of silence*: the way in which political, social and economic domination lead to passive acceptance in those who are marginalised. His study of the way in which oppression is experienced became the basis for his doctorate, which was submitted to Recife University in 1959, after which he was appointed to a chair in history and philosophy.

In 1962, Freire was invited to become director of the government's adult literacy programme in North-East State Brazil. His radical pedagogy was based on the belief that every person is capable of engaging in critical dialogue when they perceive it as relevant to their life experience. Freire gained recognition, and was invited to become director of the national literacy programme. This placed him in a powerful position to influence both educational and electoral reform (P. Taylor, 1993). Freire's insight into literacy as a vehicle for political consciousness, the links between education and power, led him to be seen as an enemy of the state. So, when the multinational-backed military coup took place in Brazil in 1964, Freire was arrested, stripped of his professorship, and imprisoned. He was seen as a threat to the *status quo* because of his intention to develop a national literacy programme that would increase literacy levels for the rural and urban poor, and so make them eligible to vote (P. Mayo, 2004). After 75 days, he was offered political asylum in Bolivia. Fifteen days later there was a coup in Bolivia, and he was, in turn, exiled to Chile where he continued his work at the Institute for Research and Training in Agrarian Reform.

This gave Freire the opportunity to experience his pedagogy from a different cultural, ideological and political perspective. He worked with "the most progressive sectors of the Christian Democratic Party Youth ... finding himself in contact with highly stimulating Marxist thought and powerful working-class organizations" (Torres, 1993, p 123). After spending some time at Harvard as visiting professor, he moved to Geneva in 1970 as principal consultant to the Department of Education of the World Council of Churches. Throughout this period, Freire's influence spread, and his critical pedagogy offered a practical tool for progressive educators engaged in political/cultural projects in many countries. The concept of *conscientização* (conscientisation) gave fresh insight into the political nature of popular education as a tool for liberation. Freire gained worldwide recognition, speaking at conferences, acting as consultant to projects throughout the developing and industrialised nations, and advising governments. It was during the first six years of his long period of exile that his most celebrated work, *Pedagogy of the oppressed*, was written and brought him acclaim as a seminal thinker of the 1970s (P. Mayo, 2004).

After his enforced 16-year exile, Freire returned to Brazil in 1980, following the amnesty of 1979. He began 'relearning Brazil' by reading Gramsci and also "listening to the *popular Gramsci* in the *favelas* [Brazilian shantytowns]" (Torres, 1993, p 135). He spent at least two afternoons a week with people in their communities, listening to their experience and analysis and, in this way, developing a *critical praxis* out of lived experience. After this, Freire worked in the Faculty of Education of the Catholic University of São Paulo. He set up *Vereda*, an educational centre that brought together people from popular education projects. He also worked with the education section of the Partido Trabalhista (the Workers' Party), which led to his honorary appointment as President of the Workers' University of São Paulo, an organisation that fosters trade union and political education.

Paulo Freire's ideas have pioneered and epitomised the concept and practice of critical pedagogy. Although his original interest was in the relevance of people's education in developing countries, particularly through literacy, health, agrarian reform and liberation theology, he also worked closely with radical educators in North America and Europe, arguing that issues of exploitation and discrimination exist everywhere. The influence of Freirean pedagogy has spread far and wide, providing a major influence for those committed to a more fair and just future. The inescapable paradox is, as Torres puts so well, that political pedagogy "in industrialized societies is nurtured by notions of education and social change developed in the Third World" (Torres, 1993, p 137).

In 1986, Elza died, and Freire lost his long-time colleague and companion. He married Ana Maria Araujo (Nita) in 1988, a friend of the family and a former student, who shared his life and his work until his death in 1997 (P. Mayo, 2004). Freire remained an active influence until his death. In the last 10 years of his life he was Secretary of Education in São Paulo (1989-91) and taught at the Pontifical Catholic University in São Paulo. He also wrote prolifically and gave inspiring talks around the world. It was at the Pedagogy of the opressed Conference, initiated by Doug Paterson at the University of Omaha at Nebraska, that I was fortunate to meet Freire with Augusto Boal and Peter McLaren in March 1996, and Ira Shor the following year, just weeks before Freire died. Both Freire and Boal were conferred with honorary doctorates by the university during the conference. This organisation, now Pedagogy and Theatre of the Oppressed, holds an annual conference in different venues in the US, developing the work of Freire, and Augusto Boal continues to run Theatre of the Oppressed workshops for practitioners.

Mayo comments that "in his later work, Freire stressed and elaborated on points that were already present in his early work … a person in process, constantly in search of greater coherence" (P. Mayo, 2004, p 79). And although his later works are important, *Pedagogy of the oppressed* remains Freire's seminal contribution. I still see his ideas exciting new readers with their ongoing relevance to oppression. Freire has always evoked extremes of passion, and I address some of the critiques of his work in Chapter Eight. His ideas were shaped by, and need to be understood in relation to, his cultural and political times. New understanding of the concept of multiple, interconnected oppressions has challenged an oppressor/oppressed analysis as simplistic, obscuring the complexity of the process. But, the profound insight of Freire still offers the conceptual tools with which to develop our ideas, and this begins with a critical rereading of his work from our many new understandings. "We can stay with Freire or against Freire, but not without Freire" (Torres, 1993, p 140). This calling for a critical rereading of Freire is echoed more and more by those critical pedagogues who see the transformative potential of his work to engage with issues of 'race', gender, age, ethnicity, 'dis'ability, sexuality and so on in all their complex intertwinings – Ira Shor, Peter McLaren, Paula Allman, Peter Mayo, Keith Popple, Kathleen Weiler and Antonia Darder, to name but a few.

Freire's work embraces an eclectic range of thinkers: he was influenced by Antonio Gramsci, Eric Fromm, Karl Mannheim, Jean-Paul Sartre, Herbert Marcuse, Mao, Che Guevara, Franz Fanon, John Dewey, Lev Vygotsky, Martin Buber, Teilhard de Chardin and Jacques Maritain, among many. From a feminist point of view, he was one of those rare male thinkers who embrace emotions, intellect and faith to provide us with a more integrated approach to praxis. He gave us confidence to believe that we develop theory in action, based on the underlying belief that we all have the right to be fully human in the world. In other words, people, when they are thinking critically, are capable of analysing the meaning of their own lives. Freire's great strength is the way that he locates critical pedagogy within an analysis of power and the way that it becomes woven into the structures of society. In this way, Freirean pedagogy is not segregated from life in the false structures of a classroom, but is all around us in the places that people live their lives; an engagement with people in context.

Freire, from his early days in Brazil, recognised the vital energy produced by using popular education for critical consciousness, because it has relevance in people's lives:

> People will act on the issues on which they have strong feelings. There is a close link between emotion and the motivation to act. All education and development projects should start by identifying the issues which the local people speak about with excitement, hope, fear, anxiety or anger. (Hope and Timmel, 1984, p 8)

People make critical connections when they link cultural, political, social and economic issues with their everyday life experience. This counters the apathy and passivity symptomatic of a *culture of silence*. Such insights into the nature of oppression, and the ways in which the traditional education system functions to maintain the obedience of paternalism, informed the development of Freire's pedagogy; a form of learning based on teaching to question rather than teaching answers. The cornerstone of his theory is that every human being is capable of critically engaging in their world once they begin to question the contradictions that shape their lives.

I witnessed Freire's critical pedagogy in action in Nicaragua in 1985, a living example of participatory democracy in process. The local Nicaraguan people I met in their own communities, often geographically isolated, felt politically engaged in the development of a democracy. Their national literacy campaign, to which Freire acted as consultant, reduced illiteracy from 50%, one of the highest in Latin America, to less than 13% within five months (Hirshon, 1983, p xi). Antonia Darder, herself a Nicaraguan, talks about the literacy campaign as one of the Sandinista government's major "ideological enterprises" (Darder, 2002, p 205). She reflects on her own political awareness as a schoolgirl being triggered by some of the most progressive Freirean thinkers in her country. His ideas have inspired such radical training texts as Hope and Timmel's *Training for Transformation*, developed out of practical experience in Zimbabwe in the 1970s (first published in 1984), which in turn have been used with great effect in the UK for two decades. His reach has been global, influencing the practice and analysis of many local projects, such as the Gorgie-Dalry Adult Learning Project in Edinburgh (Kirkwood and Kirkwood, 1989).

Finally, it is important to mention Myles Horton and the Highlander Folk School in Tennessee. Freire and Horton, from two vastly different cultures, had a similar vision of the role of popular education in the process of empowerment. The idea for Highlander was stimulated by Horton's visit to Denmark to study the Danish Folk High School movement. The following year, 1932, he started Highlander with Don West, with the broad idea of using popular education for social and economic justice. He was its director until he retired in 1972. In the early 1950s, Highlander focused its attention on racial justice, and from then it played a key reflection and action role in the emerging civil rights movement, with connections with prominent Black activists such as Rosa Parks and Martin Luther King, Jnr. A key community initiative was the development of Citizenship Schools, which concentrated on Black literacy as a route to political power. Horton and Freire eventually came together in December 1987, and Freire felt that their meeting brought him through his despair over Elza's death. The talking book they did together, reflecting on their lives and their experience of radical education, united their shared beliefs, and was published as *We make the road by walking* (Horton and Freire, 1990). A week after they met to discuss the manuscript, Horton died. Freire went on to become director of public education in São Paulo.

Freire's commitment is to the oppressed everywhere, not only in developing countries; the concept is "ideological and political, not geographic" (Mackie, 1980a, p 119). His powerful ideas have extended beyond the limits of literacy to areas such as community development, social work, liberation theology and participatory action research (Reason and Rowan, 1981; Reason and Bradbury, 2001). Indeed, Freire's connection with the liberation theology movement continued throughout his life and "in a conversation with Carmel Borg and [Peter Mayo], the then Sao Paulo cardinal, Paulo Evaristo Arns, stated categorically that, in his view, Paulo changes not only people's lives but also the Church" (P. Mayo, 2004, p 6). His vision was one of transforming humanity to a state of mutual, cooperative endeavour defined by liberation and participatory democracy.

Many criticisms have been levelled against Freire's pedagogy: he has been seen variously as a dangerous revolutionary, an eclectic philosopher, or a literacy expert. He has been accused of interrelating such a diversity of ideas in his work that it reaches the point of analytic impossibility, and of coming from an unacknowledged Christian and Marxist perspective (Leach, 1983). Nevertheless, Freire's thought is compelling:

A word of witness has its place here – a personal witness as to why I find a dialogue with the thought of Paulo Freire an exciting adventure. Fed up as I am with the abstractness and sterility of so much intellectual work in academic circles today, I am excited by a process of reflection which is set in a thoroughly historical context, which is carried on in the midst of a struggle to create a new social order and thus represents a new unity of theory and praxis. And I am encouraged when a man of the stature of Paulo Freire incarnates a rediscovery of the humanizing vocation of the intellectual, and demonstrates the power of thought to negate accepted limits and open the way to a new future. (Richard Shaull in his foreword to *Pedagogy of the oppressed*, 1972, p 11)

Let us now explore an example of a Freirean approach to community development practice.

Empowerment and the use of story

To reiterate, community development is committed to social justice through a process of critical education that begins in personal empowerment, and follows through to collective action for a more just, equal and sustainable world. The strong ideological base on which our work is founded frames the lens through which our practice is shaped, and is a key component of critical praxis. A stumbling block in the process of collective action is the move from personal, group and project stages to the full collective force that is needed for transformative change. Here I want to consider the way in which community development embraces the deeply personal and the profoundly political. Power and empowerment, poverty and privilege, nature and humanity are all inextricably linked by the interdependent web of life on earth, and the beginning of change for a just and sustainable future begins in the personal. It is this personal/political dimension that I want to focus on by linking the use of story to collective action for change.

A real narrative is a web of alternating possibilities. The imagination is capable of kindness that the mind often lacks because it works naturally from the world of Between; it does not engage things in a cold, clear-cut way but always searches for the hidden worlds that wait at the edge of things. The mind tends to see things in a singularly simple, divided way: there is good and bad, ugly and beautiful. The imagination, in contrast, extends a greater hospitality to whatever is awkward, paradoxical or contradictory. The German philosopher Hans-Georg Gadamer, in an interview shortly before his death last year, said: "The integrity of a society demonstrates itself in how that society engages with contradiction". The imagination is both fascinated and stimulated by the presences that cluster within a contradiction. It does not perceive contradictions as the enemy of truth; rather it sees here an interesting intensity. (O'Donohue, 2004, p 138)

If the stories of the people are the beginning of the process of transformative change, where does story link to the process of empowerment? Steedman (2000, p 72) says, "The past is re-used through the agency of social information, and that interpretation of it can only be made with what people know of a social world and their place within it." Life is a fiction. We tell and retell the stories of our lives differently according to our audience, our recollection and our insight; thus stories become shaped by time and space and understanding, and the telling of stories can, in turn, be the vehicle of our understanding. But, for this process to follow through to its collective potential, personal stories need to be set within a theoretical analysis that offers critical insight for action.

In relation to personal empowerment, Mo Griffiths talks about the "little stories" that link voice to narrative, making that vital connection between the deeply personal and the profoundly political "by taking the particular perspective of an individual seriously; that is, the individual as situated in particular circumstances in all their complexity [and linking this] to grander concerns like education, social justice and power" (Griffiths, 2003, p 81). Voice is an expression of self-esteem; it is rooted in the belief that what we have to say is relevant and of value. If we are not heard with respect, our voices are silenced. My point is that the simple act of listening to people's stories, respectfully giving one's full attention, is an act of personal empowerment, but to bring about change for social justice this needs to be located within wider structures.

Let us link this with Freirean thought at this point. Paulo Freire stresses that transformative theory begins in lived reality, in the stories of the people, in relations of trust, mutuality and respect, and that dialogue is the basis of this praxis. It is in these relations of trust that we share stories that are told from the heart. My point here is that giving voice to silenced voices is the beginning of emancipatory practice. People sometimes say to me that this is not viable: in these days driven by tight funding policies, there is not the time to form trusting relationships. My experience is quite different. I believe that trust embodies respect, dignity and all the other qualities that frame this approach to practice, and therefore trusting relationships are intuitive and often immediate. This act of listening from the heart is the foundation of dialogue:

> Paulo somehow connected his whole being, his reason and emotion, to the whole being of another.... His ability to listen, not just to hear the other person, but that way of listening mentioned in the [*Pedagogy of Freedom*] – also noticeable in his look signaled the moment when he accepted and gathered within himself what he was hearing from the other.... In Paulo, to touch, to look and to listen become moments of me and you in dialogue about something which he and the other person wanted to know. (Ana Araujo (Nita) Freire, cited in P. Mayo, 2004, p 80)

Feminist pedagogy, like Freirean pedagogy, is rooted in everyday stories as the beginning of a process of personal empowerment leading to a critical understanding of the nature of structural oppression. This is based on the notion that the deeply personal is profoundly political. But feminist pedagogy emphasises difference, and the complex interlinking, overlapping matrix of oppressions that shape us all according to 'race', class, gender, age, ethnicity, sexuality, 'dis'ability, and so on, rather than a simplistic dichotomous analysis of oppressor–oppressed.

From a feminist perspective, any form of emancipatory practice needs to examine the power relationship in the collaboration. For example, I continually ask myself whether I am focusing my middle-class, White, female, middle-aged, heterosexual, Northern English, Quaker gaze across difference and putting my interpretation on other lives as an outsider looking in (Weiler, 1994, 2001).

Let me give you an example of what I mean in relation to my own practice. Wendy and I found our lives woven together in 1985 when I began work as the community development team leader and community centre manager in Hattersley, Wendy's community. Wendy, who had been a community activist for a number of years, was elected chair of Hattersley Forum at the same time. This was the beginning of a seven-year partnership, and our friendship continues across the 100-mile divide that was created when I moved to Lancaster. The idea of using story in the process of empowerment (autoethnography-locating personal narratives within the historical, cultural and political structures that shape reality) as useful to emancipatory practice is captured in the following story, and in its fragile conception, where Wendy powerfully and immediately identified my 'outsider' gaze and challenged it.

In the beginning, the idea ...

The summer sunshine beamed on us. I drove, Wendy by my side, Celia and Mary in the rear, out for the day in the rugged Derbyshire countryside. Our reunions, this little group of women who had pioneered Hattersley Women for Change in the 1980s, happened at irregular intervals out of a shared history and a fondness for each other. This would be the last, the end of an era, as we were destined to find out a few months later when Celia died. Today, my head was full of ideas for a partnership with Wendy, based on collaborative research, a continuation of the political activism we had shared. We stumbled down the slope together to the wishing well, to witness where baskets of provisions had been left for the plague victims several centuries before, Mary and Celia being too infirm to make the little detour from the car. While we were alone, I gingerly broached the subject, trying to inject it with enthusiasm. "I've got an idea for some important work we could do together ..." Wendy looked ill, drawn, preoccupied, and inwardly I had nagging doubts. Was this really an opportunity for a reciprocal venture, or was I using my friendship with her to further my own academic interests? At that stage, I was acutely aware that the experiences we shared in common as women had vastly different outcomes, some of which led to her being so unwell. I had tried to avoid preformulating my ideas, asking Wendy to climb aboard my wagon, on my terms, and I stuttered, trying to communicate my good ideas in the face of her lukewarm response. She'd give it some thought, she said.

Some weeks later, we negotiated the miniature wooden bridge in dimmed light to the sound of running water and found a secluded table where we could talk. This theme pub, built at the end of the new motorway that led to Hattersley, was a landmark for passing motorists, a sign of consumerist luxury never dreamt of in my days there. Tentatively, I revisited my ideas. In my mind, this research would focus on an autoethnography that was Wendy's. It didn't occur to me that, in my intention to call the research collaborative,

I had clearly perceived the collaboration to be in the product; I failed to notice that I was levelling my middle-class gaze at her working-class story. She looked at me, *"Are you suggesting that I should be the one left standing in my underwear in public! I don't think so! You join me, and we'll stand in our underwear together"*. In those words, she located the contradiction in my ideas. I, in turn, felt exposed! This was Wendy, identifying and dislocating my power in relation to her, and presenting me with a critical insight into my own assumptions. It took me a while to respond to her challenge.

From that time on, Wendy's challenge to my consciousness and my openness to reflect on it has resulted in a much more mutual, comparative approach to our life stories in order to identify the power structures that have shaped our different experience of the world.

Self-esteem/identity/autonomy: a sense of who we are in the world

If story has a powerful potential in the process of critical practice, it is important to have a theoretical understanding that explains how it might work most effectively. Griffiths (2003) supports the idea that "little stories" restore self-respect through dignity, mutuality and conviviality – but stresses that this is not transformative until it becomes a collective process. Darder talks about the way she provides learning contexts in which she resists giving answers, but encourages people "to reach into themselves and back to their histories" (2002, p 233). Using reflective writing to explore the inner depths of memory and history, she works with her students to analyse their stories from theoretical perspectives. The focus of each reflection moves in a connected way to excavate the deepest life experiences. Take, for example, Darder's idea of *problematising* 'reading' with her students. Reflections begin with the first memory of hearing stories told by people who love us, extending by degrees to reflections on learning to read in school. By reaching inside themselves and their histories, she uses this approach with her students to develop reflection and story as a discovery of who they are and what has shaped them in their world. This is the beginning of *critical consciousness*. These stories are critical pedagogy in action, leading to personal autonomy and a collective will to act together for change.

In these ways, we begin to build theory and practice around the role of story in developing the self-esteem that leads to autonomy and the confidence to act. Most importantly, we understand the significance of beginning in the deeply personal stories that have constructed people's reality in the overall process of collective action for social justice. Stories give voice to experience, and in turn provide a structure for reflection on the world. The insight gained from this reflection reveals the political nature of personal experience and leads to critical consciousness and critical action.

This thinking is relevant to research I did with Paula Asgill, my colleague and friend for 13 years, who died prematurely in May 2005. Our lives were woven together when we became educators of community workers at St Martin's College, Lancaster in 1992. As a White woman and a Black woman reflecting on our experience in community development, we realised that there is little evidence to suggest that alliances between Black and White women are sustained beyond the immediate issue that brings them together. Often, the end of the alliance is marked by a passion fuelled by Black rage and White fear. In the course of our research over several years, we concluded that without a sense of one's own personal autonomy, collective action is weakened. In other words, without a sense of self, a pride in one's own identity in relation to the world, alliances across difference will not be sustained. Personal identity gives rise to the confidence needed to reach out in alliance for social justice, otherwise alliances break down in the face of anger, insecurity and a host of other behaviours that arise out of low self-esteem (Ledwith and Asgill, 2000; Ledwith and Asgill, in press). This research is discussed in relation to collective action in Chapter Five.

Doyal and Gough (1991) take this idea of personal autonomy even further. They suggest that autonomy of agency is a basic human need that leads to critical autonomy, and they see this as the prerequisite to critical participation in society, the basis of collective action. Expressed diagrammatically, this offers a clear structure to the development of critical practice:

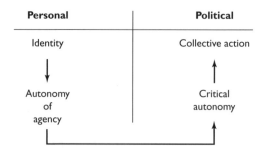

These theoretical insights link the practical strategy of reflection as story with a political discovery of who we are in the world.

Richard Winter, in his work on patchwork texts, remarks that story often starts from a personal interpretation, an 'exploring inwards':

> ... but if fiction is to be the basis for a process of reflection that is to be sustained, we need a format where questioning and exploring beyond one's initial set of ideas is made explicit and is built into the writing process itself, as well as into the discussion of the writing.... In order to sustain the reflective process, a format is needed which is flexible enough to allow different ways of writing to be combined, a format which allows the writer to move easily between description, imagination, creation and analytical commentary. (Winter et al, 1999, p 65)

He suggests that we can create a plurality of voices without false claims to a single truth: that we can present a unity of narrative out of this diversity if we are explicit about uncertainty and present possible, plural truths. In other words, it is possible to link the personal and the collective without reducing or silencing the diversity of different experiences. It is also possible to engage with paradox and contradiction as a more complex 'truth'; a counter-force to positivism, as suggested by O'Donohue (2004). You may wish to link these ideas to the feminist critiques of Freire and the argument for a Freirean-feminist pedagogy presented in Chapter Eight.

Community development always focuses on the stories of the people as the basis of action and reflection. My purpose is to locate this more rigorously as a central component of critical praxis and to define it more clearly as a way of integrating research with people in community into our praxis. I see it as a form of Freirean *problematising*, using story as a vehicle for critical consciousness.

Without an analytic commentary linking the personal to the political, stories remain subjective and without criticality. The following framework is offered as a way of working with groups in community, using story as a tool of empowerment leading to autonomy, critical consciousness and change. It is a method of working that Wendy began with *Hattersley Women Writers* in the late 1980s and early 1990s. Here, I must stress that the importance of such a model lies in its capacity to provide a structure for locating the deeply personal within the profoundly political, and thereby to move understanding from personal empowerment to collective action for transformative change.

A Freirean-feminist approach to story as personal empowerment in the process of collective action for change

- *community groups*: grounded in an ideology of equality, providing the initial context for the practice of social justice, that is trust, mutuality, reciprocity, respect, dignity, empathy in action;
- *writing and telling*: using story as reflection, as *problematising*, as noticing, as fiction, as a skill for community workers;
- *listening*: from the heart and mind, taking experience seriously as the bedrock of action/reflection, grounded in theory; story as the basis of empowerment;
- *noticing*: 'extraordinarily re-experiencing the ordinary' (Shor, 1987, p 93); feminist claiming of feelings and emotion as legitimate knowledge, alongside the intellect, as a more holistic epistemology;
- *empathising*: understanding difference – locating the interface of unity and difference in a complexity of oppressions;
- *making critical connections with the bigger picture*: identifying emergent themes; framing the story within analytical/critical comment – historical, cultural, political, social; moving from the personal to the political;
- *action plan*: coming to new ways of knowing (epistemology) and determining action for new ways of being (ontology);
- *collective action for change*: moving from groups, to projects, to movements for change; developing alliances and networks that have a local/global potential.

This model encapsulates the ideology, theory and action of community development in a framework that moves from the deeply personal story through to collective action for change.

Beginning the process

Narratives of liberation are anchored in people's stories. In this sense, what stories we decide to tell, and the way in which we decide to tell them, form the basis of critical pedagogy (McLaren and Leonard, 1993).

The initial challenge for community workers is to make contact with people wherever they happen to be, in their homes, at the shops, in the pub, launderette, or in already established groups. By identifying issues and interests that are relevant to people's everyday experience, coming together becomes less threatening. Community groups will contain all the raw emotions of life, but a culture of respect can evolve, where critical issues are explored, and where action is decided. Overcoming the apathy or anger generated by social exclusion is a crucial skill, and *relevance* is the key to this transition. The loss of self-esteem, which gives rise to apathy and anger, can be transformed into confidence and a sense of personal autonomy early on in the process if your practice is founded on the values that form the foundation of community development. This is the basis of Freirean pedagogy, and more of this approach can be found in Chapter Five. As well as an evolving critical consciousness, community action can also be triggered by a shared crisis: a death, a suicide, an external threat to the community, all factors that unite people to act together. This in itself generates an energy out of apathy and gives you the opportunity to bring people together from a critical perspective.

The basic skill is *dialogue*, a mutual and reciprocal form of communication in which the act of listening in a holistic way is valuing, and therefore liberating. Without humility on the part of the community worker, dialogue cannot happen. Communication is a key skill in community development that involves an understanding of power in relationships. When it is informed by the values implicit in an ideology of equality, it becomes that critical form of *dialogue* that is the basis of emancipatory practice. This is the foundation of praxis. The next stage in the process is problem-posing, or *problematising*, presenting an everyday reality in a symbolic form – photograph, story, cartoon, drama, music – in which it generates debate and alternative perspectives. Here, I have concentrated on the use of story in community groups as a form of *problematising*. Group discussion gradually shifts from the initial focus and assumes a more critical analysis of the situation. Developing the skills to connect the personal to the cultural and political context is central to critical practice. Without this, each personal case becomes pathological: the emphasis placed on the inadequacies of the individual rather than the inequities of the system. Our challenge is to find a strategy for locating "little stories" in the bigger picture. Action research, embedded in an emancipatory ideology, offers us the potential to look deeper into the microscope of the personal while framing it within the wider political picture. Thus, "little stories" give depth to bigger pictures, and the personal is understood as political.

FOUR

Organising in the community

> Education, or the act of knowing as Freire calls it, is an ongoing research programme into aspects of people's experience and its relationship to wider social, economic and political factors. (Kirkwood, 1991, p 103)

An integrated praxis grows through the ongoing dynamic of research, critical education and community action in symbiotic relation. It is a process of *conscientisation* through *dialogue* (Freire, 1972).

Dominant ideology is absorbed into the very fabric of people's being, influencing the way we see the world and engage with it, creating a false consciousness that does not question reality. Community development practice emerges from a strong value base founded on an ideology of equality: our trust in people, in turn, restores people's faith in themselves. In order to be a critical practitioner, it is necessary to be reflective and self-reflective, an inner and outer process of research. In the inner process, we need to be reflexive: to question our reflections, and take them to a deeper level. This is the way we challenge our own inner attitudes and prejudices. In the outer process, we need to create critical spaces where we can engage with others in building a body of knowledge that takes our collective understanding to more complex analytic levels. Critical thought is discouraged in a world that is founded on capitalism; one in which the interests of the powerful are served by the subservience of the many. Herbert Marcuse, whose thinking was formed in the 1950s and 1960s, identified structures of domination and social control that produce an advanced state of conformity: "Independence of thought, autonomy, and the right to political opposition are being deprived of their basic critical function in a society which seems increasingly capable of satisfying the needs of the individuals through the way in which it is organized" (1991, p 1). Marcuse talks about false consciousness being the conceptual repression of understanding life experience: "a restriction of meaning" (Marcuse, 1991, p 208). In this chapter, I look at the process of critical consciousness in collective, public spaces as the basis for organising in community.

Emancipatory action research as a key component of critical praxis

Research is essential to the community development process. It develops knowledge in action, and keeps it relevant to the changing political context. However, the approach to research that we adopt needs to fit the ideological base of community development, and integrate into our praxis. In order to assess the potential contradictions that might give rise to dissonance in our practice, it is important to examine the power-based approaches of traditional research.

The positivist tradition has created an approach to research that is essentially 'masculine', attempting to be objective, value-free and absolute, at the expense of feelings, paradox or imprecision. Traditional approaches to research with human beings have, therefore, carried out research *on* people rather than *with* people, creating a powerful myth around the researcher as an external, objective expert, and the only person qualified for the job. This myth is alienating and generally denying of more 'female' qualities. For example, as a community worker, I was presented with a contradiction between the emancipatory style of my practice and the pressure to adopt a research method that was 'scientific', and inevitably controlling. I was seeking a coherent methodological framework that shared my ideology. One of the key concepts here is *cultural invasion*: the "imposition of the values, belief systems, ideology, cultural norms and practices of an imperialist culture on those it has colonized and oppressed" (Southgate, 1981, p 53). It is ideological hypocrisy for community development to resort to research methods that are based on unequal, culturally invasive relationships while claiming an emancipatory approach.

One of the most formative contributions to my thinking was Rowan's Dialectical Paradigm for Research (Rowan, 1981). In his attempt to synthesise old and new paradigm research, he analyses three concepts: *alienation, social change* and *the research cycle*. 'Alienation' refers to the treating of people as fragments, as a result of which they are not perceived as an essential part of a whole. In other words, studying the way people behave without relating it to the whole person, let alone their social and political context, is a dehumanising act. People function as whole beings within a context, and we need to understand the context in order to understand people. I am, therefore, suggesting that research that is taken on without critical, ethical analysis is likely to be incomplete, oppressive and alienating. It is likely to be based on assumptions that reinforce discrimination. If we are seeking a style of research that is compatible with anti-oppressive ideology, we need to be sure that it contributes to the process of liberation from oppression. Emancipatory action research seeks to be participatory and collaborative, involving everyone in the process of change, demanding "that the investigator be as open to change as the 'subjects' are encouraged to be – only they are now more like co-researchers than like conventional subjects" (Rowan, 1981, p 97). This is a model of research that is based on collective action, with all participants acting in the interests of the whole. It begins as a response to the experience of the oppressed and is a mutual, reciprocal process of discovery "where the researcher and the researched both contribute to the expansion of the other's knowledge" (Opie, 1992, p 66).

Emancipatory action research is a form of action research that, in line with our practice, is firmly grounded in an ideology of equality. It adopts a methodology and methods that are collaborative, and in doing so commits to identifying and challenging unequal power relations within its process. It is rooted in *dialogue*, attempting to work *with*, not *on*, people, and intends that its process should be empowering for all involved. More than this, it is committed to collective action for social change as its outcome. My assertion is that not only is this approach to research consonant with the values, vision and principles of community development, but it is an essential component of its critical praxis.

The key point I am making here is that emancipatory ideology is the lens through which this research is shaped. That strongly stated value base forms the foundation of the quality and validity of the research, and provides us with a frame through which we can check every stage of the process by forming validity questions. In other words, if we claim that our work is reciprocal, collaborative, transformative and empowering, what evidence is there that this is the case? What evidence is there that what we claim to do is what we are doing? If these questions are reflectively and collaboratively developed at each stage, we will be faced with the jarring discomfort of dissonance from the answers we get if we falter from our course.

The cycle model as a model of process

Rowan's research cycle model, which I have adapted in Figure 4.1, offers a clear diagrammatic structure for stages of the process of community development, taking an emancipatory action research approach that is central to critical praxis.

The cycle model is particularly useful in integrating reflection and action in the process of community development. Although it is possible

Figure 4.1: The cycle model

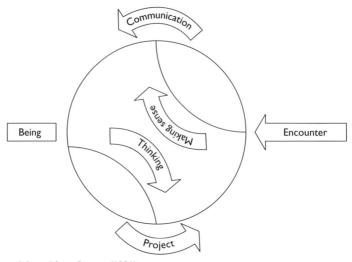

Source: Adapted from Rowan (1981)

to enter the cycle at any stage, for ease of explanation I will begin at *Being*, the stage at which we become aware of a need for change. No longer are the old ways of seeing or doing appropriate. Perhaps an issue has arisen that calls for new thinking. The cycle has an inner and outer flow. As I move into the stage of *Thinking*, the arc indicates an inward process of seeking. It is a creative process that involves talking to people, sharing ideas and experience, and finding out relevant information. At some point, thinking is not enough and I need to move outwards to the stage of *Project*, involving others as the process moves on. At this stage, we formulate a plan of action, which moves from the contradiction of the existing situation towards new practice. Continuing the outer movement, we move towards *Encounter*, the stage at which we engage in action with the wider community. The model is flexible and at any stage it is possible to flow back and forth, until we are satisfied with the relevance of our work. But, there is a point at which action needs to move inwards from *Encounter* to a stage of *Making sense*. This is the stage at which "experience turns into meaning and knowledge" (Rowan, 1981, p 100) and where a balance between achieving understandable simplicity and complex connections has to be reached. For the process to become useful, there is a need to share the experience. Following the arc outwards to the stage of *Communication* with new understanding emerging from practice, we are generating knowledge in action and need to share it so that others can learn from the experience. Community workers need to share experience by writing up projects for publication in books and journals; having dialogue with other communities; sharing ideas and experience at conferences and meetings; and using the media more effectively. In doing so, we contribute to an increasing body of community development knowledge.

At each point in the cycle I have adapted six types of question for the community worker from Rowan (1981) that help with insights into the process and also provide rigour:

i)   *positivist/efficiency* questions, which focus on validity and tighten up the research design (Is a representative sample involved? How is the information gathered?);

ii) *alienation/authenticity* questions, which highlight roles and personal commitment (Who has initiated the research? Who has defined the problem?);

iii) *political/patriarchal* questions, which look at the social context and the patterns of oppression that exist (Is the social context being taken into account? What is being studied and by whom?);

iv) *dialectical* questions, which consider the philosophical assumptions of the research (Is just one answer being sought? Is the situation being explored from more than one perspective?);

v)   *legitimacy* questions, which explore the position of the researcher in the situation while acknowledging that there may be confining structures (Is there pressure to avoid certain problems? Who is funding the research?);

vi) *relevance* questions, which consider whether the study is of use and the likelihood of the findings being acted upon (Am I doing good – or harm? Is my analysis relevant to the people who took part? How are the results disseminated? Who will use them and who will benefit?).

I have included examples to illustrate my point, but a more comprehensive guide is to be found in Rowan (1981, p 107).

All too often community development is limited by failing to share theory and practice in a wider context. It is part of the '*doing* rather than *thinking*' syndrome that results in all too few projects contributing their experience to a body of knowledge. The result is that theory is impoverished, and, as a result, fails to develop the necessary analysis for critical practice to achieve its potential for transformative change. So, I am proposing that research is an integral and essential part of the process of change, and that emancipatory action research is the approach that is consonant with community development ideology. The cycle model structures our often chaotic and tangled process in clear, diagrammatic form, representing balance and directional flow. This does not mean to say that it denies any of the complexity of the process; quite the opposite. It is of great value in offering structures within which to contain and disentangle the knots. For the community worker, I feel it represents stages of the process in relation to the whole. It reminds busy workers that practice is only effective when it is part of a balanced process of reflection, action, inquiry and communication: "seeing research as a set of phases can also help make clearer some of the problems facing community development in its work of developing alternative ways of doing research" (Graham and Jones, 1992, p 236).

The cycle does not remain isolated. It becomes part of multiple cycles in an interlocking model. These can be used sequentially to go deeper into an issue, producing a spiral, or they can be used concurrently so that the same issue is developed from diverse perspectives. An example of a spiral from my own practice would be the way that a group of women writers got involved in Hattersley Women for Change, which in turn developed Hattersley Women's Room. An example of a concurrent model would be the way that Keeping Hattersley Warm, a home insulation project, had sideways links with the precinct action group, the residents' association, and a gardening/allotments project all of which focused on different aspects of improving the quality of the environment. When developed in conjunction with reflective questions, the cycle model becomes more rigorous, and at each stage we are reminded of the anti-discriminatory, reciprocal and empowering essence of this approach. "By making each cycle fully rigorous in its own terms, we can achieve a recursive validity of a cumulative nature – yielding a deeper and more extensive truth than that given by a linear approach" (Rowan, 1981, p 105).

This collaborative approach to research sits well with community development practice and plays a key role in critical praxis by uniting theory and practice in emancipatory action. It calls for an ideological change of consciousness on the part of the researcher where the skills involve being fully present, to "suspend thinking and to stay aware of your experience in the ever-flowing present" (Reason and Rowan, 1981, p 122). Rather than the claimed neutrality of the traditional researcher, the emancipatory action researcher is involved in the process as a co-researcher in partnership with the community. To be fully present is not as simple as it sounds. It requires the community worker to operate at critical and self-critical levels of awareness, otherwise "all we are doing is opening ourselves to our most unthought-out prejudices and emotional reactions" (Rowan and Reason, 1981, p 123).

One of the most challenging concepts to emerge from this approach to research is that described by Heron as a state where there is full interpersonal reciprocity at each stage of the research action – where the researcher becomes co-subject and the subject becomes co-researcher in a truly Freirean way (Heron, 1981). This not only integrates the researcher in the process, letting go of any delusions of neutrality, but it also relinquishes power over the process and the product to achieve a more participatory experience in partnership with the community. Traditional research is epitomised by the researcher having full control and the subject having no control and often very little idea of the purpose: a model that can be invasive, exploitative and harmful. An emancipatory approach expects subjects to share control appropriately at every stage of the process, and for researchers to be participants in the research. Of course, there are many intermediate points where participants may be more involved in some stages of the research process than in others. True endogenous research is that which is generated and conducted from within the culture by people who are of that culture according to their own knowledge and values (Maruyama, 1981, p 230). This, in its strict sense, is free from cultural invasion and hegemonic exploitation and is culturally 'pure' – hard to attain, but a challenge to received academic wisdom.

The new paradigm researchers of the 1980s were profoundly influenced by Freirean pedagogy. An overt example is that of Randall and Southgate's approach to dialogical research using a *problematising* approach with community groups in a community centre (Randall and Southgate, 1981, p 349). The situation is a familiar one in community development: conflict was raging between groups who disagreed on the purpose of the centre, and they were, in turn, blaming the community workers. Using cartoons as codifications, they identified major contradictions that emerged in dialogue, depersonalising the anger and diverting the energy into forming new alliances. Emancipatory approaches to action research often start from a position of *problematising* or problem-posing – the Freirean approach to identifying an issue, which also questions the underlying causes. In developing a critical understanding of social problems and their structural causes, the possibilities for overcoming them become part of the whole. It calls for *dialogue*: a horizontal interaction between researchers and those with whom the research is conducted, embracing both action and reflection. In other words, it is committed not to abstract external knowledge, but to active, democratic participation in the process of change.

In these ways, the work of Reason, Rowan, Heron and others incorporated Freire's thought into a new paradigm for research. This is vital for community development inasmuch as: i) it makes a clear break with alienating methods based on scientific research; ii) it offers a method that moves us towards the wholeness that is necessary to heal alienating experience in everyday life; iii) it offers a holism within which to contain the fragmentation of postmodern thought; iv) it supports a critical pedagogy that is founded in collective action; and v) it offers a language and structure of research that "yield a deeper and more extensive truth" (Rowan, 1981, p 105).

Reason defines three important, interrelated aspects of this paradigmatic shift: "the move to participatory and holistic knowing; to critical subjectivity; and to knowledge in action" (Reason, 1988, p 10).

i)   *Participatory and holistic knowing* is achieved through a critical engagement in and with the world.
ii) *Critical subjectivity* is the synthesis of naïve inquiry (a knowing based on feelings, emotions and experience) and scientific inquiry, bridging the subjective/objective divide to provide an approach to human inquiry that is objectively subjective. This offers a range of possible styles, from heuristic research, "a process of internal search through which one discovers the nature and meaning of experience and develops methods and procedures for further investigation and analysis" (Moustakas, 1990, p 9) to Heron's form of cooperative inquiry, which is based on different kinds of knowledge: *experiential* (direct encounter with people, places or things); *practical* (how to do something); *propositional* (theoretical knowledge about something); and *presentational* (symbolising the knowing that we cannot put into words in movement, sound, colour, shape, line, poetry, drama and story) (Reason, 1994, p 42).
iii) Finally, *knowledge in action* is used by Reason as the term to denote a transcending of the chasm between intellect and experience in which Western consciousness has placed value on 'thinkers' at the expense of 'doers', dividing theory from practice. Knowledge in action is, therefore, engaged in the world rather than alienated from it.

> I have been much persuaded over recent months by the image that the purpose of human inquiry is not so much the search for truth but to heal, and above all to heal the alienation, the split that characterizes modern experience....

To heal means to make whole: we can only understand our world as a whole if we are part of it; as soon as we attempt to stand outside, we divide and separate. In contrast, making whole necessarily implies participation: one characteristic of a participative world-view is that the individual person is restored to the circle of community and the human community to the context of the wider natural world. To make whole also means to make holy; another characteristic of a participatory world-view is that meaning and mystery are restored to human experience, so that the world is once again experienced as a sacred place. (Reason, 1994, p 10)

Schuler's core values of the new community

In practice, I found my adaptation of Rowan's cycle model useful in the way that it focused my mind on important stages of the community development process, and helped me to see the complementary connections between different projects. I am introducing Schuler's core values model because it helped me to understand the need to pay attention to the balance of needs in the process of community development. The core values model (Schuler, 1996) does not come from a Freirean perspective, but complements the cycle model by reminding us that projects in the process of change should not be fragmented from an organic whole. Schuler sees a community as a system that he likens to a human body, each part dependent on the rest for a healthy, fully-functioning whole. If one aspect is developed without attention to the rest, the whole will not flourish. If these ideas are applied to regeneration projects that focus on economic developments in community without paying attention to well-being or culture or education, it becomes apparent that the overall process will be weakened. This is similar to understanding that life on earth is an ecosystem, which can be related to human diversity and biodiversity. In other words, if the human world and the natural world are to co-exist as a healthy functioning system, we need to pay attention to all its component parts. From this view, you can begin to see that racism or sexism diminish the fully functioning whole, in just the same way that the destruction of the environment threatens a sustainable future. Focusing on community assets rather than deficits, Schuler's model is based on *community participation* and *citizen action*. He identifies six core values, which are graphically represented in Figure 4.2.

The model captures the interrelatedness of the system, and makes it

Figure 4.2: Core values of the new community

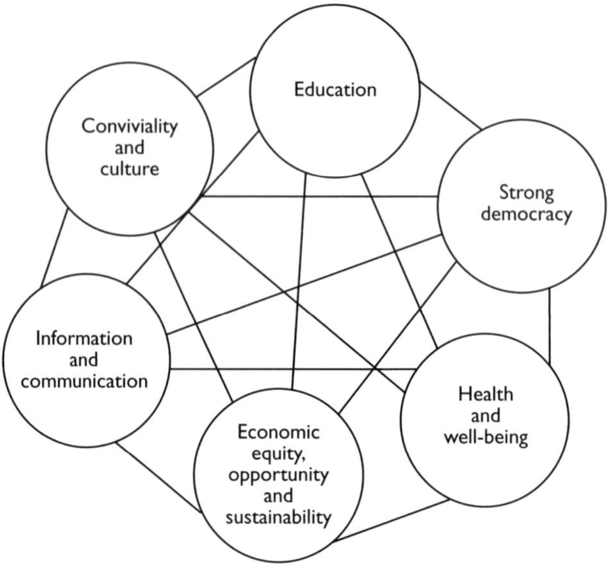

Source: Schuler (1996)

easy to see how underfunctioning in one area impacts on the whole. It moves us nearer to a model that demonstrates the interlinked nature of human needs for healthy, thriving communities. Schuler is proposing that the core values should be examined in relation to both major and minor community projects, and I would stress that this also needs analysis according to difference and diversity. By way of example, the health and well-being needs of people according to 'race', class, 'dis'ability, gender, age and so on are likely to be quite different. These critical components are kept in place if we develop effective approaches to planning and evaluation.

Achieving better community development (ABCD)

The Scottish Community Development Centre (SCDC) identified a dearth of systematic evaluation in practice at a time when policies were increasingly focusing on community development. The result was that the SCDC, with support from government departments across the UK and Ireland, were commissioned to develop a core set of indicators for the evaluation of community development. The result is the ABCD framework shown in Figure 4.3 (Barr and Hashagen, 2000), a flexible but rigorous approach to planning and evaluating community development interventions. All those involved in the process, including

Figure 4.3: The ABCD model

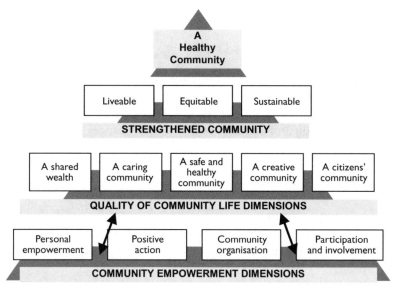

Source: Barr and Hashagen (2000)

funders, policy makers, managers, practitioners and activists, are encouraged to be clear about their goals, their approaches, and how change can be effected in the light of experience at policy, programme and project levels, with the overriding emphasis on the centrality of community.

Planning and evaluation are integral to the process of community development and play a key role in collective action. Barr and Hashagen (2000, p 17) argue that "evaluation is the key to effective practice, and that it should be conducted in accordance with the values and principles of community development itself. This means:

- working with communities to develop a shared view about what community interventions are there to do
- deciding how the community and other partners are going to work towards realising that vision
- bringing in the resources the community has itself, or can access
- providing opportunities for community members to play a direct role in the process
- ensuring the community has ownership over the outcome".

This model, a pyramid of outcomes, is a core idea in ABCD. It is founded on community empowerment with its four dimensions, all of which must be built into every community activity:

i)   personal empowerment: individual learning, knowledge, confidence and skill;
ii) positive action: work related to poverty, health, 'race', gender, 'dis'ability, and other aspects of discrimination that challenges dominant power structures;
iii) community organisation: the range, quality and effectiveness of community groups, their relations with each other and the wider world;
iv) participation and involvement: by which changes in community life are achieved.

The outcomes from these are related to:

i)   learning
ii) justice
iii) action and organisation
iv) power.

The empowerment dimensions interact with quality of life dimensions, as indicated by the arrows on the model. Quality of life dimensions are the context for change that involves central and local government agencies, and others responsible for policy, management and service delivery in social, economic and environmental areas. They are expected to engage with community in partnership through five dimensions:

i)   community economic action;
ii) social and service development;
iii) community environmental action;
iv) community arts and cultural development;
v)   governance and development.

The outcomes from this stage of the process are linked to:

i)   shared wealth;
ii) a caring community;
iii) a safe and healthy community;
iv) a creative community;
v)   a citizens' community.

These build towards a stronger and healthy community with liveability, sustainability and equitability outcomes.

   The cycle of change in ABCD is a planned process of change based on *inputs*, *process*, *outputs* and *outcomes*. I have tried to capture these stages in Figure 4.4.

Community development draws on *'inputs'*, human, financial and material resources that are identified inside and outside the community. *'Process'* is the 'bread and butter' of community work – organisational capacity, advice and support, encouraging reflection and planning, assessing power relationships and helping develop strategic thinking (www.scdc.org.uk/abcd_summary.htm). This leads to *'outputs'*, which are the tangible products, the quantitative measure of what we achieve

Figure 4.4: Community development: a model of process

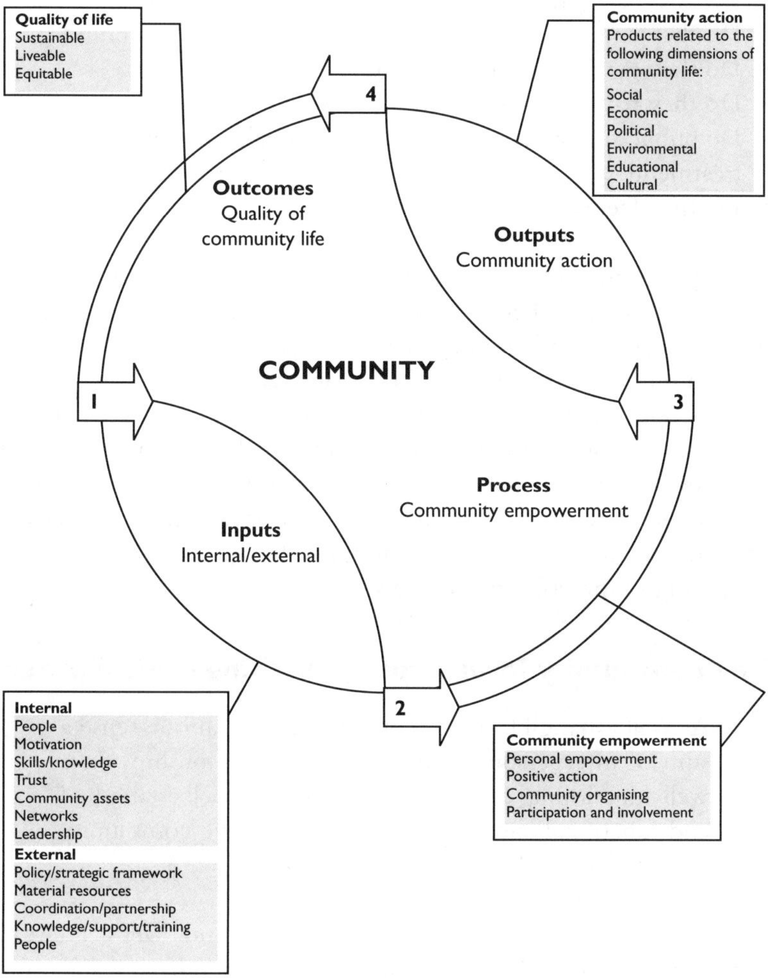

Source: Developed from Barr and Hashagen (2000)

in action. Finally, '*outcomes*' is the stage that effectively measures quality of community life against community development interventions, the less tangible results of our work that relate to social capital.

Based on the concepts of *sustainability*, *liveability* and *equitability*, Barr and Hashagen (2000) suggest developing general questions as a guideline for more specific questions which identify the quality of life outcomes of community development interventions:

- Can people meet basic needs for food, shelter and clothing?
- Do they have the opportunity for fulfilling work and leisure?
- Are they confident in themselves and proud of their identity?
- Are they in control of their lives?
- Are they safe and secure?
- Do they enjoy good relations with others in the community?
- Do they get justice and fair treatment?
- Do they have equal access to the services they need?
- Do public and private services provide equality of opportunity and treatment?
- Do they feel well and happy?

It is by framing relevant questions, questions developed with the community, that we begin to move towards a more critical approach to practice. Indicators should always be identified in partnership with the community, and they should develop measures based on changes in: i) people, ii) the community, iii) local services, and iv) policies. Effective evaluation provides the foundation for the next cycle of planning, and in this rigorous and comprehensive way, the community development process gains strength and achieves greater potential. Let us move on to look at the community forum as a structure for organising in the collective process.

The community forum: contextualising critical praxis

> As well as tangible assets, communities are in one sense a sum of interpersonal and inter-group relationships. In a well-functioning community these will be well established and functional and a crucial part of how the community actually works. (Barr and Hashagen, 2000, p 56)

In the radical community work of the 1970s and 1980s, Freirean pedagogy influenced those who sought a critical approach that located local community action within a wider social and economic analysis

(Lovett et al, 1983). Feminism's insight into the personal as political had brought new perspectives to work with women and children in community (M.Taylor, 1995).The Community Development Project's challenge to ideologies of poverty as pathology reinforced these views, calling for alliances that were capable of taking on the might of the state. As a response, alliances began to stretch outwards across community and regional boundaries.This process was supported by radical left-wing local governments in the 1980s, who developed policies of participation and empowerment, investing large budgets in both establishing community work teams, and establishing neighbourhood centres where local service provision could be located in the heart of communities. Added to this was the way in which metropolitan counties, formed in the major conurbations, strengthened innovative policies and projects. Out of this context came the community forum movement, which united communities in their struggle against poverty. For many, inspiration had come from Saul Alinsky's model of People's Organizations. The difference lay in the power and the funding rather than the structure: the Alinsky model was independently funded, whereas the community forum movement was largely supported by socialist local governments.

The roots of community associations lie in educational settlements such as Toynbee Hall, Oxford House, Friends' House and the Working Men's College, which were based on principles of democracy and participation in relation to the needs of local people.The community forum movement gained strength in the 1980s when it was adopted as a strategy for decentralisation by most left-wing local governments in the struggle against Thatcherism. It strengthened the position that local government was beginning to hold as the 'main focus of opposition to the Conservative Government after 1979' (Khan, 1989a). Khan's research into the functioning of forums in Sheffield and Islington led him to form three major conclusions for the limited success that this strategy achieved: i) lack of political will, ii) inflexibility in the operation of forums, and iii) inaccessibility for representatives from those groups that are most marginalised. Interestingly, Khan observed that, whereas the Islington policy on forums heralded a new type of local socialism that was both "bold and radical, the actual powers that were to be devolved to forums were minimal" (Khan, 1989a, p 1). There was a real danger that devolution of power in a class sense would obscure representation of differently oppressed groups.

The community forum's function is:

- to bring individuals from the community together;
- to provide an umbrella organisation for community activism;
- to provide a platform for debate and action;
- to provide critical education for democratic practice;
- to act as a pressure group for improved service delivery;
- to organise leisure and cultural activities;
- to manage the community centre;
- to provide a collective voice for the community.

In this way, the forum becomes the fulcrum of change in community. It offers a structure for organisation, where groups and projects become cross-germinating and more collective, and where networks and alliances are formed. It is a place where the conflicting interests of the community are expressed, and where the interests of the people are protected by participatory, democratic decision making. This is a public space with the potential for critical reflection and collective action, and for the deepening of consciousness.

Hierarchical models of power in society are often replicated by those who are subordinated by them, resulting in acts of *horizontal violence*. In the early days, Hattersley Forum often erupted into conflict between those seeking personal power, while those who dared to challenge were personally and vindictively attacked. The rest were silenced, uncomfortable and embarrassed. Freire and Gramsci gave me a political analysis of what would have otherwise felt like a damaging personal experience at times.

The forum meeting was held once a month, and every resident had a democratic voting right. Working together with Hattersley Forum Executive during the early period, our aim was to develop greater democratic participation. We:

- changed the physical layout of the meeting, abandoning the top table and sitting 'in the round';
- welcomed people with refreshments and made the atmosphere more congenial;
- minimised the business side of the agenda and devoted more time to relevant issues and critical debate, often using a problem-posing approach with photographs, video, story and sometimes inviting people from outside communities, agencies, or local government departments;
- held collaborative training and analysis days;
- made effective use of the local authority community development policy document as a focus for action;

- adopted a clause that community centre user-group conditions require that representatives attend monthly forum meetings;
- developed a community newsletter giving information about community projects, issues and events to encourage wider participation;
- set up a community notice board, which posed local/global issues.

Gradually, the tension of the meetings transformed and the partnership between workers and the forum executive, meeting informally on a daily basis and formally on a weekly basis, went through a political metamorphosis.

The process of *conscientisation* at forum meetings continued as an inner process at the same time as networks were formed outwardly. We became part of wider anti-poverty campaigns and protests. In these ways, the forum provided a vital link between organising in community, collective consciousness and reaching beyond the boundaries of the community in collective action.

The community forum became a focal point in decentralisation policies adopted by many left-wing councils. Khan discusses this shift of power from the parliamentary party to local government as an attempt to relocate a political nexus harnessing the left of the party with the combined energies of other disenfranchised pressure groups, such as women, minority ethnic groups, left-wing trade unionist and gay and lesbian groups (Khan, 1989b). It was received as a radical move and attracted attention because local government was seen as a site of resistance, with the community forum as the locus of struggle. It failed as a transformative, historical moment because the "collective will" in which "inner reasoning is worked out in the popular consciousness" (Gramsci, 1986, p 127) had not been achieved.

Collective will can only be achieved if community work develops a coherent theoretical basis for action, and this can only come about if critical praxis bridges the divide between theory and practice. Perhaps, in this respect, it is worth considering Saul Alinsky's approach to organising in community as a way of creating political consciousness and harnessing collective power for social justice.

Saul Alinsky: People's Organizations

> It should always be remembered that a real organization of the people, one in which they completely believe and which they feel is definitely their own, must be rooted in the experiences of the people themselves. This is essential if

the organization is to be built upon and founded upon the people. (Alinsky, 1969, p 78)

The Chicago of the 1930s, in the grips of the Depression and controlled by the Mafia, housed the Back-of-the-Yards neighbourhood, a concentration of extreme poverty set in a vast area of old stockyards. In 1938, Saul Alinsky was assigned to research the causes of juvenile delinquency as a postgraduate student. As a participant observer, he entered the world of Al Capone, an experience that led him to believe that criminal behaviour was a symptom of poverty and powerlessness. He found he could not remain a detached observer. Growing up in Chicago's Jewish ghetto, together with his mother's maxim on not walking away from what is clearly wrong, led to a passionate belief that social justice could be achieved through democracy. His methods were not theoretically founded, but based on the premise that restoring dignity to poor communities by showing them how to organise would give them a power that could strategically outmanoeuvre the powerful. These were the methods he used to create a 'backyard revolution' that spread across cities in America (www.itvs.org/democraticpromise/ alinsky.html). His vision was an 'organisation of organisations' that embraced all groups: youth committees, small businesses, trade unions and the Catholic Church. On 14 July 1939, Alinsky, Joe Meegan (an organiser with links with the Catholic Church) and Bishop Sheil convened the first Back-of-the-Yards Council meeting, which was to prove a revolutionary step in democratic participation, organising and action.

Alinsky's People's Organizations were based on the use of power, action and justice to fight racism, poverty and isolation. Jacques Maritain saw him as an authentic revolutionary of modern times, describing him as "an indomitable and dreaded organizer of 'People's Organizations' and an anti-racist leader whose methods are as efficacious as they are unorthodox" (Maritain in Doering, 1994, p xiv). Alinsky's aim was the political education of powerless people to bring about their active participation in local politics. His strategy was based on inventive, creative, non-violent conflict and disruption as a way of identifying the collective power that poor people have to force corporations and authorities to change. His belief was that grassroots political activism should bring about the reform of powerful institutions. On 13 June 1972, Saul Alinsky collapsed and died following a heart attack. He was 63 years old. His colourful character had an impact on everyone who came into contact with him, and he was described by Doering as:

> ... a gruff, rough-hewn, agnostic Jew for whom religion
> of any kind held very little importance and just as little
> relation to the focus of his life's work: the struggle for
> economic and social justice. He loved crowds, the more
> unruly the better. His gestures and language were muscular
> and he used the vernacular of a tough street fighter. His
> habitual stance seemed one of calculated, aggressive and
> imaginative irreverence. Alinsky's primary tactic was to stir
> up nonviolent conflict. (Doering, 1994, p xv)

In his own words, Alinsky's tactic for overcoming apathy was "to rub
raw the resentment of the people of the community; fan the latent
hostilities ... to the point of overt expression" (Alinsky, 1972, pp 116-
17).

Alinsky and his organisers developed community activism in many
cities across America. Bailey tells of some of the extreme reactions he
evoked: banned from Oakland, California by the city council; jailed
in Kansas; a large corporation hired detectives to watch him; and the
former editor of *The Christian Century* described him as developing a
"power structure dictatorship based on slum dwellers" (Bailey, 1974,
p 1). He also had many admirers, and one was the governor of Illinois
who said, "If I were asked to choose a single agency which most
admirably represented all that our democracy stands for, I would select
the Back-of-the-Yards Council. All that you have done for the health,
the social welfare, the economic advancement, and the happiness of
the people in your community is to me one of the most heartening
accomplishments of our time" (Bailey, 1974, p 1).

Saul Alinsky's impact has inspired community activism in the UK
since the 1970s. Although he did not claim any strong theoretical
base, his ideas are consonant with Freire: "People only understand
things in terms of their experience, which means you must get within
their experience. Further, communication is a two-way process. If
you try to get your ideas across to others without paying attention to
what they have to say to you, you can forget about the whole thing"
(Alinsky, 1972, p 81). So, let us take a closer look at what he had to say
that may be of relevance to organising in community today.

According to Alinsky:

> A People's Organization is not a philanthropic plaything
> or a social service's ameliorative gesture. It is a deep, hard-
> driving force, striking and cutting at the very roots of all
> the evils which beset the people. It recognizes the existence

of the vicious circle in which most human beings are caught, and strives viciously to break this circle. It thinks in terms of social surgery and not cosmetic cover-ups. This is one of the reasons why a People's Organization will find that it has to fight its way along every foot of the road toward its destination – a people's world. (Alinsky, 1969, p 133)

We can detect in Alinsky's words an analysis: transformative change needs to target causes not symptoms, and be not ameliorative but radical in its intention. Despite his military terminology, his model for change was based on non-violence, and his recipe for success was based in equal proportions on a formula of *agitate, antagonise, educate* and *organise*.

People's Organizations were carefully structured. One large community organisation comprised representatives from other groups in the community. In this sense, membership was not open to individuals, but to the representatives of community groups, defined as any officially organised group or business that had a minimum of 10 members or employees. If a group could not meet these criteria, it could become a cooperating agency with most of the rights of the member groups. The fundamental democratic principle was that the community organisation must be open to any community group which wanted to join. The member groups sent delegates to an annual community congress, usually a one-day event, at which officers for the coming year were elected and resolutions passed. Throughout the year, the organisation was governed by the senate, comprising delegates from each member group plus the elected officers. The senate met monthly and appointed chairs for the standing committees, each of which tackled a different community issue. The standing committees also met on a monthly basis. Multiple membership of different groups was encouraged as a strategy for avoiding inter-group conflict.

Bailey's (1974) research into the success of People's Organizations defined 'activism' as a sustained and regular level of participation in the decision-making process of the organisation as well as one's self-perception as an activist. People's Organizations were more likely to emerge under particular social conditions generated by powerlessness and alienation, but paradoxically were more effective where i) the local churches were involved and had the resources to support action and ii) residents had the resources for effective participation. There are four key features that Bailey identifies as prerequisites to success of these organisations: i) independent funds; ii) the hire of professional outside organisers with experience and knowledge of protest tactics and organisation building; iii) grassroots networks for immediate mobilisation; and iv) the use of protest with the emphasis on disruption.

"If your function is to attack apathy and get people to participate it is necessary to attack the prevailing patterns of organized living in the community. *The first step in community organization is community disorganization*" (Alinsky, 1972, p 116). As with Freirean pedagogy, Alinsky's ideas are based on personal empowerment leading to collective change. Confidence, self-esteem and personal power provide community activists with a sense of autonomy and a cause, giving them a greater stake in the community and society at large. This thinking was at the heart of Alinsky's methods of organising in community.

Horwitt (1997) considers Alinsky's ideas more important now than ever:

> In the 1940s, Alinsky organized the basic model in "the Jungle," the old Chicago stockyards neighborhood made famous in Upton Sinclair's classic muckraking work. There, he recruited and guided indigenous leaders who identified common interests that brought together previously hostile ethnic groups of Serbs and Croatians, Czechs and Slovaks, Poles and Lithuanians into a large organization, the Back of The Yards Neighborhood Council. The Council, like the handful of other large-scale organizations Alinsky organized in predominately black communities in the late 50s and 60s, was in part a pressure group, demanding and negotiating with public and private sector institutions on bread and butter issues like better schools and more jobs, and in part a self-help operation that established credit unions, built or rehabbed housing and provided social services. As important as these functions were, the greater significance of Alinsky's voluntary community organizations is that they provided a connection between the individual and the larger society. This was what made Alinsky's experiment important, Daniel Bell wrote in 1945, in his review of Alinsky's book, Reveille for Radicals, because it "attempts to give people a sense of participation and belonging [and] becomes important as a weapon against cynicism and despair".

Today, Alinsky's impact is still evident. 'Citizen activists' still use the same strategies for change in urban neighbourhoods across America.

Alinsky, known as the father of democratic radicalism, founded the Industrial Areas Foundation in 1940, and it is still effective today with 60 organisations in over 50 cities moving towards the vision Alinsky had of a large network of People's Organizations that would provide ordinary people with the power to shape their lives and communities ('The democratic promise: Saul Alinsky and his legacy', available at www.itvs.org/democraticpromise/legacy.html). Alinsky Organizers were paid for their skills and experience to support the development of other community organisations. Would this model be a possibility in the UK where the perennial dilemma for community workers is their contradictory role 'in and against the state'?

This chapter has considered the importance of a highly rigorous approach to community development where emancipatory action research plays a key role in praxis, and where models are developed to structure stages of the process. A systematic approach to planning and evaluation, which operates within the ideology of community development and which engages in authentic partnership with all players in the process, is needed for a critical approach to practice. Developing the skills to measure the quality outcomes of practice interventions is vital and poses an ongoing challenge. Community development reaches from the individual to the group, and from the group to a more coherent structure that embraces a collective consciousness and action across the wider community. A community organisation that facilitates this collective process plays a key role within communities. Let us move on to a consideration of how this process can be extended to reach beyond community, from local to global.

FIVE

Collective action for change

> When we turn from reflection to action, what happens is
> not that our minds become blank while our bodies exercise
> themselves. It is simply that the conscious intention which
> characterizes us as human beings is shifted to the outside
> world. Whereas in reflection we are engaged quite literally
> in changing our minds, in action we are engaged in
> changing the world. Action includes thought; it is not
> something which can be distinguished from thought. The
> life of reflection is not a different life from the life of action.
> It is a limitation of the life of action to one of its aspects....
> It is only when the world of thought is related to the world
> of action as mean to end, and the intention in thought is to
> use its results in action that thought is significant.
> (Macmurray, 1996, pp 75-6)

Macmurray talks about true action being conscious and intentional,
in much the same way as Freire talks about reflection without action
leading to armchair revolution (Freire, 1972). It is a vital aspect of the
community development process that we are eternally conscious of
the continuum between the personal and political, between the
individual and the collective, at levels from local to global.

It is useful to take a brief, renewed look at the process and explore
where this collective reach fits into the whole:

> Any group committed to radical social change must always
> take into account, and keep in balance, four different levels
> of need in their work:
>
> 1. the individual person
> 2. the small face-to-face group
> 3. the institution (or the structures of society)
> 4. the wider society
>
> Without concern for all four of these levels, it is impossible
> to build a strong movement and if any one of them is

> neglected the whole movement will weaken and die. (Hope and Timmel, 1984, p 21)

Every stage must include an analysis of power and disempowerment, of difference and diversity, and of anti-discriminatory practice.

I like the way that Hope and Timmel weave skills into the levels of development. It keeps our minds concentrated on the process as an integrated whole. The individual level is the foundation of our work. It is the level at which we anchor what we do in the lived realities of the people with whom we work, and which gives relevance to our work in their lives. Individual stories become collective narratives that express the hopes and fears, needs and strengths that are the basis of theory and practice. Personal empowerment through a process of *conscientisation* is the beginning stage of collective action for transformative change. Practice needs to be informed by ideas related to human needs (see, for example, Doyal and Gough, 1991), and to include such skills as listening and dialogue, which are related to an understanding of interpersonal power.

Community groups form the initial collective stage of the process where trust and cooperation create the context for reflection. The group is the basis of cultural belonging where a collective identity is formed, and from which a commitment to the process of change is much more likely to be sustained. It is a place where *problematising* teaches people to question their reality, to open their minds to altered perspectives on what is impacting on their lives. This is the bedrock of collective, critical action. At this stage, a worker needs to understand group dynamics and group leadership. Specific skills include team building, conflict resolution, planning and evaluation, set within an ideology of equality.

The dominant ideology of the powerful in society gives rise to discrimination that becomes structurally embedded in its institutions. Any change that aims to be transformative, rather than tokenistic or ameliorative, has to target the root causes of injustice not just the symptoms, and this involves structural change. Marcuse (cited in Hope and Timmel, 1984, p 21) described the revolutionary task as "the long march through the institutions" – churches, schools, trade unions, armed forces, mass media and so on – and for this we need an analysis of the role these structures play in the process of domination–subordination, for which an understanding of Gramsci's concept of *hegemony* is vital (this can be found in Chapter Six). Theories and concepts that help to make sense of the cultural, economic, political and social forces that are constantly in dynamic with community are necessary tools for the community worker. These analyses are the basis of collective action that extends beyond community to reach from local to global, and it is this level of organising that is my focus here.

This chapter moves into a consideration of structural sources of oppression and discrimination, demonstrating the need for collective action which reaches beyond community into the wider political context in a more strategic form.

Critical pedagogy

> Critical pedagogy has failed to articulate a vision for self-empowerment and social transformation; consequently, the term 'critical pedagogy' needs to have its meaning specified in more precise terms. (McLaren, 1995, p 34)

Critical pedagogy involves questioning, naming, reflecting, analysing and collectively acting in the world. It is a form of education that liberates rather than controls, in which relations are reciprocal rather than dominant, and where the humility of the educator enables a co-teacher/co-learner relationship to flourish. Critical pedagogy is a democratic process of education that takes place in community groups and forms the basis of transformation. It is founded on *conscientisation*, the process of becoming critically aware of the structural forces of power that shape our lives, and leads to action for change. *Dialogue* focuses on the stories of the people, and in *problematising* personal/local issues, exposes socially constructed identities that have been silenced: "in this respect, a postcolonial narratology encourages the oppressed to contest the stories fabricated for them by 'outsiders' and to construct counterstories that give shape and direction to the practice of hope and the struggle for an emancipatory politics of everyday life. It is a pedagogy that attempts to exorcise from the social body the invading pathologies of racism, sexism, and class privilege" (McLaren, 1995, p 105).

In other words, the community worker is a critical educator who, in the process of dealing with everyday issues, poses questions that encourage people to see their world from a critical perspective, and in turn to pose their own questions. In so doing we:

> ... free ourselves from the dead weight of dominant corporate consumer narratives. We can do this by crossing cultural boundaries and negotiating new, hybrid identities. As an initial step towards creating emancipatory social

practices in both private and public spheres we can help
our students bring a halt to the immutable constancy of
imperial identities of the patriarchal family, the authoritarian
state, and the narrative of the happy, compulsive consumer
(McLaren, 1995, p 104)

In rediscovering our histories, we reconstruct our cultural identities
and, in doing so, we create narratives of possibility for social
transformation. In these ways, critical pedagogy, locating itself both
within community and within larger contexts of global capitalism,
enables people to identify other possibilities that are based on a more
just, participatory democracy "that promotes sustainable, people-centred
development, equal opportunities and social justice" (Craig and Mayo,
1995, p 1). But for this to be effective, we need theoretical analyses
that are capable of evolving in relation to specific contexts. Let us take
a closer look at key Freirean concepts in this respect.

Key Freirean concepts

The insistence that the oppressed engage in reflection on
their concrete situation is not a call to armchair revolution.
On the contrary, reflection – true reflection – leads to action.
On the other hand, when the situation calls for action, that
action will constitute an authentic praxis only if its
consequences become the object of critical reflection....
Otherwise, action is pure activism. (Freire, 1972, p 41)

Freire achieves theoretical coherence because his work unites a
philosophy of hope with a pedagogy of liberation. The basic belief
underpinning this is that human beings are subjects, able to think and
reflect for themselves, and in doing so transcend and recreate their
world. This is set in juxtaposition to the dominant view of people as
objects, unthinkingly and unquestioningly bound to their world in
systems of power and control. Freire's quest was to identify a process
of critical discovery through which oppressed people could free their
minds and become aware that they hold the key to transformative
change. Freire identified the way in which perceptions of powerlessness
erode hope and create a *culture of silence*. In the struggle for freedom and
justice, critical pedagogy aims to restore people's full human potential:

This struggle is only possible because dehumanization,
although a concrete historical fact, is *not* a given destiny

but the result of an unjust order that engenders violence in the oppressors, which in turn dehumanizes the oppressed.... In order for this struggle to have meaning, the oppressed must not, in seeking to regain their humanity (which is a way to create it), become in turn oppressors of the oppressors, but rather restorers of the humanity of both. (Freire, 1972, p 21)

In order to examine the usefulness of such a vision to community workers, certain key concepts need to be understood. My intention here is to introduce these in a brief and coherent way.

Conscientisation is the process whereby people become aware of the political, socioeconomic and cultural contradictions that interact in a hegemonic way to diminish their lives. This awareness, which is based on critical insight, leads to collective action. The process of becoming critically aware is seen by Freire to have three levels. *Magical consciousness* refers to the level at which people are passive and unquestioning about the injustices in their lives. The harshness of their lives tends to be passively accepted, and explanations are often based on fatalism, such as suffering in the present is paying for past sins. *Naïve consciousness* involves a degree of insight into the nature of individual problems, but does not connect these with structural discrimination. At this level of consciousness, people are likely to blame themselves, and say, for example, that they are not clever enough, or they should have worked harder, or studied better at school. This individualisation of problems lends itself to the hegemonic blaming of victims, which is so much part of the market economy ideology. *Critical consciousness* is the stage at which connections are made with the way in which the structures of society discriminate, reaching into people's being, shaping their lives in prejudiced ways. The process is rooted in critical reflection and collective struggle. Its antithesis is the *false consciousness* of fatalism or individualism; the way in which subordinate groups are persuaded to accept inequalities by being passive and pessimistic. "Conscientization is the deepening of the coming of consciousness." But Freire warns that "not all coming to consciousness extends necessarily into conscientization"; without curiosity, critical reflection, rigour and humility it is not possible to reveal the "truths hidden by ideologies" (Freire, 1993, p 109). The process may remain partial.

Freire stresses the political nature of education. It is not possible for education to be neutral. It is either *domesticating* or *liberating*. In its domesticating form, the *banking* approach is used. The educator is seen as powerful and all-knowing, pouring information into the unquestioning minds of learners, who are perceived as malleable and controllable *objects*. The educator is active and the learners passive. This is the traditional, hierarchical model of education, which transmits knowledge based on dominant interests in society. Knowledge is commodified and the inequalities in society reinforced. It is based on *cultural invasion*: the imposition of the values and beliefs of a dominant culture in a way that marginalises and silences in order to dominate. Educators who are committed to liberating people from oppression provide opportunities for marginalised groups of people to value their experience, history and culture in curious, creative and questioning ways, thereby restoring confidence and giving voice. This can be achieved by using *generative themes* in a *problematising* way. A *generative theme* is a relevant issue or concern about which people will feel passionate. This is captured from people's experience and presented to the group in a form that encourages them to see it critically. Originally Freire used line drawings, but equally photographs, drama, video, story, poetry and music are effective forms of *codification*, depending on their relevance to the group. The term *codification* simply means the medium that is used to capture the essence of everyday issues and present them to the group. Taking an experience out of its context enables people to see it with fresh eyes, rather than from the taken-for-grantedness of everyday experience. The more relevant the theme, the more likely it is to generate the emotion that motivates action. To be effective, it must be *coded* in the language and culture of the people concerned, drawing on their experience and encouraging them to question. One outstanding example is the way in which the Brazilian colleague of Freire, Augusto Boal, developed *Theatre of the Oppressed* as a medium for *conscientisation*, influencing radical theatre on an international level (Boal, 1994; Schutzman and Cohen-Cruz, 1995). In Brazil, he is still involved in popular theatre as a vehicle for consciousness and a collective force for influencing national policy decisions.

A problem-posing approach, or *problematising*, is based on a horizontal model, that of equality between the *educator–learner* and the *learner–educator*. This co-learner relationship is the basis of *dialogue* and is fundamental to the process of liberation. It "strives for the emergence of consciousness and *critical intervention* in reality" (Freire, 1982, p 54) by placing educators and students together in a mutual educator–learner relationship. It is more than just a technique; it requires a belief and trust in the potential of people to be wise and thinking, with the capacity for *action and reflection*. It is a process that creates critical, inquiring and responsible citizens who "carry both the seeds of radical change and the burden of oppression" (Popple, 1995, p 64). The role of the educator in critical pedagogy is to provide the context in which shared problems can be critically questioned and analysed. It is a mutual process founded on reciprocity and humility that gets beyond the power imbalance of the traditional teacher–student relationship. The roles of educator and learner become interchangeable because the educator is open to learning as much as teaching. This is the interface of praxis at which the knowledge and theory of the educator come together with the everyday experience of the people.

Let us be more specific. For instance, a group of people may come together motivated initially by the need for safer play facilities in the community. This community group would be termed a *culture circle* by Freire. A culture circle is a community group that, in dialogue, questions an issue that is important to them. The community worker may choose to focus the group by providing overhead slides of the play areas that already exist. This would be termed a *codification*. The secret to success lies in using an appropriate form of codification that is capable of engaging the group in a way that expands consciousness. Everyday experience is too familiar to be questioned. Taking the reality and capturing it in another form enables people to begin the process of questioning. As questions are raised, the community worker responds with questions rather than answers, taking the questioning to a more critical level. Why? Where? How? Who? What? In whose interests? Why are those swings rusty and broken? Why are broken bottles lying around? Why is it so dangerous? Why is it open to the road? Successive questions probe deeper towards the source of the problem. It is a process that liberates the thinking of the group members as they become confident, analytic and creative in investigating the issue. They move towards a solution that is likely to be nearer to the root of the problem, and as they are active in the process of reflecting on the issue, they are more likely to engage in the action to tackle it. Of course, this process is not uniform; it develops at many different levels both within the group and within the lives of the individuals of that group. But, once the questioning has begun, it continues; like water flowing through a valve, it is propelled forwards. As Freire says, "*starting* with the 'knowledge of experience had' in order to get beyond it is not *staying* in that knowledge" (Freire, 1995, p 70).

Dialogue and *praxis* lie at the heart of the process of humanisation. "Only dialogue, which requires critical thinking, is also capable of generating critical thinking. Without dialogue there is no communication, and without communication there can be no true education" (Freire, 1972, p 65). Dialogue embodies the notions of human dignity and respect, encouraging people to relate to each other in ways that are mutual, reciprocal, trusting and cooperative. For Freire, this is an encounter to name the world and, as such, is a precondition for true humanisation. It involves horizontal communication between equals who are mutually engaged in a process of critical inquiry. By listening to the *narratives* of the people and engaging in *dialogue*, the community worker is able to establish strong relationships based on an understanding of local culture; in turn, local people develop a sense of confidence and trust. The opposite of this is *cultural invasion*, or *anti-dialogue*, which involves the imposition of one's assumptions, values and perceptions of the world on others, silencing and disempowering. This is a form of dominance that permeates within and between cultures. *Banking education* is a vehicle for this oppression. It is education for domination and divides people from each other and from their culture.

Praxis is rooted in dialogue, which in turn is only possible when the humility of the community worker gives rise to trust in the capacity of people to transform the world on their own behalf. It refers to the dynamic between action and reflection, building theory in action; a critical approach to practice. In making sense of experience, theory informs action and action generates theory. Both become increasingly critical in nature because they emerge from the history and culture of the people, and place people in a fundamental role in the process of transformative change. Freire sees this as the only way of truly countering oppression. Dialogical relations are the essence of freedom and provide the critical link between Freire's theory and methods. "No pedagogy which is truly liberating can remain distant from the oppressed by treating them as unfortunates....The oppressed must be their own example in the struggle for their redemption. It would be a contradiction in terms if the oppressors not only defended but actually implemented a liberating education" (Freire, 1972, p 30).

It is characteristic of oppression that the oppressed turn against each other in acts of *horizontal violence*. This is the way in which divide and rule politics erode solidarity. The oppressed, themselves the victims of hierarchical power, turn against those who are working alongside them in the struggle for change:

> Almost always, during the initial stage of the struggle, the oppressed, instead of striving for liberation, tend themselves to become oppressors, or 'sub'-oppressors. The very structure of their thought has been conditioned by the contradictions of the concrete, existential situation by which they were shaped. (Freire, 1972, p 27)

In my experience, this is characteristic of community groups. The model of power and status in Western society is one of experiencing 'success' on the back of someone else's 'failure'. It is based on arrogance rather than humility and lacks compassion and solidarity. When participation leads to new experiences of power in community, this can often result in a desire to possess it and to abuse it, according to the dominant model. This becomes an illusion of democratic power, because although it is located in community it is not representative of the community, and is destructive rather than liberating. This swing towards counter-oppression gradually stabilises if the horizontal process is eased towards mutual respect, dignity and equality. The process of *conscientisation* becomes increasingly collective, and the oppressed cease striving to oppress the oppressors, but move towards restoring humanity for both:

> Only power that springs from the weakness of the oppressed will be sufficiently strong to free both. Any attempt to 'soften' the power of the oppressor in deference to the weakness of the oppressed almost always manifests itself in the form of false generosity; indeed, the attempt never goes beyond this. (Freire, 1972, p 21)

Similarly, Freire saw the relevance but also the pitfalls of those from the dominant class who join the oppressed in their struggle – Gramsci's *traditional intellectuals*. Although acting as a catalyst in the process of conscientisation, the status and superiority that come with the role can result in an inherent distrust in the capacity of the people to think and act for themselves. A lack of trust leads to acting *for* rather than *with* the people. "They talk about the people, but they do not trust them; and trusting the people is the indispensable precondition for revolutionary change" (Freire, 1972, p 36).

Freirean pedagogy is profoundly radical. It is rooted in anti-colonial discourse and offers the basis for pedagogies of *difference*. Giroux argues that "Freire is a border intellectual, whose allegiance has not been to a specific class and culture as in Gramsci's notion of the intellectual; instead, Freire's writings embody a mode of discursive struggle and opposition that not only challenges the oppressive machinery of the state but is also sympathetic to the formation of new cultural subjects and movements engaged in the struggle over the modernist values of freedom, equality and justice" (Giroux, 1993, p 179-80). By crossing borders we can transgress cultural, theoretical and ideological boundaries, altering our perspectives and thus breaking our patterns of thought. However, if we cross borders as colonialists then we are likely to overlook the oppressive aspects of our being that we have inherited, and therefore fail to analyse situations of oppression. It is probable that we will be culturally invasive, believing that our way of seeing the world is the right way.

The need to struggle with complex ideas in dialogue is essential in making sense of our rapidly changing world. Theory has evolved in the light of postmodern and postcolonial challenges to thought, and a political context of globalisation has resulted in more complex oppressions within and between nations. In these ways, the issues of the world at large become issues for our communities. McLaren based on dialogue with Freire, cites how "Freire maintained that when presented with a difficult theoretical language, students always have the right to ask their teachers to translate their ideas. In responding to such a request, teachers have the obligation to strive to be simple, but never to be simplistic" (McLaren and Leonard, 1993, p 7). Complex ideas, in becoming 'simple but not simplistic', transcend the void between academy and community, to play a key role in developing critical praxis:

> To be a critical, empowering educator is a choice to be what Henry Giroux has called a 'transformative intellectual'. Giroux's notion of 'civic courage' and a 'pedagogy of possibility' invite educators to become change-agents in school and society, for critical thought and action, for democracy, equality, ecology and peace, against domination, manipulation, and the waste of human and natural resources. (Shor, 1993, p 34)

Collective action: local to global

Critical pedagogy is a process that begins in personal empowerment and extends to critical, collective action, from local projects to movements for change. We cannot dip in and out of Freire in this process; his pedagogy is an "indivisible totality based on assumptions and principles which are inter-related and coherent ... we cannot take hints from Freire or use bits of Freire; we must embrace the philosophy as an integral whole and attempt to apply it accordingly" (Allman and Wallis, 1997, p 113).

Collective organising in current times is faced with the resistance of a culture of individualism and a politics of consumerism. At the same time, the escalation of globalisation has complexified structures of exploitation under capitalism. Neoliberal globalisation is that form of western corporate capitalism which not only dominates the world economically, but reproduces political, cultural, racial, gendered, sexual, ecological and epistemological hierarchies on a global scale. In other words, in the name of a free market economy, the same structures of oppression that exist under Western capitalism are being reproduced on a complex global scale. "Capitalism, imperialism, monoculturalism, patriarchy, white supremacism and the domination of biodiversity have coalesced under the current form of globalisation" to form a major threat to a just, equal and sustainable future (Fisher and Ponniah, 2003, p 11). This is precisely why the practice of community development, rooted as it is in anti-discriminatory analysis, cannot justify an approach to practice that focuses on the local and overlooks global dimensions of oppression. Unregulated markets, a free market economy and globalisation do nothing to protect the natural world and the most vulnerable people from the drive of capitalism to produce at lowest cost to maximise profit:

> As the globalization project unfolds, it exposes its bankruptcy at the philosophical, political, ecological and economic levels. The bankruptcy of the dominant world order is leading to social, ecological, political and economic non-sustainability, with societies, ecosystems, and economies disintegrating and breaking down.
>
> The philosophical and ethical bankruptcy of globalization was based on reducing every aspect of our lives to commodities and reducing our identities to merely that of consumers on the global market place. Our capacities as producers, our identity as members of communities, our role as custodians of our natural and cultural heritage were all to disappear or be destroyed. Markets and consumerism expanded. Our capacity to give and share was to shrink. But the human spirit refuses to be subjugated by a world view based on the dispensability of our humanity. (Vandana Shiva, in Fisher and Ponniah, 2003, p 1)

The collective action that prevailed from the late 1960s, through the 1980s and even into the early 1990s, gave expression to identity politics and saw the rise of the new social movements. Paradoxically, the poststructuralist critiques of class metanarratives generated at this time, which gave rise to a politics of difference, have conspired to create a difficult context for collective organising. In other words, the Marxist analysis that had been the basis of community development was challenged by feminists and postmodernists because it engulfed any other aspect of difference in the name of class. Conversely, the fragmenting of class action as a form of collective organising has called for alliances across difference as a strategic alternative. In this respect, Fisher and Ponniah suggest that any counter-hegemony must tread that fine line of embracing a respect for difference at the same time as being able to create a common vision:"If the global movements are to prosper, they have to produce a vision that allows them to maintain simultaneously both their convergence and their difference" (Fisher and Ponniah, 2003, p 13). Their argument centres on the belief that another centralised global system, even one replacing a neoliberal for a social democratic ideology, would fall into the same trap of dominance over diversity. "Today's need is not for another centralized global institution but the de-concentration and decentralization of institutional power and the creation of a pluralistic system of institutions and organizations interacting with one another, guided by broad and flexible agreements and understandings" (Fisher and Ponniah, 2003, p 287).

In relation to our developing theoretical analyses in the field of critical pedagogy, Hill et al (1999), Allman (1999, 2001) and McLaren et al (1999) present a unified backlash to postmodernism, arguing that it fragments our thinking and our action, blurring our understanding of the power of capitalism in global times. Paula Allman (1999), for example, draws attention to the complex ways that global capitalism simultaneously cleaves divisions of poverty and wealth within and between countries. Global capitalism uses individualism as a smokescreen for its necessary illusion of progress, giving legitimacy to this juxtaposition of extremes of wealth and poverty. She warns that those "engaged in local struggle need to understand the global significance of what they do ... otherwise victories won are used to defuse and depoliticize the significance of the local effort" (Allman, 1999, pp 5-6). If we fix our gaze on the local, we reinforce this exploitative system by celebrating small-scale successes that give the illusion of change, but fail to challenge the wider structures that perpetuate oppressions. Critical praxis is necessary for social transformation, and Freire and Gramsci in powerful combination offer insight into the role of education in politics, and politics in education: their potential is reduced if they are used partially or fragmented (Allman, 1988, 1999). Our praxis is grounded in local reality, but needs a global connection to the whole if our analysis is to lead to transformative change. Linked to this discussion, further theoretical arguments that centre around analyses of class and difference, and those that locate the interface of social justice and environmental justice, can be found in Chapter Eight.

The challenge for community development in the context of globalisation is to find theory and practice which work at local, regional, national and global levels, where we reject a single economic and social worldview for one which embraces a 'universalism of difference' (Fisher and Ponniah, 2003, p 284). At the same time, we need to build strategies for collective action which support moving beyond the local to wider possibilities for collective strength. One model worthy of consideration is the Budapest Declaration (Craig et al, 2004) which identifies the potential of community development to build a European civil society based on the empowerment of local communities through participatory democracy.

Alliances across difference

Community development faces two major sticking points that reduce its critical potential. One is a resistance to developing theory in practice; the other is reluctance to move beyond community to harness a greater collective force for change. Alison Gilchrist identifies this dilemma when she notes that community development's principle of collective organising is "found in the rhetoric (if not the practice)" of regeneration and renewal initiatives (Gilchrist, 2004, p 43). Networks, campaigns and alliances offer structures to harness collective power outside community, but if these are to be successful we need to develop theory and skills that support working across difference. To illustrate my point, I will draw on research on alliances across difference undertaken with my late Black colleague Paula Asgill, which is explored in greater detail in other publications (Ledwith and Asgill, 1998, 2000, in press).

There are widely held assumptions that women come together 'naturally' in action for social justice. Our experience told a different story. We realised that we could not recollect instances in all our years of practice where alliances between Black and White women were sustained over time, but we had many experiences of where they collapsed in rage or fear. In the course of our research, which engaged us in dialogue on our own practice as well as interviews with Black and White women activists, we concluded that clear strategies are needed for the development of sustainable alliances. *Critical alliance* depends on the personal autonomy of Black and White women to reach out to each other in confidence and respect, and this process begins in separate groups where critical consciousness emerges from reflection on shared experiences. Pride in who we are in the world, in our separate identities, leads to more equal alliances where issues of power have been addressed.

Black rage and White fear are the emotions that characterise the breakdown of alliances. Often White women assume the power to set the agenda and invite Black women to join them. Immediately, this creates a power imbalance in the relationship. One of the reasons for this is inevitably our concentration on understanding Black oppression without at the same time developing an analysis of White power, and the subtle ways in which it gets acted out. Fine et al (1997) identify the importance of understanding White power within an anti-discriminatory analysis, otherwise while we have a greater understanding of the nature of Black oppression, we remain ignorant of the insidious ways that White power works. These realisations motivated us to approach Black women and White women across England who had experience of community activism, and 16 (eight Black and eight White) women joined us in this inquiry. In order to structure our thoughts, we developed a model based on stages that span from personal empowerment to collective action. To structure our thinking we adapted Rowan's cycle model (see Chapter Four), which gave us a greater insight into the flow from the personal to the collective, and helped us to identify the relevance of work in community that perceives the importance of personal autonomy as a prerequisite for collective action. This is a vital understanding for the development of structured practice.

There are five distinct stages in this process: i) being, ii) seeking, iii) separateness, iv) autonomy and v) critical alliance.

Being is the stage at which we begin to question our experience. Our difference becomes apparent. We begin to recognise that our Blackness or Whiteness, or age, or sexuality, or class, or culture all interact in complex ways to shape our identity. Think about this in relation to Gramsci's concept of hegemony (Chapter Six), which helps us to understand the complex ways in which the structures of society filter into our minds and the power that these ideas have to construct our worldview. This awareness causes dissonance. We can no longer carry on with the old way of seeing ourselves; it pushes us into a stage of **seeking** new ways of seeing ourselves in relation to our world. Following this we identified a need for **separateness**, a withdrawal into relationships where we feel at ease with those who are similar so that we can share ideas and make sense of our personal experience:

Every once in a while there is the need for people to … bar the doors … and say "Humph, inside this place the only thing we are going to deal with is X or Y or Z." And so only the Xs or the Ys or Zs get to come in … most of the time when people do that, they do it because of the heat of trying to live in this society where being an X or Y or Z is very difficult to say the least.… It gets too hard to stay out in society all the time.… You come together to see what you can do about shouldering up all your energies so that you and your kind can survive … that space should be nurturing space where you sift out what people are saying about you and decide who you are. (Reagon, 1983, pp 357-8)

Autonomy is the stage at which we are able to name who we are, feel confident and proud in who we are, and gain a sense of personal empowerment. Our identity is strong enough not to fear dilution. This involves unlearning internalised oppression and internalised superiority (Pheterson, 1990).

The potential for **critical alliance** emerges from this personal *autonomy*, a clearer sense of who we are in the world. From greater confidence in our own identity, we have the humility and compassion needed to understand difference not as a division but as a strength. This is the basis for joining together in sustainable alliances across difference in action for a more fair and just society.

The importance of emotion and experience as legitimate knowledge (refer to Weiler, 1994, 2001, discussed in Chapter Eight) is a theoretical link that is crucial to understanding the experience of Black rage and White fear and the way that they hinder alliances. Without this, we react in fight/flight behaviour that limits the sustainability of the collective process.

Our research as a whole supported the evidence that, despite popular beliefs in community development about women uniting across difference, there is little to prove that this is found in practice in any sustainable way. Our model provided useful ways in which to structure experience in community and provided possibilities for shifts in understanding. Sustainable critical alliance as a form of collective action offers an alternative to the unifying aspects of class solidarity. Clearly, there is a need for work on identity and autonomy in community development, despite the fact that this has largely fallen off the agenda in the last decade. Our five defined stages – i) being, ii) seeking, iii) separateness, iv) autonomy and v) critical alliance – offer a structure to community workers that helps to make sense of the staged development of work that needs to take place at a local level as the basis of collective action. (For ideas on how to use story as empowerment, see Chapter Three.) Collective action starts with women organising in their locality around their common issues, and then moving outside neighbourhoods by allying with regional and national movements for change, which in turn have the capacity to connect on a global level. Our concern is that the potential for collective action is getting stuck all too often at group or project level in local contexts. We suggest that identity and autonomy are key to unblocking this potential at a time when globalisation calls for a strongly defined self within a cultural/political analysis that attends to difference and power.

The Beijing Conference: an example of local/global action

Inspiration can be found in the Beijing Conference, 1995, as a model of collective action with a local to global reach. At this UN intergovernmental conference, the NGO (non-governmental organisation) meeting runs in a parallel but independent way. This was the context where over 30,000 women came together in Beijing, some to represent their organisations, others as individuals, but all with a commitment i) to raising awareness of the violations of rights that affect women in very similar ways but in different cultural and political contexts and ii) to forming global alliances as forces for change. At previous conferences, the NGO meeting had been known as the NGO Forum, but in Beijing this forum assumed the status of a second conference. It is important to honour that in trying to attend the conference many women had risked persecution and harm. The collective strength and unity of purpose of women the world over were expressed in a banner, capturing the essence of women's everyday lives and our wish for peace and non-violence. Many women's groups who did not get to Beijing sent their message in this way. The panels had been stitched by the local and national groups that the women represented, and were joined by the hands of the women as they snaked their demonstration of world peace and justice to the conference site (M. Page, 1997). The Women's Forum played a key role in evidencing women's common concerns across the globe. Women united across age, class, nationality, ethnicity, 'race', ability and sexuality to influence the outcome of the final recommendations of the Global Platform for Action. This document, which defines women's demands for justice, was signed by the governments of the 189 countries represented at the conference in commitment to following it through to implementation at national level (Ledwith and Asgill, in press).

The success of a global alliance is founded on grassroots organising. Many women who were involved in Beijing had been part of the NGO Forum of the Nairobi Third World Conference and were determined to bring about practical outcomes and strategies for implementation of the Platform for Action. Page's research indicates a frustration from the women at the lack of dialogue between governments and NGOs as well as a lack of consciousness and commitment to their work locally: "they spoke of building networks with NGOs in other regions and countries, and engaging in an exchange of experience and vision across constituencies and regions" (M. Page, 1997, p 5).

First, I want to trace the global developments and then look at the grassroots organisation. In Mexico City in 1975, the UN First World Conference on Women took place, and 1976-85 was declared the UN Decade for Women. In 1979, the Convention on the Elimination of All Forms of Discrimination Against Women (CEDAW) was adopted by the UN. In 1980, the Second World Conference on Women emphasised education, employment and the role of women in development. The Third World Conference on Women in Nairobi in 1985, adopted the Forward-looking Strategies for the Advancement of Women Towards the Year 2000. Then, the World Conference on Human Rights in Vienna, 1993, adopted the UN Declaration on the Elimination of Violence Against Women, which was received as a significant turning point in the development of the women's human rights movement.

Preparation for Beijing concentrated on campaigns to develop public awareness of human rights abuses against women. Success was based on strategies that linked grassroots activism through networks and alliances in a "two or three year preparatory process of negotiation and consensus building to produce a programme of action, a declaration, and recommendations for implementation. Women's international networks gathered strength through coalitions and caucuses at the Forums and conferences where women's NGOs demonstrated that 'women's concerns' must be placed at the centre of economic, social and political agendas, and can no longer be considered in isolation" (M. Page, 1997, p vi).

Regional conferences were held in preparation for Beijing throughout 1994: in Indonesia for Asia and the Pacific, in Argentina for Latin America, in Austria for North America and Europe, in Jordan for Western Asia and in Senegal for Africa. Grassroots organisations were the bedrock for this level of organisation, which, in turn, sustained the process through to a global level. In the UK, women were active at local, national and international levels across difference, involving grassroots women in the preparatory process by raising awareness about the relevance of the conference to campaigning work within the UK (M. Page, 1997).

The Platform for Action is reviewed on a five-yearly basis, and the first follow-up conference, Five Years on from Beijing happened in New York in 2000. This strategy for change, supported by national governments, represents the interests of women around the world, identifying the specific ways in which globalisation impacts on women in different cultural contexts. Developments are monitored under: health, education, participation, stereotyping and lack of access to the media, the girl child (including harmful cultural practices), violence against women, trafficking in women and sexual and reproductive health. In addition, armed conflict and a commitment to non-discrimination on the basis of 'race', age, language, ethnicity, culture, religion or 'dis'ability, or due to being indigenous people are also addressed (www1.umn/humanrts/instree/beijingmnu.htm). The challenge that the women took from Beijing was i) holding governments responsible for the implementation of the Platform for Action and ii) a commitment for developing strategies for women to work together across difference, levels of experience, degrees of power and different levels of operation to truly 'bring Beijing home' (M. Page, 1997). Women's organisations are concerned about the lack of evidence for significant progress and stress that "in order for changes to come about participation by women must happen at a local level to be effective in developing mechanisms for the advancement of women" (www.aontas.com). For further detail, see Ledwith and Asgill (in press).

For strategic organisation, effective and sustainable over time and space, community development needs to recognise the centrality of personal empowerment in the collective process. Critical pedagogy involves people coming together to explore their own identities across all aspects of *difference* in order to develop confidence in 'who they are' within the structures that define them. This leads to autonomy, a sense of who we are in relation to our world, which is the basis of collective action. Local issues are taken on as group concerns and developed into important projects within communities, but more often than not we fail to make the leap that takes our thinking and practice outside our neighbourhood to those levels that link with other communities and other countries. Local action is the basis of global action. Alison Gilchrist (2004) stresses the enormous confidence it takes to join any collective activity, and it is usual that people come along because they already know somebody who is involved. We should never underestimate this personal connection. The importance of informal social networks is that they connect people in community and sustain people in collective political activity. By understanding the relevance of personal empowerment in the process of collective action, and by developing theories that challenge our thinking, the autonomy needed to reach out across difference in sustainable alliance is seen as a continuum in community development practice.

Community development has to move beyond the local to the global in strategic forms of collective action in order to achieve transformative change for justice. This chapter has located the relevance of theory on the personal/political and local/global dimensions. It has looked at research into critical alliances, and offered a structure for moving practice from identity politics to alliances across difference. The following chapter explores the power of dominant ideas and how these are absorbed into our being.

SIX

The power of ideas

This chapter demonstrates the power of ideas in the processes of both dominance and liberation, exploring the usefulness of Gramsci's concepts of *hegemony* and the role of *the intellectuals* to radical community development praxis. Linking this to Thomson's (2001, 2003) PCS model offers insight into the way that the personal, cultural and structural contexts interact in the interests of power and privilege, in turn locating key sites of intervention for change.

Antonio Gramsci

Gramsci has much to offer critical pedagogy. His insight into the complexity of power relations in society provides a profound understanding of politics that certainly helped me, in conceptualising *hegemony*, to understand the notion of *the personal as political*. In addition, his analysis of the role of *the intellectuals* in the process of social change enables us to locate community development as a site of resistance. Paula Allman claims:

> A socially and economically just and an authentically democratic alternative to capitalism is possible, but … it can only be created by people who understand why capitalism invariably leads to crisis and why of necessity it is driven to produce wealth for a minority and either endemic insecurity or perpetual poverty and scarcity for the vast majority, and by people who also understand why its remedies for environmental destruction must be inextricably linked to profit margins. (Allman, 2001, pp 2-3)

It is precisely in Gramsci's emphasis on education as a critical, mutual process of learning to understand the forces of hegemony, the way that economic, social and political forms of domination weave through our lives and minds, that Allman locates the struggle for reform as a preparation for the critical action that leads to authentic transformation (Allman, 2001, p 139). It is in the process of critical education that these struggles take place and lead to altered consciousness. Myles Horton talks about Highlander (see Chapter Three) in the early days concluding that "reform within the system *reinforced* the system, or was co-opted by the system. Reformers didn't change the system, they made it more palatable and justified it, made it more humane, more intelligent ... so I think when Highlander was first recognized to the extent that we were invited to talk about education was after Paulo made this kind of education respectable by being a professor at Harvard" (Horton and Freire, 1990, pp 200-2). Gramsci, from his own experience, felt that the unions offered a corporate stage of consciousness, but that this was based on a limited sector of the economy that could, therefore, achieve nothing more than reformism (Forgacs, 1988). Reforms begin the process of change, but this does not become transformative unless a more collective form of revolutionary change creates an alternative worldview. Gramsci saw critical education as the key to grassroots change.

In order to examine Gramsci's relevance it is important to locate him historically and culturally. Not only does this offer a richer appreciation of his intellectual contribution, but Nairn suggests that lessons from Gramsci can only be understood in the specific light of the Sardinian and Italian historical context (Nairn, 1982, p 159). Gramsci's life was epitomised by loneliness, poverty and struggle. His life was fraught with "struggle against physical deformity and recurrent illness, the struggle against material hardship and poverty, the struggle against political adversaries and finally the psychological struggle for survival in prison" (Ransome, 1992, p 54).

The life and work of Antonio Gramsci

Gramsci was born on 22 January 1891, in Ales, Sardinia, the fourth of seven children. His father, Francesco Gramsci, was a civil servant from mainland Italy, and his mother, Guiseppina Macias, was from a moderately wealthy family by Sardinian standards. Living conditions were harsh in comparison with mainland Italy, a contrast that was to form the basis of Gramsci's ideas on injustice. He did not have an easy childhood. At the age of four, he developed a back deformity, which, at the time, was attributed to falling down stairs although this is now refuted. It is now considered likely that his condition was due to tuberculosis of the spine, and that his parents wanted to hide this due to the superstitious beliefs that were so much part of Sardinian culture (P. Mayo, 1999). It was a culture in which werewolves, ghosts and withces were feared (Davidson, 1977). "The spinal deformity that subsequently became apparent and produced a hunchback and abnormally short stature has also been attributed to tuberculosis of the spine, a condition known as Pott's Disease, with which he was diagnosed in 1933" (Kenway, 2001, p 48). Gramsci resented the fact that the power of popular superstition, which cast 'dis'abled people as possessed by evil spirits, had prevented his parents from getting the right treatment to overcome it in the early stages (P. Mayo, 1999). On the advice of a specialist, he was suspended from the ceiling in a leather corset for long periods of time in an attempt to straighten his back. The spinal deformity persisted and he became a solitary child. When he was six, his father was imprisoned for over five years, accused of fraud and embezzlement, but it is more likely that it was an act of political retribution. The family was reduced to a state of bare survival and returned to Ghilarza where his mother's strength and hard work saved the family from destitution. This was a significant turning point in Gramsci's early life. Until then he had been protected from persecution by his parents' relatively privileged position in local society. Due to his poor health and his mother's desire to protect him from discrimination, he started school late at the age of seven. His 'dis'ability and his family's reduced status, caused him to be bullied and rejected by the other children. This was a formative experience and led to his passion and commitment for all who suffer injustice (Davidson, 1977). His schooling became fragmented, he suffered from malnutrition, and by the age of 11 his father returned home and forced him to leave school to help support the family. He worked 10 hours a day for six-and-a-half days a week humping heavy ledgers around the Land Registry Office, "many a night I wept in secret because my whole body was aching" (Gramsci, 1988, p 238).

This marked the start of feelings of great resentment towards his father. His schooling was resumed once his father considered that the family was sufficiently back on its feet, and he was boarded out 11 miles away to receive what he considered an inadequate education based on principles of 'intellectual dishonesty'. His solitary nature led to a great passion for reading. Gennaro, his older brother, away in Turin on military service, started sending him *Avanti!*, the Italian Socialist Party (PSI) paper. At this time, Sardinia began to erupt in the face of the rising discontent of the poor. Fiori (1990) describes Gramsci's cultural and political times – widespread malnutrition and premature death from chronic diseases and work accidents – together with his political reading as having changed Gramsci's political perspective. His dream was of action that would lead to social justice.

His move to the lycée at Cagliari saw the dawn of his active political life. He lived with Gennaro, who introduced him to the socialist movement, and he started reading Marx. Sardinia increasingly rebelled under the weight of the abject oppression of the poor, and Gramsci's identification and involvement with the socialist movement deepened his critical consciousness.

Eventually, he was offered a scholarship to Turin where the combination of a large, industrial, working–class city and the stimulation of critical thinkers was to influence his philosophical thought. However, the transition from Sardism to socialism was lengthy and protracted. The image is one of extreme unhappiness, a man who was "too appallingly miserable for people even to want to approach him" (Davidson, 1977, p 70). The liberal intellectual Piero Gobetti saw him as "seething with resentment" and described his socialism as "first of all a reply to the offences of society against a lonely Sard emigrant" (Nairn, 1982, p 161). His compensation was, once again, found in excessive study, which, combined with poverty, increasingly damaged his health.

A turning point came in 1916. He abandoned his degree in linguistics, and his long–term ambition to become a good teacher, to work full time on the political paper *Avanti!* Turning his back on academic life, Gramsci the revolutionary political activist emerged. A simultaneous change in his personality took place. He became more happy and sociable. "He was in the process of remaking himself in what Marxists call praxis. By engaging in a practical and active rather than a contemplative life, he was purging himself of the emotional and ideological incrustation of [his] past" (Davidson, 1977, p 72). As a political journalist, he put into practice his belief in bringing theory to the workers. He saw this as the route to self-knowledge for the industrial proletariat, liberation of the mind. In a process of reflection on history, he saw the beginnings of liberation of the masses.

By early 1917, the time of the Russian Revolution, his ideology expressed through his journalism synthesised with a vision of practice located in the factory councils to offer a critical praxis with transformative potential. He was central to the development of the factory council movement in Turin and became increasingly involved in political journalism, helping to found the socialist paper *L'Ordine Nuovo* in 1919, as a tool of consciousness. Its motto spoke clearly: "Pessimism of the intellect, optimism of the will". The factory council, for Gramsci, was the initial context of praxis, the point of contact with the workers: workers' democracy organised through workers' and peasants' councils, which he saw as an educational force that would put workers in touch with their own potential political leadership.

The factory council movement spread rapidly between 1919 and 1920. The moment of crisis came when 600,000 workers from the Italian industrial cities occupied their factories. Gramsci and his friends closed the offices of *L'Ordine Nuovo* and went to live in the factories with the workers. However, as a revolution it was doomed to failure. Gramsci believed that the moment of conflict had been determined by capitalism, and that the workers were unprepared. The result was that the whole movement was premature and uncoordinated. He blamed himself for failing to understand the need for parallel growth in both theory and practice in order to achieve a *unity of praxis*. It was his belief that, had the process been critical and the timing right, it would have enabled the workers to run the new society and the party to play its key role in taking over the bourgeois state.

After the collapse of the factory council movement, Gramsci became actively involved in the formation of the Communist Party of Italy (PCI). These years saw, once again, his emotional withdrawal into a life governed by the intellect. In May 1922, he was a Communist Party delegate on the Executive Committee of the Communist Third International in Moscow. His health deteriorated while he was there and he was sent to a sanatorium near the Black Sea where he met Giulia Schucht. She was of Russian Jewish ethnicity, and a music teacher who had studied violin in Rome (Kenway, 2001, p 48). They married in 1923.

It was only over time that Gramsci realised the significance of the growth of fascism. His analysis was founded on the idea that fascism was a rural phenomenon that released suppressed passions and hatred in the masses. Politically, he saw fascism as separate from the bourgeois state because of its decadence: an uncontrollable cross-class movement dominated by the petit-bourgeoisie and characterised by legitimate violence. In 1922, Mussolini took power with his March on Rome, which marked the final death throes of the Italian proletariat drive for a Soviet-style revolution. By early 1923, communist leaders were being arrested and Gramsci sought to unite the working classes against this wave of fascism.

The volatile political climate made it unsafe for Gramsci to return to Rome until 1924, and he did so without Giulia. In the general election of April 1924, he was elected to parliament and subsequently became the general secretary of the PCI. He was committed to travelling the country subversively, addressing meetings and organising the party on the basis of workplace cells. May 1924 saw Gramsci's inaugural speech in parliament. His fearlessness was a constant threat to the fascists who determined to circumvent his parliamentary immunity and silence him. He was constantly followed around the country and eventually arrested on charges of conspiracy, agitation, inciting class war, insurrection and alteration of the Constitution and the form of the state through violence. Davidson considers his chief threat to the fascists to have been his awareness "that the main battle to overthrow fascism lay among the peasantry" (Davidson, 1977, p 118).

Gramsci returned to Moscow briefly following the birth of Delio, his first son. Between October 1925 and July 1926, Giulia joined him in Rome with Delio. She left because of the deteriorating political climate in Italy, just two months before Gramsci was arrested. Their second son, Guiliano, was born in Moscow in August 1926. Gramsci never saw him. Giulia remained the romantic love of Gramsci's life, but she suffered badly from depression, and eventually had a breakdown, never to return to Italy.

From 1926, the international political climate deteriorated and the situation "demanded a new analysis of the political and ideological resources of capitalist societies, the sources of their extraordinary resilience" (Forgacs, 1988, p 189). It was this analysis that occupied Gramsci's thoughts throughout his prison years. In November 1926, he was arrested, along with other communist members of parliament. He was moved from Rome to exile on the island of Ustica, and then to Milan to await trial. His first plan for the *prison notebooks* was formed in this period. Tatiana Schucht, Giulia's elder sister, devoted her life to supporting Gramsci in the difficult years of his imprisonment, and Gramsci became dependent on her for emotional sustenance. It is Tatiana who is responsible for ensuring that the Gramscian legacy was preserved by smuggling his letters and prison notebooks past the prison censor into the public domain. She passed a letter on to his old student friend, Piero Sraffa, who was now a Marxist economist at Cambridge, outlining the subject of his notebooks. It was Sraffa who brought Gramsci's plight to public attention in an article in the *Guardian* on 21 October 1927, but to no avail. Gramsci was transferred to Rome in May 1928. On 4 June, the prosecuting attorney, Michele Isgro, echoed Mussolini's personal instructions in declaring a need to stop Gramsci's brain from functioning for 20 years, such is the threat of powerful ideas to the status quo (Milne, undated; Davidson, 1977). Mussolini's enforcement of the 'long Calvary of Antonio Gramsci' had begun (Fiori, 1973). "His active political practice had finished. He now had four and a half thousand days to think on its theoretical implications for Marxism and revolutionary socialism" (Davidson, 1977, p 231).

In July 1928, he was transferred to a special prison in Turi, in the

South, because of his ill-health. Not until early 1929 was he given permission to write, and he started work on the first prison notebook in a school exercise book. As part of the amnesty programme for the tenth anniversary of the fascist 'revolution' his sentence was commuted to 12 years and four months. By this time his health was deteriorating rapidly. After he collapsed in his cell in March 1933, his doctor recommended that he be transferred to a clinic. This was supported by Sraffa who, as well as paying for Gramsci's supply of books, worked endlessly to help him over the years by putting moral pressure on the fascist regime. Gramsci's writing continued from the clinic at Formia until 1935, when illness forced him to stop. There were by then 2,848 tightly packed pages of his writing in 33 prison notebooks, an achievement that signifies what Henderson calls "a prodigy of will, intellect and indomitable staying power" (H. Henderson, in Gramsci, 1988, p 10). He saw this period of his life as "a time of waiting, a pause and preparation" (Lawner, 1979, p 39).

Not prepared to compromise his political position, Gramsci suffered an arduous 10-year confinement under the fascist regime in Italy, while his health slowly disintegrated. A cerebral haemorrhage killed him on 27 April 1937, six days after his freedom had been granted. Tatiana, in a letter to Sraffa on 12 May 1937, describes how, on the very day she brought him news of his freedom, he collapsed. She stayed with him the two days it took for him to die. "I kept watch over him doing whatever I thought best, wetting his lips, trying to help him get his breath back artificially when it seemed to stop. But then he took a last deep breath and sunk [sic] into a silence that could never change" (Lawner, 1979, p 280).

Tatiana saw that all his work was safely deposited at the Banca Commerciale in Rome, from where it was transferred to Moscow, and then to his friend, Togliatti. Since then, his writing continues to be analysed and published, challenging the thought and the practice of those who read it.

Gramsci's contribution to critical pedagogy

> ... the relationship between teacher and pupil is active and reciprocal so that every teacher is always a pupil and every pupil a teacher. (Gramsci, 1971, p 350)

Gramsci recognised the inadequacy of Marxist economic determinism to offer sufficient analysis for the increasing complexity of social forces in the 20th century. He reconceptualised the moral, cultural and political influences in society to offer profound insight into the pervasive nature of these forces in everyday life. Of particular relevance to critical pedagogy are his concepts of the nature of *hegemony* and the role of the *intellectuals*. Education and culture were two themes that were of constant relevance to Gramsci. Much of his early thinking was preoccupied with the problem of achieving working-class intellectual autonomy. His belief was that everyone is innately cultured and capable of intellectual thought, but that this is undisciplined and incoherent without critical education. By placing emphasis on the learner, not the teacher, a learning process can be stimulated that moves through self-knowledge to liberation (Forgacs, 1988). His influence on Freire can be seen in these ideas. Ideology, according to Marx and Engels, assumes that the class with the power to control the material forces of society also controls the dominant ideas in society, which are passively absorbed into working-class minds as the *false consciousness* of *common sense*. So, "not only does the ruling class produce the ruling ideas, in view of its control over the means of intellectual production, but the dominated classes produce ideas that do not necessarily serve their interests" (P. Mayo, 2004, p 41). Although Marx and Engels introduced the role of ideology as an instrument of class struggle, their emphasis was on the role of the party in developing consciousness. Gramsci developed a revolutionary ideology, "a theory of popular, as well as working-class, ideology of protest" to a much more sophisticated degree (Rude, 1980, p 22).

Fundamental to Gramsci's thinking is the notion of revolution as process. He rejects cataclysmic change in favour of revolution through critical education. His belief was that society can only be transformed by the systematic construction and consolidation of new social relationships. The capacity of the people to play key roles in their own destiny is central to this process. Intellectual and moral reform is Gramsci's term for what Freire would call *conscientisation*: the process whereby people critically reconceptualise their roles in society from their *false consciousness*. "The philosophy of praxis is the crowning point of this entire movement of intellectual and moral reformation, made dialectical in the contrast between popular culture and high culture" (Forgacs, 1988, p 351). Gramsci's writings offer an originality of thought and a practical base, a praxis that reflects his experience as an activist.

According to Gramsci, Lenin's belief that there can be no revolutionary movement without a revolutionary theory is of fundamental importance to understanding the function of critical education. Examining traditional working-class organisation and leadership, which had proved so ineffective in conquering capitalism while at the same time existing within it, he developed insight into the dynamics of social, political and economic relations that had never been achieved before. His vision of progressive revolutionary change was based on the role of critical education in achieving mass political consciousness with a democratic, grassroots base rather than an elite leadership.

"Classical Marxism, by emphasising the coercive nature of politics, has been correspondingly weak in analysing the problem of consent" (Hoffman, 1984, p 1). Gramsci's substantial contribution is found in his analysis of consent in relation to *hegemony*.

The concept of hegemony

Gramsci's analysis of the concept of *hegemony* is profound. Hegemony is the means by which one class assumes dominance over the masses in society. Traditional Marxism emphasised that this was achieved through coercion, the way in which the state exercised control through the law, the police and the armed forces. Gramsci extended this understanding by identifying the way in which dominant ideology, as a form of ideological persuasion, permeates our lives through the institutions of civil society. By these means, dominant attitudes are internalised and accepted as *common sense*, and thereby legitimised in the minds of people. Not only did he develop the notion of *consent* within a Marxist framework, but he analysed *hegemony* as "the entire complex of practical and theoretical activities with which the ruling class not only justifies and maintains its dominance, but manages to win the active consent of those over whom it rules" (Gramsci, 1986, p 244). This development of the cultural and moral aspects of hegemony challenges the entire Marxist conceptual analysis of the state as an instrument of coercion (Hoffman, 1984). His notion of the *historical bloc*, a term that encompasses the interrelationships of the economic, cultural and political alliances in society, is bound together by the cohesion of hegemony. Hegemonic dominance established through an intellectual and moral bloc is likely to be much more stable than power achieved through coercion. "Gramsci is very specific about this object, which is not successfully fulfilled by all parties – the establishment of an integral State, a State which has a fully developed hegemony in civil society encompassing the mass of the population and thereby cementing together a strong historical bloc" (Showstack Sassoon, 1987a, p 150). But hegemony is not a system, it is a process of constant struggle to maintain dominance over subordinate classes, which is actively maintained and modified by agents of the state – in itself a form of praxis (Ransome, 1992). So, having achieved dominance, a ruling class has a continuing need to maintain hegemonic control. The complexity of the concept of hegemony is that its structure is open to constant analysis, challenge and modification (Entwistle, 1979). It is not likely that hegemonic dominance can be maintained effectively without the collective will of the people – therefore the development of a counter-hegemony plays an essential part in the process of change. This is where Gramsci saw the importance of critical education. He also transcended the dichotomous class divide of previous Marxist thinkers by identifying potential alliances between many social groups in the process of collective action.

Gramsci saw the embodiment of social equilibrium in the interrelationship of coercion and consent. Also of central importance in this respect is the flexibility of hegemony, the way in which peripheral criticisms can be absorbed as acts of compromise. In this way, reformist measures can be negated before they threaten the bedrock of the dominant ideology. By offering such palliatives, the status quo can be maintained without resorting to the use of coercion, which is both expensive and difficult to maintain. In a similar vein, Freire refers to *false generosity*, or tokenism.

One extreme example of the use of ideological persuasion to cement cracks in a crumbling status quo could be seen in Margaret Thatcher's use of the Falklands War to unite the UK in the face of the threat from an outside enemy, namely Argentina. On the other hand, state reversion to coercion during the 1984-85 Miners' Strike, as well as ideological persuasion, aimed at the rest of civil society, that the miners were the 'enemy within' (Milne, 1994), demonstrates the might of the state when the full force of coercion and consent are used in combination. *False generosity* is used within the process of *hegemony* to create an illusion of democracy and justice. Just one example is the tokenistic way that the hegemonic education system allows individuals from some oppressed groups to flourish, while the groups as a whole remain disadvantaged. This individualises educational failure and success, creating a smokescreen for the hegemonic function of schools.

Gramsci provides community workers with insights into the way in which community groups can begin the process of transforming society for the common good. His analysis offers critical insight into the power of ideas to infiltrate the inner recesses of our being to persuade us to accept the dominant order of things unquestioningly as *common sense*. Whereas coercion is exercised overtly through the armed forces, the police, the courts and prisons, consent is subtly woven through the institutions of civil society – the family, schools, the media, political parties, unions, religious organisations, cultural, charitable and community groups – in a way that permeates our social being and asserts hegemonic control by influencing our ideas. The struggles against oppression around issues of *difference* and *diversity* are located in civil society. This places the community worker at the heart of the process. The values, attitudes, morality and beliefs that are internalised as *common sense* by the masses but serve the interests of dominant groups have to be challenged at a local as well as an institutional level. In order for this to happen in a critical way, Gramsci believed that the *false consciousness* of the subordinated classes needed to be transformed to release full potential for participation in the process of social action. This is why both Freire and Gramsci locate critical education at the heart of the process of transformative change.

Based on his political activism, Gramsci recognised that *hegemony* is a resilient and flexible force. He believed that the critical consciousness of ordinary people is vital in any effective intervention, but that this will not erupt spontaneously. External agents need to act as catalysts in this process, and he conceptualised these as *traditional intellectuals*.

The role of the intellectuals

Central to Gramsci's thought was how to raise the consciousness of oppressed people without simultaneously destroying their innate energy. He believed that without emphasis on intellectual understanding, the consciousness of oppressed people is likely to be fragmented, manifesting itself in a simple form of anti-authoritarianism – a generic hatred of the state rather than a critical analysis of power and domination. Gramsci recognised that critical consciousness could only come about through a political understanding of the illegitimate foundations of class domination. *False consciousness* is powerful and the questioning needed to reach a more critical awareness does not usually happen without external intervention.

Gramsci saw every person as having intellectual capacities for thinking and reasoning. He used the term *intellectual* to refer to people who occupy a wide range of organisational or ideological/cultural roles in society. Within this concept, *organic intellectuals* are those who emerge from their culture of origin. Every social group produces individuals who possess "the capacity to be an organiser of society in general, including all its complex organism of services, right up to the state organism, because of the need to create the conditions most favourable to the expansion of their own class" (Forgacs, 1988, p 301). *Traditional intellectuals* he saw as the product of a previous historical period, whose role has continued to exist in the present, and who are not deeply committed to a class. He particularly had in mind the Catholic Church, which at that time in Italian history had a monopoly not only of religious ideology but of education, morality and justice. *Traditional intellectuals* have an important preliminary role in challenging hegemony by acting as a catalyst in the process of transformation, unlocking mass consciousness (Boggs, 1980). They bridge the divide between theory and practice by becoming committed to social justice, and begin the process of liberation by creating the context for questioning the legitimacy of everyday experience.

Gramsci felt it ultimately essential that intellectuals should be generated from the very heart of the working class, but he saw the role of the *traditional intellectual* as one of sympathetic allegiance to justice, and vital in setting the wheels of change in motion. He was sceptical that their allegiance would be sustained; converts who do not emerge from the people, according to historical analysis, are prone to defect in the face of persecution. But, having cut the ties to their own class, *traditional intellectuals* could perform a useful role as catalysts for change. The most important function falls to the working class *organic intellectual*, a person of ideas, a person with a passion for the people that transcends the dichotomy between *knowing* and *feeling*. Without this holistic element, the struggle will remain peripheral. (The knowing–feeling divide is addressed in Chapters Seven and Eight in relation to feminism.)

Organic intellectuals remain committed to their cultural roots. They articulate new values, pose critical questions, and invite new ways of thinking about the world. The role, in its commitment to its class of origin, shares the inherent dilemmas of that class, and plays an integral part in the process of change. When *organic intellectuals* emerge from everyday life into that role, their specific purpose is raising the critical consciousness of the people; they remain central to the creation of a just society.

> The organic intellectual of the working class is a builder, an organiser, a permanent persuader so that he [sic] is able to engage in all aspects of the struggle.... These attributes, developed before the revolution, will serve after the revolution as the tasks of the organic intellectual continue in all these areas, from the organisation of socialist production to the building of a new culture ... the creation of a new intellectual begins in the heart of the old society. (Showstack Sassoon, 1987a, pp 149-50)

Organic intellectuals become leaders in the process of change, but they are not an elite. Gramsci distinguished the role by its function rather than its status. In this sense, he moves beyond a revolutionary leadership model to one where these key roles function within an overall unity that is inspired by critical consciousness. This unity can be seen in the type of socialism discussed by Fromm (1962), by which people become the conscious subjects of history, experiencing themselves as powerful, not powerless, and by such intellectual emancipation are able to free themselves from the chains of *false consciousness*. "Through a constant process of theoretical preparation and political education, members of the rank and file could develop their political capacities and eventually become leaders. In this way the necessary division between leader and led was no longer arbitrary and formal, but merely functional" (Showstack Sassoon, 1987a, p 85).

According to Gramsci, *common sense* is a collection of myths and superstitions that is resilient to spontaneous critical thought. The *traditional intellectual* unlocks popular critical consciousness by offering a coherent understanding of oppressive forces in history and society. In contrast to this initial function, the *organic intellectual* integrates this critical consciousness into everyday culture. Everyday thought and action are questioned, transformed and, in turn, collectively transform society. The organic intellectual stratum grows both qualitatively and quantitatively, for every person is innately an intellectual, and by this process *false consciousness* transforms into *critical consciousness*.

Gramsci's insight into the complex nature of *hegemony* changed the very essence of the concept by recognising that people are not only controlled by coercion, but consent to their own oppression as a result of the subtle forces of ideological persuasion. As a powerful form of control, dominant attitudes and values permeate people's lives through civil institutions – the media, the family, schools, and all other social groups that we experience. The result is *cultural invasion* (Freire, 1972): our minds become colonised with how we should think, feel and act. We are robbed of the confidence to be critical because the interests of power and privilege invade our thinking, influencing our perceptions of the world and our place in it.

Gramsci's emphasis was on praxis in the process of change. The term he frequently used in his notebooks, *philosophy of praxis*, is the concept of a unity of theory and practice. "For Gramsci the philosophy of praxis is both the theory of the contradictions in society and at the same time people's practical awareness of those contradictions" (Forgacs, 1988, p 429). bell hooks (1993, p 151) talks about making a commitment to work from a "lived understanding" of people's lives rather than accepting as authentic the distortion of a "bourgeois lens". She cites Freire's words from *Pedagogy in Process*: "authentic help means that all who are involved help each other mutually, growing together in the common effort to understand the reality which they seek to transform. Only through such praxis – in which those who help and those who are being helped help each other simultaneously – can the act of helping become free from the distortion in which the helper dominates the helped".

The rest of this chapter explores the implications of these ideas for community development practice and considers some practical interventions.

Locating and dislocating oppression

An analysis of power and the structures of discrimination is needed in order to develop practical strategies for change. This analysis needs to incorporate not only 'race', class and gender, but the whole range of patterns of power and subordination that exist. These do not operate in a discrete and exclusive way, or in a hierarchical way. In other words, a simplistic, dichotomous analysis of power in relation to oppressor/ oppressed is no longer adequate for our emerging understandings of difference and the complexity of overlapping, interlinking patterns of discrimination. This overarching emphasis on class discrimination distracted us from recognising the complexity of difference within class relations, and it was the development of feminism and postmodernism that led to the refinement of our analysis.

Discrimination as formalised oppression

An understanding of Gramsci's concept of *hegemony* is essential to this analysis. Maintaining power by persuading people that dominant attitudes are *common sense* works in a much more subtle way than a dominant group overtly coercing others into subordination. Power is located within a multidimensional system of oppressions in which we are all simultaneously oppressors and oppressed. It is essential that we see this as a complex whole that interlinks and reinforces at every level.

Ideology, the ideas that are formed around values and beliefs in society and inform the way society is organised, reinforces and justifies the divisions and power imbalances between groups in order to maintain the status quo. These ideas are difficult to change because they have been sold as *common sense* – a term that Gramsci defined as fragmented, disjointed, contradictory thinking that justifies reality for the mass of the people (Hall, 1996c). In these ways, the ideas of the most powerful in society sustain their own interests. This can be seen in relation to 'normality'. Take the issue of *the family*, which has fundamentally changed in role and structure over recent decades. A 'normal' family, despite an understanding of difference and changing structures, is still perceived in a White, Western heterosexual, fully able, middle-class way as a man and a woman living together with their two perfectly formed children. Anything different is 'other', deviant and undesirable, and therefore undermining of the moral base of society. This thinking in turn justifies policy decisions that target groups that do not conform to this norm – and, ironically, this constitutes the majority of people in society. But, due to the power of dominant thinking, it is perceived as a statistical norm rather than an ideological norm (Thompson, 2001), with the result that the *deviant* label is perceived as *common sense*.

Ideology does not only define what is *normal*, but also what is *natural*. Discriminatory ideas become embedded in the structures of society and accepted as *common sense*, so not questioned (Thompson, 2003). The way in which biological or medical determinism is used to justify *normal* stereotypical roles in society (women as natural carers; Black people as less intelligent; old people as feeble; 'dis'abled people as dependent) presents a false logic; what Thompson (2001) terms the *logic of discrimination*. These are powerful ideas, appealing to a *common sense* of what is normal and natural, which, in serving the interests of the *status quo*, not only subordinate, but diminish life chances by creating poverty, poor health and reduced opportunities. This terrain of ideological struggle is where prejudice, discrimination and oppression interact to weave power relationships into everyday lives. By locating the sites of prejudice and discrimination, we are also locating the most powerful points of intervention and transformation.

The first step in locating power and control is to understand the ways in which the legitimising of power is achieved. By this, I mean that prejudiced social attitudes reflect social divisions in society and help to reinforce them. *Prejudice* is an irrational thinking that primarily operates at a personal level, but reflects structural discrimination. It is often based on *stereotypes*, and works in a way that limits people's potential (as in the case of 'dis'abled or older people being treated as dependent), and at worst is life-threatening (as in domestic violence and racist attacks). *Discrimination* defines the way in which *prejudice* is structured in society by powerful and privileged dominant groups exploiting and subordinating groups who are less powerful, and therefore less able to act in their own interests. *Oppression* refers to the subordination, marginalisation and exclusion from society of these groups, thereby denying them social justice, citizenship and full democratic rights to participate in society. *Empowerment* is a term that is easily abused and difficult to define. As Barr states (1995, pp 121-2) "we need to be clear about the framework of reference within which we use the term because different agencies, and within them different actors, appear to have different expectations of empowerment and there is often a credibility gap between aspirations of communities and actual achievements". In radical community development, this concept links to the process of *conscientisation*, that of critical questioning and analysis as the basis of social change. Empowerment is therefore the ability to make critical connections in relation to power and control in society in order to identify discrimination and determine collective action for change.

An excellent model, which is widely used in community development practice, is Thompson's (2001, 2003) PCS model (Figure 6.1). Three concentric rings indicate levels of interaction between the individual and society. It is particularly helpful because it symbolises the ways in which these different levels mutually reinforce each other. Too often, analysis stops at the P-level – that of individual, personal prejudice. Challenging sexist comments, or even tackling the behaviour of racist groups in community, will never be enough to redress the problems of inequality in society. It will not even be enough to stem the tide of discrimination that constantly reinforces attitudes by permeating our thoughts and actions in the most subtle of ways.

Figure 6.1: The PCS model

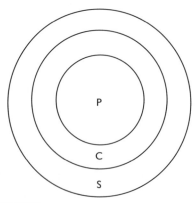

Source: Thompson (2001, 2003)

Thompson, in a simple but effective way, provides a tool that embeds the P-level (the personal or psychological – a level of thoughts, feelings, attitudes, action and prejudice) within the C-level (that of the cultural, shared ways of seeing, thinking and doing – a level of commonalities, consensus and conformity); this, in turn, is set within the S-level (the structural level where social divisions are sewn in to the fabric of society and oppression and discrimination become institutionalised – the sociopolitical power base) (Thompson, 2001). All these levels interact in ways that mutually reinforce prejudice and discrimination. This understanding is essential. It indicates why it is impossible to counter oppression by targeting one level at the exclusion of the others. This dynamic is so powerful that it negates any action that fails to address the whole. In this way, individual prejudice can only be understood within the cultural context, which in turn needs to be made sense of in relation to the structural context. These levels can never be seen in isolation from one another simply because they form an interactive dynamic that constantly maintains social divisions and serves the power relations in society. The PCS model offers an analysis that helps us to see the need for action to extend beyond community to address change at all levels, in order to bring about transformative social change.

A critical approach to community development calls for anti-discriminatory practice to be set within the social and political context. The first step to this is an openness to exploring attitudes, values and beliefs in ways that are both critical and self-critical. Out of this comes the courage to experience challenge and a willingness to understand different ways of engaging with the world. We have to become 'border-crossers', that is, we have to let go of the cultural, theoretical and ideological parameters that enclose us and offer us the security of 'home'; the familiar and the known. "To move away from 'home' is to question in historical, semiotic and structural terms how the boundaries and meanings of 'home' are constructed in self-evident ways often outside of criticism" (Giroux, 1993, p 179). Becoming 'homeless' in this sense is to shift to a space where life can be seen more critically, and possibilities for change can be explored. This is why creating contexts for critical debate in public spaces is a vital concept for the community worker; by decontextualising the taken-for-grantedness of everyday life we see things from another perspective. From here we can focus on the individual in relation to the cultural and political context. And this is exactly what the PCS model, in all its simplicity, helps to locate: it is a structure that represents the embeddedness of discrimination at every level of society.

Making even more critical connections

The strength of the PCS model is that it takes community workers beyond a simplistic notion that we can change the world by challenging oppressive behaviour on a personal or even community level. The limitations of this model are that it does not offer critical connections with the complex interweavings and intertwinings of oppressions in a multidimensional structure needed to move Gramscian/Freirean thinking from dichotomy into complexity. In relation to classroom teaching, Magda Lewis captures this complexity as follows:

> Pedagogical moments arise in specific context: the social location of the teacher and students; the geographic and historical location of the institutions in which they come together; the political climate within which they work; the personalities and personal profiles of the individuals in the classroom; the readings selected for the course; and the academic backgrounds of the students all come together in ways that create the specifics of the moment. (Lewis, 2000, p 104)

Gramsci's contribution to action can be seen in the way that he refocuses our attention from the state to civil society, and the way in which it serves the interests of the state. Community, in this analysis, becomes not only a site for critical education, but also a site for critical action. Gramsci's use of military terminology is unfortunate, but this should not detract from the conceptual insight it offers. He warned against a *war of manoeuvre*, a targeting of the state apparatus, in the first instance at least. Instead, he saw revolution as a process of consciousness rooted in popular adult education in the context of civil society. Gramsci's *war of position* involves linking all manner of social organisations in alliance, and, importantly, identifies a space for the role of new social movements in this process (P. Mayo, 1999). Community work has always paid attention to networking and alliances, but we now need more complex levels of action. In global times, the dynamic between the local and the global challenges reflection and action that is preoccupied with neighbourhood as the definitive site of community work.

Yes, Gramscian and Freirean thought are both limited by dichotomous analyses, and by a failure to fully understand the complexity of difference within a class analysis. Our responsibility is to wrestle with these ideas with the privilege of our new understandings to re-vision the insights they offer within an analysis of difference. "Gramsci's specters are whispering to us, reminding us that the struggle ahead is a politics of passionate remembrance, of re-visiting anti-fascist struggles of the past, of recognizing the lessons embedded in history's dreams and nightmares, of moving forward into the new millennium with renewed hope and an optimism of the will" (McLaren et al, 1998, p 30).

Finally, let us move on to explore some practical possibilities for working in these ways in community.

Practical feminist approaches to dislocating oppression

Hustedde and King cite Dillard's feminist spirituality approach to individual and collective inner journeys to the soul, which help to dislocate prejudice that is held deep inside us. The move is an inner rather than outer spirituality; one in which the concrete realities of our lives remain the focus of our attention: "when individuals and communities go within they meet the violence and terror within themselves that they project on to others. We hate others because we can't face the enemy within; so we project that enemy onto people of other races and classes or other institutions and communities" (Hustedde and King, 2002, p 341).

The tools that they offer community development for undertaking this approach are based on story as a route to engaging community in self-inquiry and self-knowledge: "the telling of a story slows the mind down and lets the story sink underneath the skin to reveal something of the spirit" (2002, p 342). They also emphasise the importance of rituals to community as "part of the search for who we are and the search for meaning as a community ... community rituals can provide stability and continuity and can promote a sense of solidarity and cohesion" (2002, p 343). The process takes communities forward as the creators of their own futures. This has clear links to the use of story that I discuss in Chapter Three.

They identify the following:

i) **Rituals of transition** create order out of the chaos of change. The Native American tradition of acknowledging seven generations of community takes the past–present–future dimension from solid historic connections through to marking change and planning directions for the future. This could be a valuable approach where family, community and tradition have gone through massive transition at the hands of unregulated economic forces. Another example they use is the Samoan Circle (developed by Lorenz Aggens in Chicago in 1970) where everyone is allowed to speak in turn in a safe, democratic listening environment, not led or chaired. This has been found to be effective if there are controversial issues to be tackled by a large group of people, as everyone has a stake in the success of the meeting. Conflict is more likely to be resolved because people are giving others their full attention.

ii) **Rituals of healing** are based on empathy, compassion, forgiveness, and justice. Community healing rituals can be used for reconciliation and dialogue. The authors give an example of the way that a unity candle was used in a public meeting in a community torn apart by land disputes and coal mining. The meeting opened with community leaders and coal mine operators symbolically lighting candles to indicate their willingness to talk, and then lighting one unity candle together to symbolise their desire to find a common resolution to their differences. This set the tone for cooperation as a value for healing divisions. Other examples include the Vietnam War Memorial in Washington and the AIDS quilt.

iii) **Rituals of celebration** build on common solidarity and cohesion by expressing gratitude, joy and a sense of belonging. They focus on abundance rather than poverty, on strengths rather than weaknesses. Festivals celebrate the roots of a community, generating a sense of pride, confidence and belonging. They can also bring people from all walks of life together to learn and to negotiate differences. Two examples that come to mind for me are i) the Bristol Festival Against Racism (Gilchrist, 2004, p 64) and ii) the annual world Credit Union Day celebrations in Hattersley.

Gramsci's concept of *hegemony* is powerful in its simplicity, helping us to understand the power of ideas and the ways in which our minds are colonised unquestioningly by dominant attitudes. It provides the basis for developing more complex anti-discriminatory analyses based on a plurality of oppressions, and set within the wider political context of globalisation. The next chapter explores critiques of Freire and Gramsci in order to arrive at a critical perspective from which to re-vision a pedagogy for our times.

SEVEN

Critiques of Freire and Gramsci

This chapter takes thinking from the class-based dichotomous analysis of Freire and Gramsci into the insights into difference and diversity offered by feminism and postmodernism. I demonstrate the ways that making sense of the world through a dichotomous analysis reduces life experience to an either/or, 'this' or 'that', binary simplicity, which is only capable of defining something in relation to its 'Other' (for example male/female, Black/White, young/old) thus denying the complexity and plurality of oppressions. It was the predominant emphasis on a class analysis that subsumed women's experience within the working-class struggle. In turn, the same dichotomous thought blinkered White women to see women's experience as a male/female analysis, overlooking the interlinking nature of multiple oppressions and the need for a politics of difference. Today, we are much more aware of the complex nature of oppressions linked to social justice, and the ways in which these engage with environmental justice. Here, I examine an analysis of difference and I explore the interface of social justice and environmental justice, to identify the current challenges for community development in terms of both theory and action:

> Freire's original work emphasized class while ignoring gender … [he] did conceive his pedagogy in singular 'class terms' growing out of his experiences among peasants and workers in impoverished Brazil. Therefore, as feminist educators have proposed, his foundational work from forty years ago needs correction for a theme like gender, among others. Freire himself acknowledged this missing dimension; he also urged educators to avoid copying him and to develop pedagogy suitable for their local situation. (Shor, 2000, p 6)

I want to begin my inquiry by relating it to my own community development practice. The period from the 1970s to the early 1990s was an inspiring time for community workers, which emerged from the optimism of the 1960s. "Freirean and feminist pedagogies emerged at about the same time … just after the activist 1960s, when dissent and participation were ideas whose time had come ... that legendary age of civil rights actions, student protests, anti-war campaigns ..." (Shor, 2000, p 2). This was the birthing ground for new social movements and the time when Freire made a massive impact on emancipatory practice – and in this I include liberation theology, radical community development and human rights activism. Second-wave feminism, and other new social movements, emerged from grassroots dialogue and changed our understanding of the world – anti-racist, Black women, green, lesbian and gay, 'dis'ability, grey power and so on – and we began to stretch our minds from the limitations of either/or dichotomous thought, framed by Enlightenment's search for a single truth, into the complexities of postmodernism and difference.

Freirean pedagogy has been the biggest single influence on radical community work theory and practice in the UK from the early 1970s. Emphasising *dialogue* as a critical encounter between people, and the centrality of *praxis* in that process, he located theory in everyday experience. More than this, he helped community workers to understand that the practice of social justice is rooted in its ideology of equality. In this way, democratic values create a frame for the way we see the world, analyse experience of the world and challenge the world. Beginning with every encounter, we learnt that true reflection leads to action: that personal consciousness is the basis of collective action for change, but that "action is human only when it is not merely an occupation but also a preoccupation, that is, when it is not dichotomized from reflection" (Freire, 1996, p 35). This period saw community development redefine itself as a radical emancipatory practice based on critical pedagogy.

There was an immediate feminist backlash against Freirean pedagogy, initially because of his use of dominant male language in *Pedagogy of the oppressed*. Since then the feminist critique has developed a wider analytic perspective, which offers insight into the limitations of Freire and the benefits of a feminist re-visioning of his work. Freirean pedagogy and feminist pedagogy have had a rocky ride in relation to each other, but they have much in common. Beneath the surface commonalities lies a tangled web of what Shor terms "conflict and convergence" (2000, p 3), and it is that web that I want to explore here.

Critiques of Freire and feminism

> The desire for transformation and the critique of inequality are ... common ground shared by Freire-based critical

pedagogy and feminist pedagogy, two dissident schools of thought with a close and troubled relationship in recent years. (Shor, 2000, p 2)

I have been profoundly influenced and inspired, in theory and practice, by Paulo Freire, and I witness the ways in which he continues to have that same impact on practitioners in community development today. I want to begin this critique by exploring why a Brazilian man should continue to attract feminist attention.

Feminist pedagogy, like Freirean pedagogy, is founded on grassroots education for critical consciousness as a tool for understanding the nature of structural oppression. Crucial to this understanding is an awareness that emancipatory potential lies in collective action for change for a just and sustainable world. Feminist and Freirean pedagogies converge in their fundamental assumption that dominant ways of knowing need challenging, and that all people have a basic human right to be valued and active in their world. Freire, in offering a praxis of liberation that involves an understanding of the nature of oppression, the process of *conscientisation*, and the importance of culture and history in the struggle for transformative change, complements feminism. Feminist pedagogy diverges from Freire, however, in its challenge to patriarchy as a fundamental oppressive structure that echoes through women's lives, complexified by difference.

Feminism has had a powerful influence on community development. The ways in which women at grassroots level have demonstrated that *the personal is political* have been transformative for both theory and practice. Prior to this, women's experience, in the home and community, was seen as 'soft' and apolitical. These altered perspectives led to an analysis of the way in which the public–private divide has oppressed women for generations by creating the myth that politics stops at the parameters of our communities, and certainly at the thresholds of our homes. Let us apply this thinking to a practical issue. This way of seeing things was so deeply entrenched in the public psyche that such injustices as the police refusing to intervene in incidents of domestic violence led to women being denied the protection that was their human right. The women's refuge movement, pioneered by Erin Pizzey in the 1970s, shunted domestic violence into public awareness. Yet, domestic violence remains a worldwide problem, transcending all aspects of difference. In 1990, in my practice in Hattersley, Janice came to see me. "My ex-husband came round the house and started knocking me around. I managed to get him out and lock the door, but I was terrified for my life, so I called 999. They took me seriously until I gave them my Hattersley address: 'If you live there you must be an old slag, and you're getting no more than you deserve!' – and they put the phone down on me." These are the types of experience that feminists challenge as hidden from view by a class analysis.

In these ways, we begin to understand why, despite Freire's compatibility with second-wave feminism's emphasis on the personal as political, he received harsh criticism from feminists. His pedagogy is based on a universal analysis (oppressor/oppressed) that denies the complexity of different experiences of oppression. His sexist language, evident in his early work, was also seized upon as evidencing an unconsciously gendered approach to his pedagogy. His response was that *Pedagogy of the oppressed* needs to be set in its historical and cultural context. It cannot be read as if it were written yesterday and retrospectively criticised, with the benefit of hindsight, using conceptual tools that were not available at the time it was written (Freire and Macedo, 1993). The influences of postmodernism and an increased understanding of *difference* have challenged the assumptions of metanarratives that are based on a universal, collective experience as reducing the nature of lived experience to a naïvely simplistic unity. A theory of liberation that glosses over divisions in society, attempting to universalise experience shaped by gender, 'race', ethnicity, age, sexuality, 'dis'ability and so on entrenches those divisions still further.

bell hooks poses an interesting contradiction. She states that Freire offered her a structure within which she could define her own experience of racism on a global level, when "the radical struggle of Black women to theorize our subjectivity" was not welcomed by early, White, bourgeois feminist thinkers (hooks, 1993, p 151). hooks refers to Freire's 'blind spot' to questions of gender, and his failure to acknowledge the specific gendered nature of oppression. Nevertheless, his pedagogy gave her the conceptual tools with which to analyse her own oppression as a Black American woman, helping her to see herself as a subject in resistance. Here we identify a contradiction between White Western feminism and the critical pedagogy of a Third World man.

Freire emphasises that we all have a right and a duty to participate in the transformation of society because the struggle belongs to us all, wherever its specific location. He stresses that his pedagogy is not universal, that it emerged from his own experience, and needs to be adapted for other contexts. Engaging in different cultural contexts, in a climate of political change, calls for critical questioning as the basis of an ongoing analysis. Freire was clear that giving answers, rather than asking questions, is "the castration of curiosity" (Freire and Faundez, 1992, p 35). hooks challenges feminist thinkers who separate feminist pedagogy from Freirean pedagogy: "For me these two experiences converge.... I have taken threads of Paulo's work and woven it into that version of feminist pedagogy I believe my work as a writer and teacher embodies" (hooks, 1993, p 150).

Feminist pedagogy, like Freirean pedagogy, places everyday stories at the heart of the process of critical consciousness. The notion that the deeply personal is profoundly political leads to a critical understanding of the nature of structural oppression, and the way that we are shaped in all our difference by structures of power that permeate our lives. By exploring the political nature of everyday encounters, we move towards the critical consciousness necessary to demystify the dominant hegemony and to change oppressive structures.

In much the same way as the universality of Freire's theory was challenged by feminists, White feminist analysis was challenged by Black women on the grounds of difference. In other words, White feminists stood accused of defining 'woman' from a White perspective, which overlooked other aspects of difference. This is a consequence of the dichotomous thinking that epitomises Western ideological thought. In this respect, early second-wave feminists had defined 'woman' in relation to 'man'. Stereotypes, or controlling images, mystify the nature of social relations and confound the ways in which 'race', class and gender intersect with each other. These images are "key in maintaining interlocking systems of race, class and gender oppression" (Hill Collins, 1990, p 68).

Western consciousness in its "despiritualisation of the universe" (Richards, 1980, p 72), a consequence of materialism, required the separation of the 'knowing self' from the 'known object'. Inevitably, in a subject/object analysis, those who are seen as 'Other' are subordinated to 'object' because their reality is named by those who have the power to locate themselves as 'subject'. This power relationship dehumanises people as objects rather than subjects in control of their own lives (Freire, 1972). In our unravelling of the nature of oppressions, it is easy to see how readily we fall into the trap of this dichotomy at successive stages of our understanding. Criticising the universality of Freire, second-wave feminism failed itself by overlooking the different experience of Black women. Our current challenge is to focus our analysis on the insidious nature of White power, rather than continuing our preoccupation with what it is to be Black and subordinated (Fine et al, 1997). This represents a subtle shift of gaze that takes us firmly into the need for *problematising* power, not only powerlessness, in the struggle for liberation.

In order to get to grips with justice and sustainability, there is a need for a sudden and dramatic shift in Western epistemology, a way of seeing the world from a dominant perspective that denies indigenous and subordinated worldviews:

> This interdependent world system is based on the exploitation of oppressed groups, but the system at the same time calls forth oppositional cultural forms that give voice to the conditions of these groups. White male bourgeois dominance is being challenged by Black people, women and other oppressed groups, who assert the validity of their own knowledge and demand social justice and equality in numerous political and cultural struggles. In the intellectual sphere, this shifting world system has led to a shattering of Western metanarratives and to the variety of stances of postmodernist and cultural-identity theory. A major theoretical challenge to traditional Western knowledge systems is emerging from feminist theory ... [which] like other contemporary approaches, validates difference, challenges universal claims to truth, and seeks to create social transformation in a world of shifting and uncertain meanings. (Weiler, 1995, p 23)

Dichotomous thought, based on oppositional difference, is a simplistic analysis for complex social hierarchies, hiding as much as it reveals. Domination based on difference results in a hierarchy of fragmentation: an incompleteness held together by relationships of superiority/ inferiority. Within this concept, "as the 'Others' of society who can never really belong, strangers threaten the moral and social order. But they are simultaneously essential for its survival because those individuals who stand at the margins of society clarify its boundaries" (Hill Collins, 1990, p 68). Hill Collins suggests that African-American women stand at the convergence of a series of the inferior halves of these dichotomies and that this is central to the understanding of their subordination (Hill Collins, 1990).

Angela Davis vividly captured the dangers of dichotomous thought in relation to the way that class can fragment Black women's activism:

> Black women scholars and professionals cannot afford to ignore the straits of our sisters who are acquainted with

the immediacy of oppression in a way many of us are not. The process of empowerment cannot be simplistically defined in accordance with our own particular class interests. We must learn to lift as we climb. (Davis, 1989, p 9)

In these ways, we are able to see that feminism, as a political movement, powerfully placed patriarchy as an oppressive force alongside that of class. However, because its analysis was dichotomous, it focused on 'woman' as a unitary category in relation to its 'Other', 'man', as if all women had the same experience in relation to ethnicity, class and culture. This is not a simple oversight. It represents a struggle of consciousness that, in focusing on this essentialist analysis of patriarchy, fails to offer an adequate explanation of the complex oppressions that construct female identities, including historical and cultural dimensions of gender relations. Gender inequality is not a singular experience, but the complex interplay of any number of political, cultural and historic dimensions. The social construction of gender is immensely complex, but our limited consciousness often traps us into dichotomous explanations rooted in the assumptions of a White unitary experience (Amos and Parmar, 1984). The endemic racism of White feminism not only failed to recognise the anti-racist struggle as central to feminism, but also overlooked the way it pathologises Black people in relation to sexuality and family relations (Anthias and Yuval-Davis, 1992).

So, while Freire is criticised for not dealing with the specific nature of the subordination of women within a class analysis, early second-wave feminism is criticised for not dealing with the issue of racism within a feminist analysis. The assumption of a universal sisterhood rendered Black women invisible. This ethnocentric approach overlooked cultural and historic relations, and in its preoccupation with the male/female dichotomy became oblivious of the hegemonic White, female, often middle-class focus (Anthias and Yuval-Davis, 1992). We need to develop critique in order to understand the complex interactions of 'race', class and gender and other aspects of difference, rather than move from one form of fragmented consciousness to another. For instance, Anthias and Yuval-Davis (1992, p 102) illustrate how struggles cannot be based on one major identity: 'Black' and 'White' women cannot be understood as essentially fixed oppositional categories.

Reflecting on the process of my own consciousness, I am aware that I owe my altered perceptions of social reality to Freire. His pedagogy equipped me with the conceptual tools necessary for my own struggle, and in turn this gave me the confidence to grapple with understandings that were outside my own specific experience. Despite the fact that feminist critiques accuse him of what bell hooks (1993, p 148) terms a "phallocentric paradigm of liberation – wherein freedom and the experience of patriarchal manhood are always linked as though they are one and the same", it is not useful to dismiss him. Like hooks, I believe that it would be a mistake to reject such profound insight out of hand when it has so much to offer feminist praxis. Without a critical understanding of *praxis* in the process of change, it is likely that I would have remained an academic observer, ignorant of just how necessary it is that "our lives must be a living example of our politics" (hooks, 1993, p 148).

From a feminist perspective, the problem with Freire is that he fails to include women's experience by subsuming gender within class, and does not recognise the patriarchal assumptions of the European intellectual tradition from which his own thought emerged. His early use of dominant masculine pronouns could be dismissed as a sign of the times, but feminists feel it reflects deeper assumptions about men and women. For instance, he refers to 'feminists' as though they are one voice or a single movement. Many feminists see Freire as offering a generalised and abstract analysis of dichotomous struggle where he presents himself as the heroic teacher. His sense of the revolutionary hero, imagined as male and solely existing in the public world, is problematic to the woman educator who is working with the *authority* of the teacher role and the subordination of 'woman' at one and the same time (Weiler, 2001). His later work became more inclusive and made fewer claims to revolutionary transformation, but he never critiqued the revolutionary leader and so his male assumptions failed to locate the teacher as positioned, in respect of 'race' and gender, at intersections of the private/public divide, in a matrix of interlocking oppressions.

Similarly, his assumption that liberation takes place in the public world led him to overlook the importance of the personal domestic world, thus reinforcing the public/private divide that creates the dichotomy between rationality and emotion. The contradiction here, as with Gramsci, is that he consistently recognised the influence of women in his life. Elza his first wife, he always acknowledged in terms of intellectual debt. He was a man for whom personal relationships were central to his flourishing and whose work was driven by passion and a love for people. He had qualities that inspired:

> Words seem not [to] be good enough to evoke all that I
> have learned from Paulo. Our meeting had that quality of

sweetness that lingers, that lasts for a lifetime, even if you never speak to the person again, see their face, you can always return in your heart to that moment when you were together and be renewed – that is a profound solidarity. (hooks, 1993, p 154)

He identifies love for humanity as the foundation of critical education, yet fails to elaborate fully on these dimensions in his theoretical analysis. He has a resistance to sexism or patriarchy, yet the contradiction remains that it is precisely because his work is so decontextualised and his claims so sweeping that so many can identify with his pedagogy.

Despite the range of criticism that Freire generates among feminists, we continue to be moved by his visionary humanity, humans as subjects making our own history. But, in global times, it is more apparent than ever that a pedagogy of liberation founded on class power and privilege is incomplete without an analysis of 'race', ethnicity, gender and all other aspects of difference that construct vastly diverse life experiences and life chances. The essence of feminist critiques of Freire is that he did not understand the complex nature of patriarchal privilege or the complexities of overlapping oppressions (Weiler, 2001).

Critiques of Freire from a class perspective

Postmodernism and an analysis of difference engendered a backlash from those critical pedagogues who believe that "postmodernism is an obstacle to the formation of open and radical perspectives which challenge inequalities and the deepening of the rule of capital in all areas of social life" (Rikowski and McLaren, 1999, p 1). Their concern is that "for postmodernists, all concepts are decentred (fragmented, splattered) and all dualisms (such as the Marxist notion of two major social classes) deconstructed" (Rikowski and McLaren, 1999, p 2). Their driving preoccupation is that postmodernism, in attempting to negate the Enlightenment project's emphasis on reason, rationality and a single truth, results in the search for meaning becoming so hopelessly fragmented that it offers a smokescreen for the Radical Right and its continuing path as the 'Third Way' (Hill, 2000).

Jenny Bourne expresses the dangers of relocating 'race' and 'gender' analyses from their sometimes violent and crushing everyday realities, where grassroots feminism emerged, to an elite position in the academy, not only removed from real life but relocating power in the hands of the already powerful (Bourne, 1999). She identifies the way in which "the 'personal is political' concurrently shifted the centre of gravity of struggle from the community and society to the individual", thus replacing action ("What has to be done?") with the reflection ("Who am I?") of identity politics. Her claim is that *identity* and *difference* have created a fragmentation; a view of society that cut through the "horizontal divisions of class [with] vertical divisions of gender, sexuality, ethnicity, religion, etc." (Bourne, 1999, p 137). This, of course, is problematic for community development when its process rests on collective action. Conversely, Spretnak (1997) suggests that while modernity sees the world as a collection of objects, and deconstructionist postmodernism dissipates this into an aggregate of fragments, ecological postmodernism offers a community of subjects, which are community-based, but structured politically in a model that embraces a community of communities of communities. The pendulum swings back in this way to offer us insight into the relationship between difference and collective action. The position of the class backlash is that "unless feminism and identity politics cultivated in the soil of poststructuralism ally themselves more squarely with a politics of class struggle, their contributions will not nourish the revolutionary praxis necessary in the struggle ahead" (McLaren et al, 1999, p 213). We are in a context of globalisation where more than half of the largest economies in the world are multinational corporations, not countries, which exploit the most vulnerable people and resources around the world in the name of capital. While critical pedagogy must engage with a politics of difference, we must at the same time situate this in a larger collective movement for liberation that focuses on the new oppressions created by globalisation:

> My activism can never become dissociated from my theoretical work; on the contrary, the former has its tactics and strategies formulated on the latter. The moment we recognize that food production around the world could be sufficient to feed twice its population, it is desolating to realize the numbers of those who come into the world but do not stay, or those who do but are forced into early departure by hunger. My struggle against capitalism is founded on that – its intrinsic perversity, its antisolidarity nature. (Freire, 1972, p 88)

Lockhart (1999, p 92) claims that there is no evidence that Freirean pedagogy is capable of transformative social change; that he was "always more important in terms of educational method than 'revolutionary futurity'". This is a position hotly contested by Paula Allman, who attributes the dilution of Freire's potential to the way he is often reduced to a technique by pedagogues; we cannot be partially Freirean she warns (Allman, 1999). Peter McLaren also warns of the dilution of Freire:

> Contemporary critical pedagogy needs to rescue Freire's work from the reformists who wish to limit his legacy to its contribution to consciousness-raising. Reformists are often victims of a subjectivism that occurs when people verbally denounce social injustice but leave intact the existing structures of society. (McLaren, 2000, pp 192-3)

Allman (1999, 2001) and McLaren (2000) both challenge the potential of a critical pedagogy that is based on reformism, within rather than against the existing structures of society, and emphasise that Freirean concepts disjointed from the whole pedagogy simply give the illusion of addressing capitalist social relations. However, "reform, and struggling for it, is crucial both because we must attempt to make life more palatable for those suffering the harshest consequences of capitalism and because we must try to forestall environmental collapse. But it is also important as well as essential because it is through and within the struggles for reform – the shop floor, the community, the environment or any other site where the ramifications of capitalism are experienced – that critical revolutionary praxis develops" (Allman, 2001, p 139). McLaren warns of setting class relations against cultural insights, and advocates a rereading of Marx with the insights of identity politics if we are to attain any coherent theoretical challenge to globalisation. Knowledge, he says, is transformed through an epistemological critique, which not only examines the content of knowledge, but also the way in which we produce and reproduce that knowledge. He calls for greater collective links between critical educators and students, community activists and the people, to come together in a dialogical relationship in the process of collective action for social change, in praxis.

Paula Allman (2001) poses some crucial questions for our time. How does capitalism seduce us into accepting massive contradictions of suffering and excess as natural and inevitable? How has it managed to win widespread consent at the same time as creating a culture of constant discontent? Her thesis is that a Marxist analysis provides the most complete interpretation of the nature of capitalism, and that the greatest barriers to our understanding remain a misinterpretation of his work. Praxis, for her, embraces all thought and action, not merely the application of theory to practice. Uncritical praxis has the potential for reproducing the conditions for capital to flourish; critical praxis has the infinite possibility to transform our engagement with the world. By exposing the ways in which global capitalism has been internalised and integrated into everyday subjective awareness, we thus begin a process that becomes ever critical and self-critical.

Both McLaren's and Allman's arguments are based on the premise that we remain uncritical as long as our practice relocates us within the same social relations. Praxis only assumes its critical potential when we become aware that ideological statements are partial truths that, in turn, partially distort the truth they are based on, thus reducing our understanding at the same time as convincing us that the version of reality they portray is the real truth. Capitalism, Allman stresses, cannot be reformed; the only way forward is a new worldview founded on justice, both within humanity and between humanity and the natural world. The fundamental role of critical education in this process is in *problematising* reality, constantly probing into how we know and feel. While acknowledging the contribution of the 'new antagonists' – environmentalists, feminists, human rights organisations and other new social movements – she claims that these can do no more than shake capitalism. Her criticism is that some of our finest minds remain trapped within the parameters of capitalism and liberal democracy.

According to Allman, critical pedagogy that has transformative potential needs to be informed by Marx's theory of consciousness, in which principled ethics of compassion and social justice reach out in a form of social interdependence based on a rereading of class relations. She envisages collective action for change in the form of an international alliance. This strategy is based on an analysis of the way that capitalism cleaves social divisions based on racism, homophobia, environmental destruction, gender disparity and so forth, and so recognises that capitalism is the common enemy, that oppression has a common core. From grassroots organisations, she sees this alliance gradually growing into a global movement (Allman, 2001).

Freire was always very clear that his pedagogy needed to be adapted to, not superimposed on, different political and cultural contexts, yet Blackburn (2000) sees weaknesses in Freirean pedagogy around its potential for ideological manipulation. Any pedagogy can only be as effective as the integrity and vigilance of its practitioners. While we need to be critical in re-visioning Freire in relation to our rapidly changing world and our equally rapidly changing understanding, maybe we also need to get better at practising Freire. Arguably, we are all inextricably trapped in our experience of the world, struggling for an uncluttered, unambiguous clarity. While the criticisms levelled at Freirean thought should be taken seriously, they also give it increased strength. As we push beyond the parameters of the dichotomous thinking that formed Freire's worldview, we are beginning to grapple at the edges of complexity, and develop his pedagogy in accordance with these new awarenesses. Although Freire is hailed for his pedagogy as opposed to his theory, many criticise his lack of guidance on how to become a critical practitioner. McLaren counters this, stating that:

> It is precisely his refusal to spell out in a 'bag of tricks' fashion alternative solutions that enables his work to be re-invented in the contexts in which his readers find themselves, thereby enjoining a contextually specific translation across geographic, geopolitical, and cultural borders. It also grants to Freire's corpus of works a universal character, as they are able to retain their heuristic potency (much like the works of Marx) such that they can be conscripted by educators to criticize and to counterpoint pedagogical practices worldwide. In fact, Freire urged his readers to reinvent him in the context of their local struggles. (McLaren, 2000, p 164)

Gramsci and feminism

Paradoxically, yet unsurprisingly, the personal sustenance of Gramsci during his prison years and the survival of his contribution to thought in the form of his prison notebooks were due to his sister-in-law, Tatiana Schucht; yet any political analysis of her 11 years of commitment to him was overlooked by Gramsci. Holub (1992, p 195) reminds us that we should not "assiduously polish the tainted mirrors of theoretical heroes". By the same token, it is equally important not to dismiss significant contributions to the development of our own thought, as women, out of hand. This, too, would create a paradox. As with Freire, Gramsci's thinking was historically and culturally specific, and it is therefore hardly surprising that it fell foul of the public/private divide. His thinking did not benefit from the coherent feminist awareness that has developed over the last few decades. The deep affection and admiration he felt for his mother, his sister Teresina, his wife Giulia and his sister-in-law Tatiana are well-documented and undisputed. There is also evidence that this extended to Nina Corrias, a feminist activist of his time (Kenway, 2001). There seem to be some contradictory issues here: Gramsci accepted as 'natural' the roles of the women in his personal life without recognising their political implications. However, there is a glimpse that he was aware at some deeper level of the complex subordination of women. In 1916, Gramsci's first public address was on the emancipation of women "taking as his cue Ibsen's play 'The Doll's House'" (Hoare and Smith, in Introduction to Gramsci, 1971, p xxxi). In his discussion of Americanism and Fordism he not only acknowledges women's exploitation in the public domain, but also recognises our vital function in the reproduction of the workforce, thereby identifying sexuality as a locus of oppression (Gramsci, 1986). However, "although Gramsci supported women's rights and saw sexuality as a basic aspect of emancipation, women's issues were not central to his thought" (Kenway, 2001, p 56). Indeed, his analysis was preoccupied with the role of sexuality in economic production. Holub points to an inherent contradiction in his thinking from a feminist perspective: "Gramsci insists on the centrality of sexuality, a woman's rights over her body, when it comes to the emancipation not only of women, but of society as a whole", but this is contradicted by the way his analysis is limited to "the need to discipline women's sexuality for economic and political purposes" (Holub, 1992, pp 197-8).

Holub (1992, p 196) is right in reminding us that within Gramsci's critical theory his concept of hegemony offers profound insights into the nature of power relations that bridge the divide of the public/ private spheres. Hence, it is not surprising that Gramsci was able to connect gender with the realms of production from both a political and a moral perspective. By gaining insight into the subtle ways in which power transcends the divide from public to private through the institutions of civil society – religion, education, the family and other forms of daily life – Gramsci offers understanding of the ways in which domination permeates the most intimate aspects of our being. This is the basis for Gramsci's acknowledged contribution to feminist thought through his concept of hegemony, which has provided a tool of analysis for understanding the sites of gendered oppression in society. Yet, Gramsci himself failed to do justice to his own concept in this respect. Subsequently, feminists have found the concept of hegemony to be a powerful conceptual tool. For instance, Arnot in the early 1980s argued that male hegemony consists of a multiplicity of moments that have persuaded women to accept a male-dominated culture and their subordination within it. The result is a constructed reality that is qualitatively different from that of men (Kenway, 2001). In understanding the nature of consent, we come to see that hegemony is always in process, in continuous struggle, and we begin to see that feminist consciousness has grown through questioning the nature of consent in relation to women's lives.

Holub's (1992, p 197) interpretation of Gramscian feminism is that he saw economic independence as only part of the story; true emancipation involves freedom of choice in relation to sexual relationships. What he referred to as a "new ethic" (Gramsci, 1986, p 296) is the transformative moment gained from a war of position that frees women in a truly liberatory way. Gramsci's feminist consciousness therefore connects women's sexual rights not only with women's liberation, but with the total transformation of society as a whole. Gramsci in this sense gives us a model of the way in which the *personal* is fundamentally *political*. Disappointingly, he loses credibility by calling for a sexual discipline that serves the economy:

> So the promising concessions Gramsci makes to the liberation of feminine sexuality are severely curtailed by his deterministic view of progress, his belief in the liberatory potential of industrialisation and above all his uncritical deployment, indeed, his 'forgetting', of one of his own powerful analytical tools in the demystification of power: the ubiquitous operations of hegemony, of certain ways of seeing and validating relations in multiple sites of political and social relations, in the public, but above all in the private sphere, in political, but above all in civil society, in the social, in the cultural, in the micro-spaces of everyday life. (Holub, 1992, p 198)

So, while Gramsci helps us to understand that without consent then the whole nature of domination is weakened, he failed to do justice to his own analysis of the issue of female liberation. His concept of hegemony, however, remains a critical analytic tool, which, combined with current understanding of the nature of social control, equips us well in our quest for transformative change.

Patti Lather in her work in the mid-1980s drew on Gramsci's notion of the *war of position* and the role of the *intellectuals* in relation to feminist political action. She chooses to substitute 'counter-hegemony' for 'struggle', inasmuch as it shifts the emphasis onto ideological alternatives. Lather takes Gramsci's belief in everyone's innate capacity to be philosophers and considers this in relation to the way that women have documented experience-based knowledge and acted to become prominent in all social institutions, claiming that this constitutes a *war of position*: "many small revolutions ... many small changes in relationships, behaviors, attitudes and experiences" (Kenway, 2001, p 59). She places particular emphasis on the role of the intellectuals in the tide of developing critical consciousness, but raises issues around the role of women educators in the process of transformation. The criticality of this role is dependent on the critical consciousness of its occupier. This debate is relevant to community development, and any other site of critical pedagogy. Critical approaches will inevitably falter away from liberation towards domination if the role of the *intellectual* is not conducted in an eternally critical and vigilant manner. And praxis is the core of that critical process.

Jane Kenway calls for a renewed Gramscian perspective from which we could engage with the big issues of our times:

> From a regenerated Gramscian perspective today, feminists might rework such politics in critical proximity to the new paradigms of governmentality associated with educational restructuring in the context of global economic and cultural restructuring. Further, just as feminists deconstructed and reworked the academic canons of the seventies, eighties, and nineties, so too must they now deconstruct the commodified 'informational' canons that increasingly predominate. These include commercialized knowledge in the global intellectual bazaar. And they include the canons associated with screens and machines, bits, bytes, and networks; digital entrepreneurialism (and the management theories that are organic to it); and, more generally, the tyranny of the ideology of the 'virtuous' circle between capital and technology. (Kenway, 2001, p 62)

Certainly, Gramscian and Freirean thought are both limited by dichotomous analyses, and by a failure to understand the complexity of difference – although Freire did address these issues increasingly in his later work. Peter Mayo points out that "one has to go beyond Gramsci to avoid Eurocentrism and beyond both Gramsci and Freire to avoid patriarchal bias" (P. Mayo, 1999, p 146). However, together Gramsci and Freire present a profundity of thought that offers us the basis for a critical approach to community development. "And where they relate most clearly is in Freire's consideration of the political nature of education and in Gramsci's consideration of the educational nature of politics" (Allman, 1988, p 92). Our responsibility is to wrestle with these ideas with the privilege of our new understandings.

We must hold this vision in a past–present–future dynamic, "moving between present and past with a view to contributing towards a transformed future" (P. Mayo, 1999, p 147). Throughout their radical past, Freire and Gramsci have inspired community work and popular education. Peter Mayo explores the complementarity of Gramsci and Freire coherently and confidently from Malta (1999), making a massive contribution to the Gramsci–Freire project. This, linked to the work of the British and the North American critical pedagogues provides a critical body of thought that offers a new possibility for radical community development theory.

Social justice, environmental justice and sustainability

> Unless development leads to greater equality, environmentally sound outcomes, and improved opportunities for human growth it cannot meet the goals of sustainable development. (Gamble and Weil, 1997, p 220)

From an environmental justice perspective, Freire and the Freirean movement stand accused of neglecting both globalisation and the environmental crisis (Bowers and Apffel-Marglin, 2004). The argument is that Freire's emphasis on critical consciousness in relation to class liberation, most particularly through literacy, is founded on Western assumptions that subordinate indigenous belief systems. In these ways, Freire is accused of failing to understand the cultural implications of the ecological crisis the world faces. In fact, some level the challenge that Freire's cultural assumptions reflect the cultural dominance that gave moral legitimacy to capitalism and continues to give economic superiority in the process of globalisation. Ecological thought emphasises that diverse indigenous cultures have evolved in harmony with their natural environments. Cultural diversity thus becomes essential for biological diversity, and histories based on local economic development offer alternatives for the future that reflect values other than consumer lifestyles: a harmonious co-existence between social justice and environmental justice.

Gamble and Weil spell out how vital it is that we understand the unity of social justice and environmental justice as: "the concept of sustainable development now functions as a unifying concept in several ways. It connects local and global perspectives; it provides a focus on protection of both the physical environment and human populations; it imposes a long-term view of the consequences of present-day activities; it can serve the goals of gender equity; and it provides a way effectively to integrate social and economic development" (Gamble and Weil, 1997, p 211).

They cite Estes' seven fundamental concepts as a frame for analysis and action:

i)   the unity of humanity and life on earth;
ii)   the minimisation of violence;
iii) the maintenance of environmental quality;
iv)   the satisfaction of minimum world welfare standards;
v)   the primacy of human dignity;
vi)   the retention of diversity and pluralism;
vii) universal participation.

Ecofeminism's embrace of the environment and sustainability arises from a critical connection between the 'death of nature' and the rise of patriarchy, and can be explored through the work of such people as Charlene Spretnak, Carolyn Merchant and Vandana Shiva. The central argument from ecofeminism is that "a historical, symbolic and political relationship exists between the denigration of nature and the female in Western cultures" (Spretnak, 1993, p 181). Ecofeminism is rooted in principles of "harmony, co-operation and interconnection" that challenge the perceived male principles of competition, "discrimination, extremism and conflict" (Young, 1990, p 33). This competitive worldview elevates men over both women and the natural world in a system of ranked order importance, deifying a male God, and downplaying the femininity of God, illustrating how organised religion plays a key hegemonic role in legitimising the common sense of subordination (McIntosh, 2001). Women continue to be active in organising and theorising an alternative worldview based on harmony and cooperation, non-violence and dignity, a view that embraces both public and private, local and global, humanity and the natural world in equal measure. It reflects women's concerns for preserving life on earth over time and space. Our dominant hegemony, a positivist worldview, equips us with a divided way of seeing the world that results in physical and spiritual alienation. It is founded on a complex system of domination and subordination that is resistant to reform. This calls for a new way of seeing the world:

> We need, I believe, a way of knowing which helps us to heal this split, this separation, this alienation. We need a way of knowing which integrates truth with love, beauty and wholeness, a way of knowing which acknowledges

the essential physical qualities of knowing. We need a new story about our place in the scheme of things. (Reason, 1994, p 14)

In relation to the interface of social justice and environmental justice, Cresy Cannan stresses that not only is the environmental crisis a crisis for us all, but it disproportionately affects both the poor and the South and so "intensifies forms of inequality and threatens collective goods – thus it is a human crisis as well as a threat to the entire planet" (2000, p 365). Her argument is linked to the impact of globalisation and she cites Rees' evidence on a fivefold increase in economic growth since the Second World War at the same time as poverty gaps between nations and within nations have doubled. This argument is central to sustainability. We cannot operate on a naïve interpretation of social justice that aims to lift the standards of living of the poorest in line with the artificially created greed of the rich. Current standards of consumption are not only creating global ecological degradation but massive inequalities. The problem lies in the individualist/consumerist ideology created by Western capitalism. A simplistic notion of raising the levels of consumption of the poor to those of the rich escalates the sustainability crisis, questions practice for social justice and forces us to analyse the ways in which quality of life is not simplistically linked to rising income levels, but is much more complex. Our challenge is to change the unsustainable living habits of the West while reducing the disparity between rich and poor, both in and between countries. Sustainability and social justice involve the wealthy examining the destructive nature of consumer lifestyles, in much the same way as anti-discriminatory practice involves Whites understanding the nature of White power and privilege.

An alternative ideology, based on the principle of common good rather than individual greed, raises questions about a drive for profit that holds no accountability for human or environmental well-being. The problems that we face today around health, poverty, inequality, education and the environment have become perceived as inevitable rather than as a consequence of capitalism. Community development practice needs to develop strategies that challenge this consciousness and balance the needs of business against the needs of local communities.

One example of the ways in which this understanding can be incorporated into our practice is by developing a system of community accounting that checks a wide range of environmental and social justice issues. "The enterprise paradigm has established an accounting system that measures revenue, costs and incomes for enterprise owners. A new community paradigm must do the same for communities ... if there is to be a shift in viewpoint, a system will have to be set up that looks at matters that usually escape individual enterprise accounts. This assumes a moral and not a mechanical universe" (Roxas in Douthwaite, 1996, p 336). The thinking implicit in this idea is that of a new worldview, one in which the economy is not elevated over other aspects of life, but where the emphasis is on harmony, sustainability and justice. Such a profit and loss balance for a community would include employment, goods and services versus unemployment, ill-health, inequality, crime, noise, pollution and use of natural resources, as a holistic overview. Any model of development that fails to see community needs as a balanced system will fail to understand the way that every aspect is in symbiotic relationship to the whole, much the same as Schuler's thinking in Chapter Four.

The Sustainable Seattle project, set up in 1980, developed indicators based on a range of measures that affect the quality and sustainability of human life. These ideas have been taken on board by the UK, driven largely by the developments inspired by the UN Earth Summit in Rio in 1992, and which reach from central to local government level in the form of Local Agenda 21. This is another reflection of New Labour's partnership approach based on local participation. (The government guidelines for developing indicators can be found at www.sustainable-development.gov.uk/indicators.) However, Douthwaite argues, "the market economy relies on competition to control the way businesses behave. As this will not work in a community economy, new approaches and attitudes need to be found" (Douthwaite, 1996, p 332).

Competition driven by profit is increasing as a result of globalisation, therefore the power of communities to argue for the common good will diminish, despite the fact that business continues to be "subsidized on a massive scale by taxpayers, society and the environment" and thus has a massive social and environmental obligation (Douthwaite, 1996, p 341). This is where we start to see the essence of Allman's (1999, 2001) and McLaren's (2000) arguments that reformism will not work within a system that flourishes on exploitation. An example of the challenge of a new worldview is illustrated by the case study of Dorrit Seemann. She struggled for five years to make her shop viable based on competitive economic principles. Eventually she developed the idea of inviting her customers to take out a monthly subscription to give her an income and cover her overheads, which in turn meant she was able to offer them goods at cost price. "Enough people took up the idea to make it work; this radically altered her relationship with those she supplied because instead of setting her prices at the highest level she felt her customers would tolerate, the challenge was now to buy as well as she could on her subscribers' behalf and to make the shop and its services as attractive and convenient for them as possible" (Douthwaite, 1996, p 343). Douthwaite is optimistic that if we can get enough communities to develop independent, parallel economies and to become mutually supportive in the process, the swing from global to local will increase our chances of a sustainable future.

Community development has taken more interest in the environment over recent years, particularly with the development of Local Agenda 21 programmes. The challenge for community development praxis is that our analysis of social justice should not compromise the life chances of future generations or the lives of those in the Third World. Social justice and environmental justice come together in community development in places where we offer alternatives to the values of capitalism. Fair Trade, LETS (Local Exchange [or Economic] Trading Systems) and credit unions are examples of how an alternative local economy can place cooperation rather than competition at the heart of new approaches to community, changing fundamental core values (for information contact the New Economics Foundation). The community gardens movement is an example of how economic factors can be linked to other aspects of well-being. I was involved in research in a traditional mining community in North-West England, and witnessed the impact of their community garden. A patch of derelict land marked the site where several houses had disappeared into a mine shaft when the ground subsided, and which had become a place for dumping, drug dealing and other depressing activities. It has been transformed into an oasis in the midst of all the tightly packed terraced houses, with its central social space surrounded by a range of different planted areas, including a market garden. It has provided a sanctuary for reflection; it nurtures people when they feel they cannot face the hardship of their lives. It has provided a place where people come together for barbecues, carol services and other community events. People gather there and get to know each other, and it cheers people up. Vegetables are harvested and sold locally. In these ways, we see how a simple idea contributes to the health, liveability and the economy of the community.

If we insist on placing poverty at the top of our agenda, we may fall into the trap of overlooking wider quality of life issues, and it is quality of life on earth that is the common ground between environmental justice and social justice. Research by Burningham and Thrush (2001) investigated the perceptions of environmentalism and the environmental concerns of marginalised groups in the UK. Importantly for community development, their findings emphasise that "many small problems are symptoms of deeper and more complex social and economic issues. Sustainable solutions to local environmental problems require these wider issues to be addressed" (Burningham and Thrush, 2001, p 44). In these ways, we tease out the links between environmental and social justice, and local to global action.

Critiques of Freire and Gramsci from coherently argued perspectives provide us with the basis for extending community development theory into more adequate analyses of *difference* in relation to social justice and *sustainability* in relation to environmental justice. Within this, it is important to take into account critiques of capitalism as a system capable of reform (Allman, 1999, 2001; McLaren, 2000), and the call for a new worldview, one that is based on an ideology of cooperation rather than competition (I.M. Young, 1990; Spretnak, 1993; Reason and Bradbury, 2001; Reason, 2002). *Praxis* is the bedrock of this process: theory in action, building a body of knowledge based on experience. The collective struggle for social justice and environmental justice is the basis for alliances between community workers and environmental activists in global times. In fact, many community workers are seeing this as a natural extension of their traditional work. However, Hillman (2002) raises concerns that the naïve belief that sustainability can be achieved within the current economic system deradicalises the environmental movement. The local/global dynamic is vital here: local people experience the impact of environmental degradation most immediately, and action is more relevant when it begins in people's communities as part of the process of critical consciousness and grassroots action (Burningham and Thrush, 2001). From local participation, this reaches out beyond community to engage with collective action that takes on global issues of justice and sustainability.

The environmental justice movement was formed over the last 20 years as a response to the disproportionate environmental problems experienced by already disadvantaged communities and poorer nations. This has created a tension between what are perceived as top-down issues (for example climate change, endangered animal and plant species, pollution and degradation of land and water resources) and grassroots action; a tension between strategy and participation. Cannan (2000) suggests that by identifying links between environmental justice and social justice, we can move into new areas of action and development. She includes vertical and horizontal links between grassroots participation and social movements that overcome divisive strategies of state control by concentrating on alliances as the basis of organising collective action for a sustainable and just society.

Any effective action calls for an altered consciousness. Fisher and Ponniah (2003) emphasise the need for challenging the supremacy of the market economy in Western consciousness:

> Sustainability requires putting the environment and society above the market. To make progress towards sustainable societies requires policies based on the inclusion of all races and cultures, equity and solidarity among societies, and cooperation among governments. The first step in meeting this challenge is repairing the environment and society. (Fisher and Ponniah, 2003, pp 127-8)

And one way of moving into such an alternative worldview is to develop a Freirean-feminist pedagogy fundamentally rooted in an ideology of cooperation, where a desire for peace and non-violence forms the basis of the will to see new possibilities. This is the subject of the next chapter.

EIGHT

Towards a Freirean-feminist pedagogy

Feminism's emphasis on *difference* has given profound insight into the complexity of lived experience, which places us all within a matrix of oppressions, variously positioned as both victims and perpetrators. Similarly, feminism's emphasis on non-hierarchical structures of peace and non-violence has developed altered views on both human rights and environmental justice. The challenge is now to develop an integrated praxis that informs a pedagogy for our times.

bell hooks challenges feminists who separate feminist pedagogy from Freirean pedagogy:

> Unlike feminist thinkers who make a clear separation between the work of feminist pedagogy and Freire's work and thought, for me these two experiences converge. Deeply committed to feminist pedagogy, I find that, much like weaving a tapestry, I have taken threads of Paulo's work and woven it into that version of feminist pedagogy I believe my work as writer and teacher embodies. (hooks, 1993, p 150)

Male-centred models of reality, however much they offer conceptual tools that radicalise feminist consciousness, continue to validate a male way of knowing the world. Feminist approaches attempt to place women's ways of knowing at the centre of knowledge generation, not to exclude men, but because "by looking at human experience from the point of view of women, we can understand male experience and the whole of cultural history with greater depth" (Callaway, 1981, p 460). This constitutes a critical repositioning that embraces a multiplicity of ways of knowing the world, challenging gender and cultural dominance. Within this frame, "the act of looking back, of seeing with fresh eyes, of entering an old text from a new critical direction" (Adrienne Rich cited in Callaway, 1981, p 457) allows us to 're-vision' Freire and Gramsci, using the analytic tools they offered us to expand our feminist consciousness in the first place. Looking back with our new awarenesses offers new ways of exposing the contradictions embedded in the taken-for-grantedness of daily life, and, in turn, "the imaginative power of sighting possibilities and thus helping to bring about what is not (or not *yet*) visible, a new ordering of human relations" (Callaway, 1981, p 457).

This chapter will re-vision Freire from a feminist perspective in order to move towards a critical pedagogy of difference for community development practice in our current political times.

Freirean pedagogy and feminist pedagogy

> If all people's identities are recognised in their full historical and social complexity as subject positions that are in process, based on knowledges that are partial and that reflect deep and conflicting differences, how can we theorise what a liberatory pedagogy actively struggling against different forms of oppression might look like? How can we build upon the rich and complex analysis of feminist theory and pedagogy to work toward a Freirean vision of social justice and liberation? (Weiler, 1995, p 35)

Weiler (1994, p 18) asks a central question for activists seeking an integrated praxis: "Where are we to look for liberation when our collective reading of the world reveals contradictory and conflicting experiences and struggles?" Transformative change is rooted in collective action, yet the consumerist individualism that characterises neoliberalism has shifted us away from a sense of the collective. Freire vehemently reminds us that liberation is a collective experience:

> I don't believe in self-liberation.... Liberating education is a social process of illumination.... Even when you individually feel yourself *most* free, if this feeling is not a *social* feeling, if you are not able to use your *recent* freedom to help others to be free by transforming the totality of society, then you are exercising only an individualist attitude towards empowerment or freedom. (Freire, in Shor and Freire, 1987, p 109)

Pedagogy of the oppressed continues to offer critical pedagogues around the world hope, passion and theoretical justification for their work. How, then, is it possible to address the problems it presents to feminist pedagogy? The major problem lies not so much in its sexist language, which was addressed in Freire's later work, but in its failure to fully engage with difference, overlooking the "possibility of simultaneous contradictory positions of oppression and dominance" (Weiler, 1995, p 27). However, Freire was emphatic that his work should always be open to critique and re-vision based on his experience, the experience of others, and changing contexts:

> Many things that today still appear to me as valid (not only in actual or future practice but also in any theoretical interpretation that I might derive from it) could be outgrown tomorrow, not just by me, but by others as well. The crux here, I believe, is that I must be constantly open to criticism and sustain my curiosity, always ready for revision based on the results of my future experience and that of others. And in turn, those who put my experience into practice must strive to recreate it and also rethink my thinking. In doing so, they should bear in mind that no educational practice takes place in a vacuum, only in a real context – historical, economic, political, and not necessarily identical to any other context. (Freire, 1985, p 11)

Let us engage with that challenge!

My proposal is that Freirean pedagogy and feminist pedagogy are powerful and complementary in their potential for critical practice in global times. In support of this claim, I will explore the development of feminist pedagogy and consider the similarity of process and goals. The political activism of the women's movement of the 1960s and 1970s developed out of a challenge to a dominant way of seeing the world based on patriarchy and pragmatism, which denies the validity of *experience* and *feeling*. Women rose to claim the *personal as political*. There was a groundswell of grassroots activism in which women came together in leaderless groups to explore consciousness from our own experience, making feminist theory in action. We translated this into collective action for change based on a vision of peace and justice. An outstanding example of the collective potential of this movement is the way in which, in August 1981, a group of women who had never been involved in political action before marched from Cardiff to Greenham Common to protest against the siting of cruise missiles in Britain. This marked the beginning of the Greenham Women's Peace Movement, which "highlighted the development of a new strand of community action" (Dominelli, 1990, p 119). A praxis began to evolve with emphasis on lived experience as the basis of theoretical understanding.

Many poststructuralists and postmodern feminists criticise *patriarchal* analyses of gender as *essentialist* – the assumption that there is an *essential* difference between men and women that is fixed and natural and that clearly defines a commonality and unity of experience. That is, by constructing *woman* as 'Other' than *man*, there is a risk of seeing this as the only way of defining women's experience of oppression. Gore (1993) warns that essentialism can be both silencing and empowering; that discourse based on the authority of a dominant experience can silence a different sort of experience. On the other hand, Sylvia Walby (1992, 1994) argues that some postmodernists not only reject the concept of patriarchy but also that of 'woman', to the extent that they could be considered anti-feminist. She suggests that one of the limitations of poststructuralism and postmodernism is "a neglect of the social context of power relations" (1992, p 16). Her argument is that postmodernism has fragmented the concepts of 'race', class and gender by focusing on complexity, and that while the social relations have changed, postmodernists have gone too far by denying racism and patriarchy as "virulent social divisions". Whereas Marxism subsumed all forms of discrimination under class, postmodernists have swung with the pendulum to disintegrate the concepts altogether. She illustrates the dangers of this in relation to Black women who raise three important aspects of analysis for them: i) racist structures within the labour market; ii) ethnic experience and racism; and iii) locating the intersection of ethnicity and gender, both culturally and historically. Disintegration overlooks these patterns of 'race', class and gender oppressions and their local/global dimensions. For instance, the feminisation of labour in the UK is not only the result of industrial restructuring here, but the British economy also depends on the exploitation of Third World women, thus "there is a strong case for the interconnectedness of the exploitation of First and Third World women by patriarchal capitalism" (Walby, 1994, p 232). Walby cites Swasti Mitter's call for a "common bond on women in the newly globalised economy" (1994, p 234) within a recognition of difference.

A single essential identity, 'woman', never existed; it was a socially constructed illusion. Our particular social and historical identity is constantly moulded by the changing state of other socially defined identities. These unfolding insights enable us to work with *conscientisation* from a wider perspective. Expanded awareness of our individual histories and of ourselves in process equips us with an ever-unfolding theoretical understanding that, in its validation of difference and analysis of power, moves the dynamic of praxis further towards achieving a shared vision of freedom.

In these ways, Freire and feminism enrich each other in the struggle for transformative social change. Together, they provide a pedagogy with which to denounce social injustices in all their complexity, "for to be utopian is not to be merely idealistic or impractical but rather to engage in denunciation and annunciation" and dialogical praxis is the "act of analyzing a dehumanizing reality, denounce it while announcing its transformation" (Freire, 1985, p 57).

The most compelling analysis of Freire from a feminist perspective continues, for me, to come from Kathleen Weiler. She profoundly influenced my thinking with her challenge to engage with "Freire and a feminist pedagogy of difference" (Weiler, 1995, p 23). Her point is that collective action will not emerge naturally from contradictory histories and experiences. We need to engage with the contradictions of privilege, oppression and power by acknowledging our own histories and selves in process from an "acute consciousness of difference" in order to move more critically towards our "goals of social justice and empowerment" (Weiler, 1995, p 35). She calls for a feminist pedagogy that enriches and re-visions Freirean goals, but is framed more specifically in the context of feminist struggle. In this sense, the concept of *denunciation* suggests that we need to develop better strategies to help us name and analyse our new understanding of a multiplicity of oppressions; and *annunciation* suggests the need for new forms of action across difference that unite us in mutual struggle. In other words, we have to develop analyses that deal with the complexity of simultaneous and contradictory forces of oppression, at the same time as we develop appropriate collective action that does not subsume difference.

Weiler offers three key areas of analysis with which to extend Freirean pedagogy into feminist pedagogy: the role and authority of the teacher; experience and feelings as sources of knowledge; and the question of difference.

The role and authority of the teacher

While Freire emphasises the horizontal, reciprocal role of the educator as a co-teacher/co-learner, he fails to address issues of power according to ethnicity, gender and status. Weiler suggests that *authority* can be problematic. The vision of a mutual, reciprocal, non-hierarchical way of working can be driven by hope rather than reality if issues of power, hierarchy and culture are overlooked. Women in community are not a homogeneous group, they are diverse. They are also situated within a competitive and individualistic culture. As feminist community workers, we are vested with the role, authority and status that render us different.

If we are working towards consciousness and collective action for change with groups within which issues of power and hierarchy are ignored, we are not likely to be successful. However, it is possible for the feminist educator, through the process of *conscientisation*, to name difference and reach a shared critical understanding of the forces that have shaped that difference and, in doing so, move towards greater unity for change.

Experience and feeling as sources of knowledge

We need to identify a feminist knowledge of the world as the basis for social change. Freirean pedagogy stresses the questioning of their experience by the oppressed in order that they come to an understanding of their own power if they are to transform their world: in knowing it they can recreate it. In this way, feminist knowledge of the world is the foundation for action. Belenky et al (1997) have made an immense contribution through their research into *Women's ways of knowing*. They emphasise the quest for self and voice, which plays a key role in the process of transformation for women. The self, in an inner and outer process, is transformed: "weaving together the strands of rational and emotive thought and of integrating objective and subjective knowing ... these women used themselves in rising to a new way of thinking" (Belenky et al, 1997, pp 134-5). Traditionally, *feeling* has been seen as the domain of women, as of the private domain and not a reliable basis for rational action. Women are denied the value of their being in the world by a positivist, patriarchal system that places emphasis on science, on rationality, on pragmatism rather than emotion, experience or feeling. In feminist analysis, universal truths about human behaviour are challenged and increasingly *feeling* has contributed to feminist pedagogy as a balance between the inner self and the outer world, between the public and private, the personal and political. Audre Lorde captures the essence of feelings as a guide to analysis and action, keeping us in touch with our humanity:

> As we begin to recognise our deepest feelings, we begin to give up, of necessity, being satisfied with suffering and self-negation, and with the numbness which so often seems like their only alternative in society. Our acts against oppression become integral with self, motivated and empowered from within. (Lorde, 1984, p 58)

There are strong links here with Freirean emphasis on humanisation as a way of being in the world. In identifying the ways in which our experience of power relationships is structured, the act of knowing, of critical insight, generates energy and motivation for action. Out of a state of dehumanisation, we are freed to humanise ourselves, creating alternative worldviews based on justice.

The question of difference

The assumption made by White feminists of a universal sisterhood rendered Black women invisible. The racism inherent in White feminism not only failed to recognise the anti–racist struggle as central to feminism, but also overlooked the way Black people were pathologised in relation to sexuality and family relations. Black feminists and postmodern feminists challenged the unitary and universal category *woman* as fundamentally racist on one hand and socially constructed and shaped on the other. Feminist pedagogy has focused on narratives of lived experience as a participatory strategy with groups of women to identify the social and historical forces that have shaped these narratives. For instance, Weiler (1994, p 31) cites Sistren, a "collaborative theatre group made up of working-class Jamaican women who create and write plays based upon a collaborative exploration of their own experiences". The collective sharing of experience is the key to the knowledge of our socially and politically given identities. It is the process by which we discover our power as subjects in active, creative process in our world, rather than as objects that are fixed, defined and static. The Combahee River Collective argue that "the most radical politics come directly out of our own identity, as opposed to working to end someone else's oppression" (Weiler, 1994, p 32).

In 2001, Weiler offered a further critical rereading of Freire, emphasising that we need to pay attention to: i) the nature of women as learners, ii) the gendered nature of accepted knowledge, iii) the role and authority of the teacher, and iv) the epistemological source of knowledge and truth claims of men and women. This takes us nearer to the cutting edge of feminism in a postmodern world. She flags up the dangers of discourse that rests on social and cultural definitions of men's and women's natures as some *given truth*. Difference between men and women is useful in thinking about feminist knowing, but must not be seen as innate. Failing to acknowledge the social and historical construction of the idea of women's natures would be to subscribe to Western patriarchy's *male rationality* versus *female nurturance* dichotomy. Weiler advocates the need to write from a discourse of *feminist rationality*. By this, she means that women have the capacity to think in rational and abstract ways: women's knowledge is not solely defined by emotion.

Gloria Anzaldua's conception of the *new mestiza* as a postcolonial feminist emphasises that set patterns of women's behaviour are invasions of the self, and that any critique of patriarchy must include Western conceptions of: i) linear rationality, ii) White privilege, and iii) assumptions of universal truths. Anti-racist feminist educators have "stressed that critical and feminist pedagogies, whilst claiming an opposition to oppression, are in danger of taking a kind of imperial and totalizing stance of knowing and 'speaking for' those who are to be educated into truth" (Weiler, 2001, p 72). Weiler raises *social identity* and *authority* in speaking for silenced others. Are we acting out privilege by taking on an unquestioned authority in speaking? Adopting a position of humility, she asks, "Given the complexities of feminist educational thinking, how then do I, a white woman from the US, approach the work of a Brazilian man who spoke for the subjugated and oppressed?" (Weiller, 2001, p 73).

Sylvia Walby: patriarchal sites of oppression

At this point, I want to return to the ideas of Sylvia Walby (1992, 1994) and examine their specific use in relation to a Freirean-feminist pedagogy.

Clearly Walby feels that postmodernism has gone too far in fragmenting concepts of class, 'race' and gender, denying the overarching theories of capitalism, racism and sexism as significant power structures in society. Her emphasis is on the centrality of patriarchy as a prime oppressive force. She agrees that postmodernists are right to identify the weaknesses of metanarratives. This has helped us gain insights into the way that unitary concepts can hide more than they reveal. For instance, in the UK the home is often the prime site of Asian women's oppression but often a site of resistance against racism for African-Caribbean women, with White women coming somewhere in between. Clearly, within categories of Black and White we need subdivisions of analysis. Walby's argument is that patriarchy, as a blanket theory, denies the complex ways in which women's experience varies across difference. Her solution is to identify six structures of analysis within which to analyse patriarchy: i) paid work, ii) housework, iii) sexuality, iv) culture, v) violence, and vi) the state. She suggests that the interrelationships between these elements create different forms of patriarchy. This lends itself to a model based on her six categories

Table 8.1: Patriarchal sites of oppression

Causal elements

Paid work
- Employment: unemployment
- Structural changes
- Conditions of employment
- Patterns of employment
- Training opportunities
- Affordable childcare
- Power, authority and status

Unpaid work
- The family
- Reproduction
- Care of the family/home
- Power, authority and status
- Voluntary work
- Social networks of care

Culture
- History and tradition
- Gender
- Class
- 'Race'
- Ethnicity
- Age
- 'Dis'ability
- Religion

Sexuality
- Femininity
- Masculinity
- Heterosexuality
- Homosexuality

Violence
- Domestic violence
- Child abuse
- Workplace harassment
- Street violence
- Suicide
- Abuse of the natural world/environment

The state
- Welfare
- Education
- Employment
- Housing: homelessness
- The family
- The law: policing
- Health
- Poverty
- Human rights
- The natural world/environment

that would help to expand our analysis of patriarchy for community development practice. The basis of it might look something like the model shown in Table 8.1.

Walby contests that the shift from a Marxist class analysis to postmodernism has failed to reveal any pattern other than disintegration. If we fail to theorise new patterns of gender, ethnicity and class oppressions, our practice will be uncritical. For example, while the feminisation of poverty continues to be a concern within the UK, on a global level consumer-driven profit under capitalism is dependent on the exploitation of women and children in the Third World who are becoming the new industrial producers and suppliers of some of the cheapest goods for Western markets. Walby concludes that the concept of 'patriarchy' is a vital component of gender inequality, and we ignore it at our peril. Postmodernist arguments that it is founded on naïve essentialism, that it defines women's experience as universal and unified in relation to men, are "insensitive to the range of experiences of women of different cultures, classes and ethnicities"

(Walby, 1992, p 2). Patriarchy as a concept and theory is essential to "capture the depth, pervasiveness and interconnectedness of different aspects of women's subordination" and can be developed in this way to take account of the different forms of gender inequality over time, class and ethnic group" (Walby, 1992, p 2).

These are some of the ideas that have influenced feminist pedagogy. I will now move into an argument in support of a Freirean-feminist pedagogy that engages with the multiplicity of oppressions that diminish life on earth.

Towards a Freirean–feminist pedagogy: loci of oppressions

Radical community development, and by this I mean a critical approach to practice that locates it at the heart of a movement for social and environmental justice, calls for a pedagogy of difference for our times. I see Freirean pedagogy and feminist pedagogy as a powerful combination in the development of a pedagogy of difference, and so will refer to this as a Freirean-feminist pedagogy. Such a pedagogy needs to be informed by analyses of class, patriarchy and racism as overarching structures of oppression that intertwine with each other to exploit and oppress in the most insidious of ways. These forces are woven into the fabric of life through different contexts at different levels, cleaving power that exploits and oppresses in a complex system of domination and subordination. This is absorbed in the public psyche as *common sense*, and thus legitimate. A Freirean-feminist pedagogy is also profoundly concerned with other aspects of difference and diversity, seeking a worldview that is equal, harmonious and respectful of all life on earth. Exploring the ideas of Allman, McLaren and Hill from a class perspective and Spretnak and Shiva from an ecofeminist perspective, this worldview is not possible within a system of capitalism that is built on domination and exploitation for profit. In other words, capitalism is inherently incapable of reform because its success depends on exploitation and profit, and, within this, class, 'race' and gender are prime forces of exploitation that serve its interests. Douthwaite (1996), commenting on the supremacy of the market, reminds us that the elevation of the economy over the common good justifies a drive for profit that holds no accountability for human or environmental well-being, giving rise to the illusion that the problems we face in relation to justice and sustainability are inevitable rather than a consequence of capitalism.

A Freirean-feminist pedagogy for radical community development practice thus needs a critical approach that is informed by analyses of power taking our thinking and practice from a local to a wider collective potential for change.

A three-dimensional model might be useful here; one that moves through i) **difference** ('race', class, gender and so on) on one axis, through ii) **context** (family, workplace, schools and so on) on another, and between iii) **levels** (local, national, global and so on) on a third to form a complex set of interrelationships that interweave between axes, but also intertwine on any one axis. Figure 8.1, using just a few possible examples, demonstrates how to begin to use this flexible approach to identify the complex intersections of power and discrimination.

The elements are not fixed, they are interchangeable on each face: the model is designed to probe critical thinking, stimulating questions rather than offering definitive answers. Students have said it helps to imagine this as a Rubik's cube, each section capable of changing and being re-examined in relation to the whole. It is only by struggling to locate these complex intersections that we begin to understand the root causes of oppression, and in doing so locate potential sites of

Figure 8.1: Loci of oppressions matrix

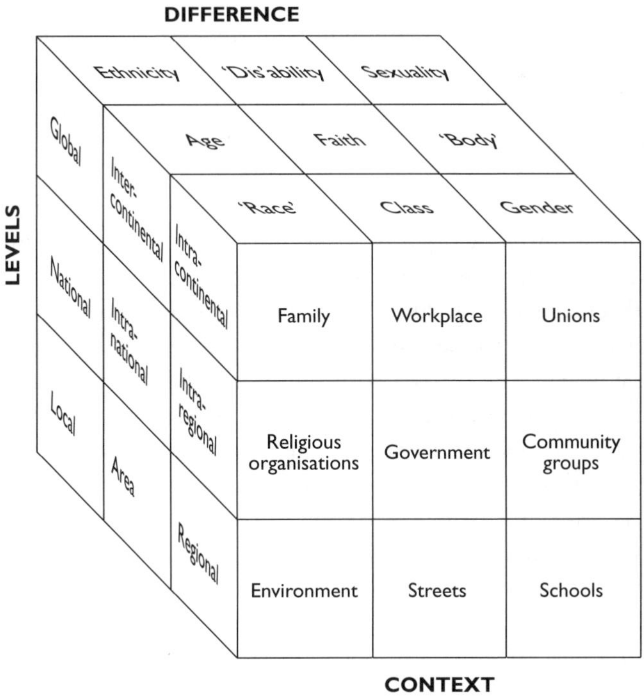

resistance. So, for example, the model not only helps us to explore the interrelatedness of 'race' and gender on one face, but to locate this within an environmental context, and on a community level. Then, if the level is shifted from local to, say, global, different but related issues emerge. The purpose of the model is to stretch our thinking in a multidimensional way by locating the interface of different dimensions of oppressions, and, in doing so, pose questions that deepen our analysis and make our practice more critical.

The critical potential of this model is that it teaches us to question in the most complex of ways. Beginning in an aspect of everyday reality, using problem-posing as part of this multidimensional model, could open us to new understandings and new forms of action. The dialogue is kept critical by using Hope and Timmel's (1994, Book 1, p 58) six stages of questioning:

i)   description (what?)
ii) first analysis (why?)
iii) real life (where?)
iv) related problems (what else?)
v)   root causes
vi) action planning.

Working with people in a community group, we could *problematise* a local issue by using a photograph as a *codification*, capturing the essence of this issue from the reality of their lives. The 'description' stage is merely asking what the photograph depicts. What is in the photo? What do you see? What do you think they are doing? What are they feeling? This moves into 'first analysis', which questions why this thing is happening, thus moving from observing the photograph to thinking about it. As confidence grows, and the group gets more involved, ask "Does this happen in 'real life'?" If you have chosen a generative theme, one that is relevant to the everyday lives of the people, and captured it well, it will generate a passionate response: "It happens to me!" "It happens every day in our community!" "This is the way it is here!" In this way, the outward focus on the codification, in this case a photograph, shifts inward to the group and critical dialogue is generated by the relevance the issue has to the reality of its members. Curiosity and mutual inquiry will often stimulate the group to identify 'related problems'. In this way the group moves beyond the concrete situation, making connections across difference, time and space. Your role is to probe in a *problematising* way. If you challenge the group to take its analysis to a deeper level, the inquiry will go beyond the symptoms to the root causes of the problem, which truly pushes towards *critical consciousness*. New ways of knowing are explored. Social relations are transformed as people experience each other differently. There is a move towards critical thought for transformative action.

Try experimenting with some of your own experiences to see if this model extends your analysis. Consider how, on one axis, difference is compounded by, say, 'race', gender and faith to give us profoundly different experiences of being a 'woman' according to a Pakistani-British Muslim identity contrasted with that of a White-Irish Catholic identity. If we then consider how this is further compounded by context, say, the public world of work as opposed to the private world of family, further patterns of difference emerge. Finally, if we follow this through to make global links with local experiences, we can begin to see realities that are constructed by the interaction of these forces. By struggling to analyse these complex intersections, we get nearer to understanding the root causes of oppression, and in doing so locate potential sites of resistance. Because the elements are not fixed, the model becomes adaptable to multiple possibilities.

If you begin to see more complex connections through the matrix, consider using it as a structure for teaching to question with your community groups. Reflect on the nature of your own power, status and authority as an educator in relation to the difference represented in your group. This may operate in half-hidden, subtle ways. How do you see the interaction of power and difference within the group? What evidence is there of different ways of knowing within the group, for example emotionality and rationality? Is your way of knowing different from that of the group? How do you see your own status, power and difference in relation to the group? You have to be deeply reflexive, learning as much from the people as you have to teach them, a co-teacher/co-learner in process. Explore the gendered, racialised nature of accepted knowledge, and discover ways in which dominant views of the world and the nature of truth may not be the same for men and women, or for different cultures. This takes us nearer to the cutting edge of a pedagogy of difference.

The matrix offers a focus for investigation of the many possible interlinked sites of oppression and deepens an awareness of the ways in which these are structurally reinforced at different levels. As the group grows in confidence and awareness, they own the process in a mutual and reciprocal way. *Critical consciousness* is an outward-flowing energy. Personal empowerment involves a sense of self in the world that gives rise to personal autonomy. This process becomes collective when critical consciousness leads to critical autonomy. Links are made with other groups in the community and alliances are formed with groups outside the community, generating a collective energy for change that has the potential to connect through levels from local to global. A coherent and strategic Freirean-feminist pedagogy offers community development a radical possibility.

> In terms of crossing paths, Freirean and feminist approaches are immediately convergent in that both privilege subjectivity and personal experience as sources of curricular themes – 'the personal is political' as a feminist orientation and the 'generative theme' method of Freire, which seeks issues for problem posing from the students' everyday lives. (Shor, 2000, p 3)

Freirean pedagogy and feminist pedagogy have shared principles. They are both rooted in a vision of transformative social change and take as their starting point lived experience. They both operate from a non-hierarchical, reciprocal model. They are both committed to social justice through critical consciousness and collective action. A re-visioning of these two powerful perspectives offers the potential to contribute to critical analysis and action for change for a peaceful, just and sustainable future.

NINE

The way forward

My message is simple.

Community development has been involved in decades of action against injustice, challenging patriarchal, racist and heterosexist traditions that erode human rights and undermine democracy. This has involved campaigns against violence towards women and children, against poverty, against the corporate degradation of the environment, against homophobia, racism and sexism, against deportation of asylum seekers, and much more. At the same time practice has focused on the development of cooperative local economies, healthy convivial communities, educational equity and employment opportunities.

This has not been enough. We have allowed theory and practice to become dislocated from each other, rendering us vulnerable to dilution and diversion. Simultaneously, social divisions have escalated within and between countries, creating unstable societies and an unstable world. Radical community development is committed to social and environmental justice. Its vision is that of a peaceful, just and sustainable world. Its practice is critical pedagogy, which is based on a "profound love for the world and for people" (Freire, 1996, p 70), and "because love is an act of courage, not of fear, love is commitment to others" (Freire, 1996, p 70). The process of liberation begins in dialogue, a critical encounter that enables people to speak their word and name their world. Freire was clear that "to speak a true word is to transform the world" (Freire, 1996, p 68).

Dialogue is a mutual process of action and reflection, which engages with deeply personal experiences and the profoundly political structures that have shaped them. It is the beginning of humanisation, becoming more fully human in the world. But a dialogue of equals cannot happen without humility and criticality on the part of the community worker. Belief in people and an analysis of power are the basis of a critical approach to community development. Founded on a well-defined value base that informs every aspect of the process, this ideological frame provides a system of checks and indicators that ring the bells of dissonance whenever the frame has slipped out of place!

Transformative change cannot be achieved without a constant preoccupation with action *and* reflection; theory in action. "Only dialogue, which requires critical thinking, is also capable of generating critical thinking. Without dialogue there is no communication, and without communication there can be no true education" (Freire, 1996, pp 73-4). But, "action is human only when it is not merely an occupation but also a preoccupation, that is, when it is not dichotomized from reflection" (Freire, 1972, p 29). Here I stress that the dichotomy between theory and practice, action and reflection, which continues to exist in community development, reduces its potential, at best, to a self-help, local activity.

Critical approaches to community development call for anti-discriminatory analyses that reach from the personal to the political, from the local to the global, as tools for emancipatory practice. Based on these analyses, strategic networks and alliances unite people across difference to provide the greatest possible collective strength for change. But understanding how diverse people identify common interests and struggle across their differences to unite against discrimination is crucial to the process, and does not happen spontaneously. Collective action for sustainable change involves harnessing collective power beyond neighbourhoods to national and global levels. It is essential that we see our practice move beyond local issues to engage with wider movements for change. Here I repeat the words of Sivanandan, which I introduced earlier, simply because they capture the essence of radical practice, expressing that global action begins in critical compassion, by being sensitive to:

> ... the oppression of others, the exploitation of others, the injustices and inequalities meted out to others – and to act on them, making an individual/local case into an issue, turning issues into causes and causes into movements and building in the process a new political culture, new communities of resistance that will take on power and capital and class. (Sivanandan, cited in Cooke, 1996, p 22)

The ideas are complex. But, when they are set within clear structures of analysis they assume a relevance that locates the complex thinking we need within grassroots practice.

Critical praxis would benefit from a re-visioning of Freire and Gramsci from a feminist perspective. Seeing these ideas with fresh eyes from female experience is not to ignore the interests of men but to offer a critical repositioning that embraces a multiplicity of ways of knowing the world, challenging all forms of domination. Dislocating White male supremacy aims for the heart of capitalism and the ruthlessness of a competitive, exploitative worldview that survives on domination and subordination. Feminism seeks to create the possibility of a worldview where cooperation and participation respect diversity. This offers not only new ways of seeing the world, but the key to what is "not yet visible, a new ordering of human relations" (Callaway, 1981, p 457). This is precisely why praxis is at the heart of a critical approach to community development, building new epistemologies, new ways of seeing the world, which in turn lead to new ontologies, new ways of being in the world:

> Liberation is a praxis; the action and reflection of men and women upon their world in order to transform it. (Freire, in A. Freire and D. Macedo, 1998, p 73)

This reaches to the heart of the challenge!

A pedagogy of difference re-visions Freire and Gramsci in our current context of difference and globalisation – two concepts that are vital to a critical approach to community development. From a Black feminist perspective, bell hooks illustrates the contradictory nature of ideas in process that lead to new possibilities:

> Freedom and the experience of patriarchal manhood are always linked as though they are one and the same. For me this is always a source of anguish for it represents a blind spot in the vision of men who have profound insight. And yet, I never wish to see a critique of this blind spot overshadow anyone's (and feminists' in particular) capacity to learn from the insights. This is why it is difficult for me to speak about sexism in Freire's work; it is difficult to find a language that offers a way to frame critique and yet maintain the recognition of all that is valued and respected in the work. It seems to me that the binary opposition that is so much embedded in Western thought and language makes it nearly impossible to project a complex response.... It is feminist thinking that empowers me to engage in a constructive critique of Freire's work (which I needed so that as a young reader of his work I did not passively absorb the worldview presented) and yet there are many other standpoints from which I approach his work that enable me to experience its value, that make it possible for that work to touch me at the very core of my being. (hooks, 1994, p 49)

Feminism has transformed the world with its emphasis on peace, harmony and non-violence, a vision of humanity in symbiotic respectful relation within itself and with the natural world. Set against the backdrop of globalisation, which seeks out the most vulnerable people and resources in the world to meet the demands of Western markets, world crises of justice and sustainability escalate as new and complex forms of discrimination emerge.

These are difficult times, but they are also times of hope and possibility. New understandings of difference, in this context of globalisation, call for a coherently articulated *critical pedagogy*, "that particular type of pedagogy which is concerned with issues concerning *social difference, social justice* and *social transformation*" (P. Mayo, 1999, p 58). The loci of oppressions matrix is a tool of analysis that locates intersections between interlinking oppressions, the contexts in which they touch people's lives, and the levels at which they get embedded structurally. These levels of analysis are needed for community development to restate its radical purpose, and for it to become central to an emerging world movement where alliances are forming at grassroots level and intellectual thought is calling for a new worldview:

> One can discern two trajectories in current history: one aiming toward hegemony, acting rationally within a lunatic doctrinal framework as it threatens survival; the other dedicated to the belief that 'another world is possible', ... challenging the reigning ideological system and seeking to create constructive alternatives of thought, action, and institutions. (Chomsky, 2003, p 236)

It is this latter perspective to which radical community development is dedicated, a worldview based on social and environmental justice through sustainability and participation. This is a time of hope for community development. We have no choice: "unhopeful educators contradict their practice. They are men and women without *address*, and without a destination. They are lost in history" (Freire, 1998a, p 107). Yet, hope can only transform reality when it is based on criticality, a constant questioning:

> We cannot continue to deny the gravity of the situation, yet to revise our view so that we experience ourselves fully as participants on this planet and with each other provides for new inspirations. In the end, we have no choice but to engage with these issues sooner or later. If we do so sooner we can do so with more dignity and more hope. (Reason, 2002, p 15)

Bibliography

Albrecht, L. and Brewer, R. (eds) (1990) *Bridges of power: Women's multicultural alliances*, Philadelphia: New Society.

Alinsky, S. (1969) *Reveille for radicals*, New York: Vintage Press.

Alinsky, S. (1972) *Rules for radicals*, New York: Vintage Press.

Allman, P. (1988) 'Gramsci, Freire and Illich: their contributions to education for socialism', in T. Lovett (ed) *Radical approaches to adult education*, London: Routledge.

Allman, P. (1999) *Revolutionary social transformation: Democratic hopes, political possibilities, and critical education*, Westport, CT: Bergin & Garvey.

Allman, P. (2001) *Critical education against global capitalism: Karl Marx and revolutionary critical education*, Westport, CT: Bergin & Garvey.

Allman, P. and Wallis, J. (1997) 'Commentary: Paulo Freire and the future of the radical tradition' in *Studies in the education of adults*, vol 29, pp 113-20.

Amos, V. and Parmar, P. (1984) 'Challenging imperial feminism', *Feminist Review*, vol 17, pp 3-19.

Anthias, F. and Yuval-Davis, N. with Cain, H. (1992) *Racialized boundaries: Race, nation, gender, colour and class and the anti-racist struggle*, London: Routledge.

Anzaldua, G. (1990) 'Bridge, drawbridge, sandbar or island: lesbians-of-color hacienda alianzas', in L. Albrecht and R. Brewer (eds) *Bridges of power: Women's multicultural alliances*, Philadelphia: New Society.

Archbishop of Canterbury's Commission on Urban Priority Areas (1985) *Faith in the city*, London: Church House.

Bailey, R. (1974) *Radicals in urban politics: The Alinsky approach*, Chicago/London: University of Chicago Press.

Barr, A. (1991) *Practising community development: Experience in Strathclyde*, London: Community Development Foundation.

Barr, A. (1995) 'Empowering communities – beyond fashionable rhetoric? Some reflections on the Scottish experience', *Community Development Journal*, vol 30, no 2, April, pp 121-32.

Barr, A. and Hashagen, S. (2000) *ABCD handbook: A framework for evaluating community development*, London: Community Development Foundation.

Belenky, M., Clinchy, B., Goldberger, N. and Tarule, J. (1997) *Women's ways of knowing: The development of self, voice and mind* (2nd edn), New York: Basic Books.

Berger, P. (1966) *Invitation to sociology*, Harmondsworth: Penguin.

Berner, E. and Phillips, B. (2005) 'Left to their own devices? Community self-help between alternative development and neo-liberalism', *Community Development Journal*, vol 40, no 1, January, pp 17-29.

Beveridge Report (1942) *Social insurance and allied services*, London: HMSO.

Blackburn, J. (2000) 'Understanding Paulo Freire: Reflections on the origins, concepts and possible pitfalls of his educational approach', *Community Development Journal*, vol 35, no 1, pp 3-15.

Blagg, H. and Derricourt, N. (1982) 'Why we need to reconstruct a theory of the state for community work', in G. Craig, N. Derricourt and M. Loney (eds) *Community work and the state*, London: Routledge and Kegan Paul.

Blair, T. (1998) *The third way: New politics for the new century*, London: The Fabian Society.

Boal, A. (translated by Jackson, A.) (1994) *The rainbow of desire: the Boal method of theatre and therapy*, London: Routledge.

Boggs, C. (1980) *Gramsci's Marxism*, London: Pluto.

Bourne, J. (1999) 'Racism, postmodernism and the flight from class', in D. Hill, P. McLaren, M. Cole and G. Rikowski (eds) *Postmodernism in educational theory: Education and the politics of human resistance*, London: The Tuffnell Press.

Bowers, C.A. and Apffel-Marglin, F. (eds) (2004) *Re-thinking Freire: Globalization and the environmental crisis*, Mahwah, NJ: Lawrence Erlbaum Associates.

Bradshaw, J. (1999) 'Comparing child poverty', *Poverty*, Journal of the Child Poverty Action Group, no 104, Autumn.

Burningham, L. and Thrush, D. (2001) *Rainforests are a long way from here: The environmental concerns of disadvantaged groups*, York: Joseph Rowntree Foundation.

Burton, P. (2003) 'Community involvement in neighbourhood regeneration: stairway to heaven or road to nowhere?', available at <www.neighbourhoodcentre.org>

Calder, G. (2003) 'Communitarianism and New Labour', available at <www.whb.co.uk/socialissues>.

Callaway, H. (1981) 'Women's perspectives: research as re-vision', in P. Reason and J. Rowan (eds) *Human inquiry: A sourcebook of new paradigm research*, Chichester: Wiley.

Calouste Gulbenkian Foundation (1968) *Community work and social change: A report on training*, London: Longman.

Calouste Gulbenkian Foundation (1973) *Current issues in community work: A study by the Community Work Group*, London: Routledge and Kegan Paul.

Campbell, B. (1993) *Goliath: Britain's dangerous places*, London: Methuen.

Cannan, C. (2000) 'The environmental crisis, Greens and community development', *Community Development Journal*, vol 35, no 4, October, pp 365-76.

Chomsky, N. (2003) *Hegemony or survival: America's quest for global dominance*, New York: Metropolitan.

Cockburn, C. (1977) *The local state*, London: Pluto.

Cohen, R., Ferres, G., Hollins, C., Long, G., Smith, R. and Bennett, F. (eds) (1996) *Out of pocket: Failure of the Social Fund*, London: The Children's Society.

Collins, T. (2002) 'Community development and state building: a shared project', *Community Development Journal*, vol 37, no 1, January, pp 91-100.

Commission for Social Justice (1994) *Social justice: Strategies for national renewal*, London: Verso.

Community Development Project Working Group (1974) 'The British National Community Development Project, 1969-1974', *Community Development Journal*, vol 9, no 6, October, pp 162-84.

Cooke, I. (1996) 'Whatever happened to the class of '68? – the changing context of radical community work practice', in I. Cooke and M. Shaw (eds) *Radical community work: Perspectives from practice in Scotland*, Edinburgh: Moray House.

CPAG (1994) *Social justice for families and children in poverty*, London: Child Poverty Action Group.

Craig, G. (undated) 'Social justice', available from <g.craig@hull.ac.uk>.

Craig, G. (1998) 'Community development in a global context', *Community Development Journal*, vol 33, no 1, pp 2-17.

Craig, G. and Mayo, M. (eds) (1995) *Community empowerment: A reader in participation and development*, London: Zed Books.

Craig, G. and Taylor, M. (2002) 'Dangerous liaisons: Local government and the voluntary and community sectors' in C. Glendinning, M. Powell and K. Rummery *Partnerships, New Labour and the governance of welfare*, Bristol: The Policy Press.

Craig, G., Derricourt, N. and Loney, M. (eds) (1982) *Community work and the state: Towards a radical approach*, London: Routledge and Kegan Paul.

Craig, G., Gorman, M. and Vercseg, I. (2004) 'The Budapest Declaration: building European civil society through community development', available from Community Development Exchange at <www.cdx.org.uk>.

Darder, A. (2002) *Reinventing Paulo Freire: A pedagogy of love*, Boulder, CO: Westview.

Davidson, A. (1977) *Antonio Gramsci: Towards an intellectual biography*, London: Merlin Press.

Davis, A. (1989) *Women, culture and politics*, New York: Random House.

Deakin, N. (2001) *In search of civil society*, Basingstoke: Palgrave.

Dixon, J., Dogan, R. and Sanderson, A. (2005) 'Community and communitarianism: a philosophical investigation', *Community Development Journal*, vol 40, no 1, January, pp 4-16.

Doering, B. (1994) *The philosopher and the provocateur*, London: University of Notre Dame Press.

Dominelli, L. (1990) *Women and community action*, Birmingham: Venture Press.

Dominelli, L. (1994) 'Women, community work and the state in the 1990s', in S. Jacobs and K. Popple (eds) *Community work in the 1990s*, Nottingham: Spokesman.

Dominelli, L. (1995) 'Women in the community: feminist principles and organising in community work', *Community Development Journal*, vol 30, no 2.

Dominelli, L. (1997) *Sociology for social work*, London: Macmillan.

Donnison, D. (1998) *Policies for a just society*, Basingstoke: Macmillan.

Dornan, P. (ed) (2004) *Ending child poverty by 2020: The first five years*, London: Child Poverty Action Group.

Douthwaite, R. (1996) *Short circuit: Strengthening local economics for security in an unstable world*, Dartington: Green Books.

Doyal, L. and Gough, I. (1991) *A theory of human need*, London: Macmillan.

Entwistle, H. (1979) *Antonio Gramsci: Conservative schooling for radical politics*, London: Routledge.

Etzioni, A. (1995) *The spirit of community: Rights, responsibilities and the communitarian agenda*, London: Fontana.

Etzioni, A. (1997) *The new golden rule: Community and morality in a democratic society*, London: Profile.

Fergusson, D.A.S. (1992) *John Macmurray in a nutshell*, Edinburgh: Handsel Press.

Fine, M., Weiss, L., Powell, L. and Mun Wong, L. (1997) *Off White: Readings on race, power and society*, New York: Routledge.

Fiori, G. (translated by Nairn, T.) (1990) *Antonio Gramsci: Life of a revolutionary*, London: Verso (first published as *Vita di Antonio Gramsci*, Bari: Laterza, 1965).

Fisher, W.F. and Ponniah, T. (2003) *Another world is possible: Popular alternatives to globalization at the World Social Forum*, London: Zed Books.

Flaherty, J., Veit-Wilson, J. and Dornan, P. (2004) *Poverty: The facts*, (5th edn) London: Child Poverty Action Group.

Forgacs, D. (ed) (1988) *A Gramsci reader*, London: Lawrence & Wishart.

Frazer, E. (1999) *The problem of communitarian politics: unity and conflict*, Oxford: Oxford University Press.

Freire, P. (1972) *Pedagogy of the oppressed*, Harmondsworth: Penguin.

Freire, P. (1976) *Education: The practice of freedom*, London: Writers and Readers.

Freire, P. (1985) *The politics of education: Culture, power and liberation*, London: Macmillan.

Freire, P. (translated by Macedo, D.) (1993) *Pedagogy of the city*, New York: Continuum.

Freire, P. (translated by Barr, R.) (1995) *Pedagogy of hope: Reliving Pedagogy of the oppressed,* New York: Continuum.

Freire, P. (1998a) *Pedagogy of the heart*, New York: Continuum.

Freire, P. (1998b) *Pedagogy of freedom: Ethics, democracy and civic courage*, Oxford: Rowman and Littlefield.

Freire, P. and Faundez, A. (1992) *Learning to question: A pedagogy of liberation*, New York: Continuum.

Freire, P. and Macedo, D. (1993) 'A dialogue with Paulo Freire', in P. McLaren and P. Leonard (eds) *Paulo Freire: A critical encounter*, London: Routledge.

Freire, A. and Macedo, D. (eds) (1998) *The Paulo Freire reader*, New York: Continuum.

Fromm, E. (1962) *Beyond the chains of illusion*, London: Abacus.

Gamble, D.N. and Weil, M.O. (1997) 'Sustainable development: the challenge for community development', *Community Development Journal*, vol 32, no 3, July.

George, V. and Wilding, P. (1994) *Welfare and ideology*, Hemel Hempstead: Harvester Wheatsheaf.

Giddens, A. (1998) *The Third Way: The renewal of social democracy*, Cambridge: Polity Press.

Gilchrist, A. (2004) *The well-connected community: A networking approach to community development*, Bristol: The Policy Press/Community Development Foundation.

Giroux, H. (1993) 'Paulo Freire and the politics of postcolonialism', in P. McLaren and P. Leonard (eds) *Paulo Freire: A critical encounter*, London: Routledge.

Giroux, H.A. and McLaren, P. (1994) *Between borders: Pedagogy and the politics of cultural studies*, London: Routledge.

Goodman, A., Johnson, P. and Webb, S. (1997) *Inequality in the UK*, Oxford: Oxford University Press.

Gordon, D. and Pantazis, C. (1997) 'Breadline Britain in the 1990s: the full report of a major national survey on poverty', *Poverty*, Journal of the Child Poverty Action Group, no 98, Autumn, pp 21-2.

Gordon, D., Adelman, L., Ashworth, K., Bradshaw, J., Levitas, R., Middleton, S., Pantazis, C., Patsios, D., Payne, S., Townsend, P. and Williams, J. (2000) *Poverty and social exclusion in Britain*, York: Joseph Rowntree Foundation.

Gore, J. (1993) *The struggle for pedagogies: Critical and feminist discourses as regimes of truth*, London: Routledge.

Graham, H. and Jones, J. (1992) 'Community development and research', *Community Development Journal*, vol 27, no 3, July.

Gramsci, A. (edited and translated by Q. Hoare and G.N. Smith) (1971) *Selections from prison notebooks*, London: Lawrence & Wishart.

Gramsci, A. (edited by D. Forgacs and G. Nowell-Smith) (translated by W. Boelhower) (1985) *Selections from cultural writings*, London: Lawrence & Wishart.

Gramsci, A. (translated and introduced by H. Henderson) (1988) *Gramsci's prison letters*, London: Zwan.

Gregg, Paul, Harkness, Susan and Machin, Stephen (1999) 'Poor kids: trends in child poverty in Britain, 1968-96', *Fiscal Studies*, vol 20, no 2, June.

Griffiths, M. (2003) *Action for social justice in education: Fairly different*, Maidenhead: Open University Press.

Hall, S. (1996a) 'The meaning of new times', in D. Morley and K.-H. Chen (eds) *Stuart Hall: Critical dialogues in cultural studies*, London: Routledge.

Hall, S. (1996b) 'What is this "black" in black popular culture', in D. Morley and K.-H. Chen (eds) *Stuart Hall: Critical dialogues in cultural studies*, London: Routledge.

Hall, S. (1996c) 'Gramsci's relevance for the study of race and ethnicity', in D. Morley and K.-H. Chen (eds) *Stuart Hall: Critical dialogues in cultural studies*, London: Routledge.

Hawtin, M., Hughes, G. and Percy-Smith, J. (1994) *Community profiling: Auditing social needs*, Buckingham: Open University Press.

Henderson, P. and Thomas, D. (1980) *Skills in neighbourhood work*, London: Unwin Hyman.

Heron, J. (1981) 'Experiential research methodology', in P. Reason and J. Rowan (eds) *Human inquiry: A sourcebook of new paradigm research*, Chichester: Wiley.

Hill, D. (ed) (2000) *Education, education, education: Capitalism, socialism and 'The Third Way'*, London: Cassell.

Hill, D., McLaren, P., Cole, M. and Rikowski, G. (eds) (1999) *Postmodernism in educational theory: Education and the politics of human resistance*, London: The Tuffnell Press.

Hill Collins, P. (1990) *Black feminist thought: Knowledge, consciousness and the politics of empowerment*, London: Unwin Hyman.

Hillman, Mick (2002) 'Environmental justice: a crucial link between environmentalism and community development?', *Community Development Journal*, vol 37, no 4, October, pp 349-60.

Hills, J. and Stewart, K. (2005) *A more equal society: New Labour, poverty, inequality and exclusion*, Bristol: The Policy Press.

Hines, C. (2000) *Localization: A global manifesto*, London: Earthscan.

Hirshon, S. with Butler, J. (1983) *And also teach them to read*, Westport, CT: Lawrence Hill and Co.

Hoffman, J. (1984) *The Gramscian challenge: Coercion and consent in Marxist political theory*, Oxford: Blackwell.

Holland, J., Blair, M. and Sheldon, S. (eds) (1995) *Debates and issues in feminist research and pedagogy*, Clevedon: Multilingual Matters/Open University.

Holub, R. (1992) *Antonio Gramsci: Beyond Marxism and postmodernism*, London: Routledge.

Home Office (2004) *Building civil renewal: Government support for community capacity building and proposals for change*, London: Civil Renewal Unit.

hooks, b. (1984) *Feminist theory: From margin to center*, Boston: South End Press.

hooks, b. (1993) 'bell hooks speaking about Paulo Freire – the man, his work', in P. McLaren and P. Leonard (eds) *Paulo Freire: A critical encounter*, London: Routledge.

hooks, b. (1994) *Teaching to transgress: Education as the practice of freedom*, London: Routledge.

Hope, A. and Timmel, S. (1999) *Training for transformation: A handbook for community workers* (Book 4), London: ITDG Publishing.

Hope, A. and Timmel, S. with Hodzi, C. (1984) *Training for transformation: A handbook for community workers* (Books 1-3), Zimbabwe, Gweru: Mambo Press.

Horton, M. and Freire, P. (edited by Bell, B., Gaventa, J. and Peters, J.) (1990) *We make the road by walking: Conversations on education and social change*, Philadelphia: Temple University Press.

Horwitt, S.D. (1997) 'Alinsky: more important now than ever', in *LA Times*, available at <www.tresser.com/alinsky.htm>.

Howarth, Catherine, Kenway, Peter, Palmer, Guy and Miorelli, Romina (1999) *Monitoring poverty and social exclusion 1999*, York: Joseph Rowntree Foundation/New Policy Institute.

Hustedde, R. and King, B. (2002) 'Rituals: emotions, community faith in soul and the messiness of life', *Community Development Journal*, vol 37, pp 338-348.

International Women's Tribune Centre (1996) 'How it happened – from day to day: excerpts from global FaxNet Bulletins, April 3-September 25, 1995', *Women's Studies Quarterly*, vol xxiv, nos 1 and 2, Spring/Summer, pp 18-39.

Jacobs, S. (1994) 'Community work in a changing world', in S. Jacobs and K. Popple (eds) *Community work in the 1990s*, Nottingham: Spokesman.

Jacobs, S. and Popple, K. (eds) (1994) *Community work in the 1990s*, Nottingham: Spokesman.

Joseph Rowntree Foundation (1995) *Inquiry into income and wealth, volumes 1 & 2*, York: Joseph Rowntree Foundation.

Kenway, J. (2001) 'Remembering and regenerating Gramsci', in K. Weiler (ed) *Feminist engagements: Reading, resisting, and revisioning male theorists in education and cultural studies*, London: Routledge.

Khan, U.A. (1989a) 'Is the red flag flying here?', *Going local*, Bristol: School for Advanced Studies, University of Bristol.

Khan, U.A. (1989b) 'Neighbourhood forums and the "New Left": Representation beyond tokenism?', paper presented to the Annual Conference of the Political Studies Association, April.

King, A.D. (ed) (1991) *Culture, globalisation and the world-system*, London: Macmillan.

Kirkwood, G. (1991) 'Freire methodology in practice', in *Roots and branches*, (series of occasional papers), vol 1: Community development and health education, Milton Keynes: Open University Health Education Unit.

Kirkwood, G. and Kirkwood, C. (1989) *Living adult education: Freire in Scotland*, Milton Keynes: Open University Press.

Kuenstler, P. (ed) (1961) *Community organization in Great Britain*, London: Faber and Faber.

Lather, P. (1995) 'Feminist perspectives on empowering research methodologies', in J. Holland, M. Blair and S. Sheldon (eds) *Debates and issues in feminist research and pedagogy*, Clevedon: Multilingual Matters/Open University.

Lawner, L. (introduced, selected and translated) (1979) *Letters from prison by Antonio Gramsci*, London: Quartet Books.

Leach, Tom (1983) 'Paulo Freire: dialogue, politics and relevance', *International Journal of Lifelong Education*, vol 1, no 3, pp 185-201.

Ledwith, M. and Asgill, P. (1998) 'Black and White women working together: Transgressing the boundaries of sisterhood' in M. Lavalette, L. Penketh and C. Jones (eds) *Anti-racism and social welfare*, Aldershot: Ashgate.

Ledwith, M. and Asgill, P. (2000) 'Critical alliance: Black and White women working together for social justice', *Community Development Journal*, vol 35, no 3, July.

Ledwith, M. and Asgill, P. (in press) 'Feminist, anti-racist community work: critical alliance – local to global', in L. Dominelli (ed) *Communities in a globalising world: Theory and practice for community empowerment*, Aldershot: Ashgate.

Lees, R. and Mayo, M. (1984) *Community action for change*, London: Routledge and Kegan Paul.

Lewis, M. (2000) 'Interrupting patriarchy: politics, resistance, and transformation in the feminist classroom', in I. Shor and C. Pari (eds) *Education is politics: Critical teaching across differences, postsecondary*, Portsmouth, NH: Heinemann.

Lister, R. (2005) 'The links between women's and children's poverty', in V. Sharma (ed) *Women's and children's poverty: Making the links*, London: Women's Budget Group/Fawcett Society.

Lockhart, J. (1999) 'Re-examining Paulo Freire and his relevance for community intervention: the source of my "surprise"', in D. Scott and T. Ireland (eds) *'Vidas secas: Lutas fecudas' Community and development in the Brazilian Northeast*, London: Whiting & Birch.

Lorde, A. (1984) *Sister outsider*, New York: The Crossing Press.

Lovett, T. (1982a) 'Community education and community action', in T. Lovett (ed) *Radical approaches to adult education: A reader*, London: Routledge.

Lovett, T. (ed) (1982b) *Radical approaches to adult education: A reader*, London: Routledge.

Lovett, T., Clarke, C. and Kilmurray, A. (eds) (1983) *Adult education and community action*, London: Croom Helm.

Lupton, R. and Power, A. (2005) 'Diasdvantaged by where you live? New Labour and neighbourhood renewal', in J. Hills and K. Stewart (eds) *A more equal society? New Labour, poverty, inequality and exclusion*, Bristol: The Policy Press.

Mack, J. and Lansley, S. (1985) *Poor Britain*, London: George Allen and Unwin.

Mackie, R. (1980a) 'Contributions to the thought of Paulo Freire', in R. Mackie (ed) *Literacy and revolution: The pedagogy of Paulo Freire*, London: Pluto.

Mackie, R. (ed) (1980b) *Literacy and revolution: The pedagogy of Paulo Freire*, London: Pluto.

Macmurray, J. (selected and introduced by Conford, P.) (1996) *The personal world: John Macmurray on self and society*, Edinburgh: Floris Books.

McIntosh, A. (2001) *Soil and soul: People versus corporate power*, London: Aurum.

McLaren, P. (1995) *Critical pedagogy and predatory culture: Oppositional politics in a postmodern era*, London: Routledge.

McLaren, P. (1996) 'Unthinking Gabachismo, rethinking democracy: critical citizenship in postmodern "predatory" times' (unpublished), Graduate School of Education and Information Studies, University of California at Los Angeles.

McLaren, P. (2000) *Che Guevara, Paulo Freire and the pedagogy of revolution*, Oxford: Rowman and Littlefield.

McLaren, P. (2002) 'Afterword: a legacy of hope and struggle', in A. Darder *Reinventing Paulo Freire: A pedagogy of love*, Boulder, CO: Westview.

McLaren, P. and Leonard, P. (eds) (1993) *Paulo Freire: A critical encounter*, London: Routledge.

McLaren, P., Hill, D. and Cole, M. (1999) 'Postmodernism adieu: towards a politics of human resistance', in D. Hill, P. McLaren, M. Cole and G. Rikowski (eds) *Postmodernism in educational theory: Education and the politics of human resistance*, London: The Tuffnell Press.

McLaren, P., Finschman, G., Serra, S. and Antelo, E. (1998) 'The specters of Gramsci: revolutionary praxis and the committed intellectual', *Journal of Thought*, Winter, pp 1-33.

Marcuse, H. (1991) *One-dimensional man* (2nd edn), London: Routledge.

Maruyama, M. (1981) 'Endogenous research: rationale', in P. Reason and J. Rowan (eds) *Human inquiry: A sourcebook of new paradigm research*, Chichester: Wiley.

Mason, J. (2002) *Researching your own practice: The discipline of noticing*, London: Routledge.

Mayo M. (ed) (1977) *Women in the community*, London: Routledge and Kegan Paul.

Mayo, M. (1994) *Communities and care*, London: Macmillan.

Mayo, M. (1997) *Imagining tomorrow: Adult education for transformation*, Leicester: NIACE.

Mayo, P. (1999) *Gramsci, Freire and adult education: Possibilities for transformative action*, London: Zed Books.

Mayo, P. (2004) *Liberating praxis: Paulo Freire's legacy for radical education and politics*, London: Praeger.

Milne, S. (undated) 'Fifty years on, Labour discovers a guru', *Guardian*.

Milne, S. (1994) *The enemy within: MI5, Maxwell and the Scargill affair*, London: Verso.

Mongella, G. (1996) 'Beijing and beyond: toward the twenty-first century of women', *Women's Studies Quarterly*, vol xxiv, nos 1 and 2, Spring/Summer, p116.

Morley, D. and Chen, K.-H. (eds) (1996) *Stuart Hall: Critical dialogues in cultural studies*, London: Routledge.

Morris, L. (1994) *Dangerous classes: The underclass and social citizenship*, London: Routledge.

Moustakas, C. (1990) *Heuristic research: Design, methodology and applications*, London: Sage.

Nairn, T. (1982) 'Antonu su gobbu', in A. Showstack Sassoon (ed) *Approaches to Gramsci*, London: Writers and Readers.

Novak, Tony (1988) *Poverty and the state*, Milton Keynes: Open University Press.

O'Donohue, J. (2004) *Beauty, the invisible embrace: Rediscovering the true sources of compassion, serenity and hope*, New York: Harper Collins.

Oakley, A. (1992) *Social support and motherhood*, Oxford: Blackwell.

Office for National Statistics (1996) *Social focus on ethnic minorities*, Basingstoke: Palgrave Macmillan.

Office of Population Censuses and Surveys (1995) *Conceptions in England and Wales, 1992*, London: OPCS.

Ohri, A., Manning, B. and Curno, P. (eds) (1982) *Community work and racism: Community work seven*, London: Routledge and Kegan Paul/ Association of Community Workers.

Opie, A. (1992) 'Qualitative research, appropriation of the "other" and empowerment', *Feminist Review*, no 40, Spring.

Oppenheim, C. (ed) (1998) *An inclusive society: Strategies for tackling poverty*, London: Institute for Public Policy Research.

Oppenheim, C. and Harker, L. (1996) *Poverty: The facts*, London: Child Poverty Action Group.

Page, D. (2000) *Communities in the balance: The reality of social exclusion on housing estates*, York: Joseph Rowntree Foundation.

Page, M. (1997) *Women in Beijing one year on: Networks, alliances, coalitions*, London: Community Development Foundation.

Pakulski, J. and Waters, M. (1996) *The death of class*, London: Sage.

Paulo (2003) 'National occupational standards for community development work', available at
<www.communitydevelopmentlearning.org.uk>.

Pheterson, G. (1990) 'Alliances between women: overcoming internalized oppression and internalized domination', in L. Albrecht and R. Brewer (eds) *Bridges of power: Women's multicultural alliances*, Philadelphia: New Society Publishers.

Platt, L. (2005) *Discovering child poverty: The creation of a policy agenda from 1800 to the present*, Bristol: The Policy Press.

Popple, K. (1995) *Analysing community work: Its theory and practice*, Buckingham: Open University Press.

Power, A. and Tunstall, R. (1995) *Swimming against the tide: Polarisation or progress on 20 unpopular council estates, 1980-1995*, York: Joseph Rowntree Foundation.

Preston, G. (ed) (2005) *At greatest risk: The children most likely to be poor*, London: Child Poverty Action Group.

Putnam, R. (2000) *Bowling alone: The collapse and revival of American community*, New York, NY: Simon and Schuster.

Putnam, R.D. (2002) *Democracies in flux: The evolution of social capital in contemporary society*, New York: Oxford University Press.

Quick, A. (1991) *Unequal risks: Accidents and social policy*, London: Socialist Health Association.

Quick, A. and Wilkinson, R. (1991) *Income and health*, London: Socialist Health Association.

Randall, R. and Southgate, J. (1981) 'The troubled fish: barriers to dialogue', in P. Reason and J. Rowan (eds) *Human inquiry: A sourcebook of new paradigm research*, Chichester: Wiley.

Ransome, P. (1992) *Antonio Gramsci: A new introduction*, London: Harvester Wheatsheaf.

Rawls, J. (1971) *A theory of justice*, Oxford: Oxford University Press.

Rawls, J. (2001) *Justice as fairness: A restatement*, Boston, MA: Harvard University Press.

Reagon, B. (1983) 'Coalition politics: turning the century', in B. Smith (ed) *Home girls*, New York: Kitchen Table – Women of Color Press.

Reason, P. (ed) (1988) *Human inquiry in action: Developments in new paradigm research*, London: Sage.

Reason, P. (1994a) 'Future participation', in P. Reason (ed) *Participation in human inquiry: Research with people*, London: Sage.

Reason, P. (1994b) 'Inquiry and alienation', in P. Reason (ed) *Participation in human inquiry: Research with people*, London: Sage.

Reason, P. (ed) (1994c) *Participation in human inquiry: Research with people*, London: Sage.

Reason, P. (2002) 'Justice, sustainability and participation: inaugural lecture', available from <p.w.reason@bath.ac.uk>.

Reason, P. and Bradbury, H. (eds) (2001) *Handbook of action research: Participative inquiry and practice*, London: Sage.

Reason, P. and Rowan, J. (eds) (1981) *Human inquiry: A sourcebook of new paradigm research*, Chichester: Wiley.

Ridge, T. (2004) 'Putting children first: addressing the needs and concerns of children who are poor', in P. Dornan (ed) *Ending child poverty by 2020: The first five years*, London: Child Poverty Action Group.

Rikowski, G. and McLaren, P. (1999) 'Postmodernism in educational theory', in D. Hill, P. McLaren, M. Cole and G. Rikowski (eds) *Postmodernism in educational theory: Education and the politics of human resistance*, London: The Tuffnell Press.

Robson, T. (2000) *The state and community action*, London: Pluto.

Rowan, J. (1981) 'Dialectical paradigm for research', in P. Reason and J. Rowan (eds) *Human inquiry: A sourcebook of new paradigm research*, Chichester: Wiley.

Rowan, J. and Reason, P. (1981) 'On making sense', in P. Reason and J. Rowan (eds) *Human inquiry: A sourcebook of new paradigm research*, Chichester: Wiley.

Rowbotham, S. (1973) *Hidden from history*, London: Pluto.

Rowbotham, S. (1992) *Women in movement: Feminism and social action*, London: Routledge.

Rowbotham, S. (1994) 'Interpretations of welfare and approaches to the state, 1870-1920', in A. Oakley and A.S. Williams (eds) *The politics of the welfare state*, London: Routledge.

Rude, G. (1980) *Ideology and popular protest*, London: Lawrence & Wishart.

Rutter, M. and Madge, N. (1976) *Cycles of disadvantage*, London: Heinemann.

Schuler, D. (1996) *New community networks: Wired for change*, New York: ACM Press.

Schutzman, M. and Cohen-Cruz, J. (eds) (1995) *Playing Boal: Theatre, therapy, activism*, London: Routledge.

Scottish Education Department (1975) *Adult education: The challenge of change* (Alexander Report), Edinburgh: HMSO.

Seebohm Report (1968) *Local authority and allied personal social services*, London: HMSO.

Shaw, M. (2004) *Community work: Policy, politics and practice*, Hull: Universities of Hull and Edinburgh.

Shor, I. (1992) *Empowering education: Critical teaching for social change*, London/Chicago, IL: University of Chicago Press.

Shor, I. (1993) 'Education is politics: Paulo Freire's critical pedagogy', in P. McLaren and P. Leonard (eds) *Paulo Freire: A critical encounter*, London: Routledge.

Shor, I. (2000) '(Why) education is politics', in I. Shor and C. Pari (eds) *Education is politics: Critical teaching across differences, postsecondary*, Portsmouth, NH: Heinemann.

Shor, I. and Freire, P. (1987) *A pedagogy for liberation: Dialogues on transforming education*, London: Bergin & Garvey.

Shor, I. and Pari, C. (eds) (2000) *Education is politics: Critical teaching across differences, postsecondary*, Portsmouth, NH: Heinemann.

Showstack Sassoon, A. (ed) (1982) *Approaches to Gramsci*, London: Writers and Readers.

Showstack Sassoon, A. (1987a) *Gramsci's politics* (2nd edn), London: Hutchinson.

Showstack Sassoon, A. (1987b) *Women and the state*, London: Hutchinson.

Shropshire, J. and Middleton, S. (1999) *Small expectations: Learning to be poor?*, York: Joseph Rowntree Foundation.

Skeffington Report (1969) *People and planning*, London: HMSO.

Smith, B. (ed) (1983) *Home girls*, New York: Kitchen Table – Women of Color Press.

Southgate, J. (1981) 'The troubled fish: barriers to dialogue', in P. Reason and J. Rowan (eds) *Human inquiry: A sourcebook of new paradigm research*, Chichester: Wiley.

Spretnak, C. (1997) *The resurgence of the real: Body, nature and place in a hypermodern world*, Harlow: Addison-Wesley.

Steedman, C. (2000) *Landscape for a good woman: A story of two lives* (2nd edn), London: Virago.

Strinati, D. (1996) *An introduction to theories of popular culture*, London: Routledge.

Sullivan, H. and Skelcher, C. (2002) *Working across boundaries: Collaboration in public services*, Basingstoke: Palgrave Macmillan.

Taylor, M. (1995) 'Community work and the state: the changing context of UK practice', in M. Mayo and G. Craig (eds) *Community empowerment: A reader in participation and development*, London: Zed Books.

Taylor, M. (2000) *Top down meets bottom up: Neighbourhood management*, York: Joseph Rowntree Foundation.

Taylor, M. (2003) *Public policy in the community*, Basingstoke: Palgrave Macmillan.

Taylor, P. (1993) *The texts of Paulo Freire*, Buckingham: Open University Press.

Thomas, D. (1983) *The making of community work*, London: George Allen and Unwin.

Thompson, N. (2000) *Theory and practice in human services* (2nd edn), Buckingham: Open University Press.

Thompson, N. (2001) *Anti-discriminatory practice* (3rd edn), Basingstoke: Palgrave Macmillan.

Thompson, N. (2003) *Promoting equality: Challenging discrimination and oppression in the human services* (2nd edn), London: Macmillan.

Timmins, N. (1996) *The five giants: A biography of the welfare state*, London: Fontana.

Torres, C.A. (1993) 'From the Pedagogy of the opressed to a luta continua', in P. McLaren and P. Leonard (eds) *Paulo Freire: A critical encounter*, London: Routledge.

Townsend, P. (1979) *Poverty in the UK*, Harmondsworth: Penguin.

Townsend, P. (1988) *Inner city deprivation and premature death in Greater Manchester*, Ashton-under-Lyne: Tameside Policy Research Unit.

Townsend, P. (1995) 'Poverty: home and away', *Poverty*, Journal of the Child Poverty Action Group, no 91, Summer.

Townsend, P. and Davidson, N. (eds) (1990) *Inequalities in health: The Black Report*, Harmondsworth: Penguin.

Townsend, P., Phillimore, P., Beattie, A. and Helm, C. (1988) *Health and deprivation: Inequality and the North*, London: Croom Helm.

Twelvetrees, A. (1991) *Community work* (2nd edn), London: Macmillan.

Twelvetrees, A. (ed) (1998) *Community economic development: Rhetoric or reality*, London: Community Development Foundation.

Waddington, P. (1979) 'Looking ahead – community work into the 1980s', *Community Development Journal*, vol 14, no 3, October, pp 225-36.

Waddington, P. (1994) 'The values base of community work', in S. Jacobs and K. Popple (eds) *Community work in the 1990s*, Nottingham: Spokesman.

Walby, S. (1992) *Theorizing patriarchy*, Oxford: Blackwell.

Walby, S. (1994) 'Post-postmodernism? Theorizing gender', in *The Polity reader in social theory*, Cambridge: Polity Press.

Weiler, K. (1994) 'Freire and a feminist pedagogy of difference', in P. McLaren and C. Lankshear (eds) *Politics of liberation: paths from Freire*, London: Routledge.

Weiler, K. (1995) 'Freire and a feminist pedagogy of difference', in J. Holland, M. Blair and S. Sheldon (eds) *Debates and issues in feminist research and pedagogy*, Clevedon: Multilingual Matters/Open University.

Weiler, K. (ed) (2001) *Feminist engagements: Reading, resisting, and revisioning male theorists in education and cultural studies*, London: Routledge.

Williams, F. (1989) *Social policy: A critical introduction*, Cambridge: Polity Press.

Wilson, M. and Wilde, P. (2001) *Building practitioner strengths*, London: Community Development Foundation.

Winter, R., Sobiechowska, P. and Buck, A. (eds) (1999) *Professional experience and the investigative imagination: The art of reflective writing*, London: Routledge.

Witte Garland, A. (1988) *Women activists: Challenging the abuse of power*, New York, NY: The Feminist Press.

Young, A. (1990) *Femininity in dissent*, London: Routledge.

Young, I.M. (1990) *Justice and the politics of difference*, Chichester: Princeton University Press.

Younghusband, E. (1959) *Report of the working party on social workers in the local authority health and welfare services*, London: HMSO.

Index